# Psychoanalytic Assessment Applications for Different Settings

In this edited book, expert assessors illustrate through case examples how they apply psychoanalytic theory to different clinical settings. These settings include private practice, neuropsychological, medical, forensic, personnel, custody, school, and psychiatric-residential.

*Psychoanalytic Assessment Applications for Different Settings* allows the reader to track the assessor's work from start to finish. Each chapter presents a description of the clinical setting in which the assessment occurred; a detailed review of the referral and patient history; test selection and test findings with supporting data drawn from self-report, and cognitive and personality performance-based measures; psychiatric and psychodynamic diagnoses; implications and recommendations; discussion of the feedback process; and assessor-self reflections on the case. Throughout the book, psychodynamic concepts are used to help understand the test data. The authors are experts in the psychodynamic assessment of clients in private practice, educational, medical, neuropsychological, and forensic settings. The findings are derived from methods particular to each setting, with supporting data highlighted and woven throughout the interpretive process.

Students, educators, practitioners, and the professionals who collaborate with assessors will benefit from this book's offerings.

**Jed A. Yalof, PsyD**, ABPP, ABAP, ABSNP, ABP, is a professor of Psychology at Immaculata University, USA; training and supervising analyst at the Psychoanalytic Center of Philadelphia; and a neuropsychologist at the Austen Riggs Center.

**Anthony D. Bram, PhD**, ABAP, FABP, is a psychologist and child and adult psychoanalyst in private practice in Lexington, MA, USA, and is on faculty at Cambridge Health Alliance/Harvard Medical School and the Boston Psychoanalytic Society and Institute. He is co-author of *Psychological Testing that Matters: Creating a Road Map for Effective Treatment*.

# Psychoanalytic Assessment Applications for Different Settings

Edited by Jed A. Yalof
and Anthony D. Bram

Routledge
Taylor & Francis Group

LONDON AND NEW YORK

First published 2021
by Routledge
2 Park Square, Milton Park, Abingdon, Oxon OX14 4RN

and by Routledge
52 Vanderbilt Avenue, New York, NY 10017

*Routledge is an imprint of the Taylor & Francis Group, an informa business*

*British Library Cataloguing-in-Publication Data*
A catalogue record for this book is available from the British Library

*Library of Congress Cataloging-in-Publication Data*
Names: Yalof, Jed A., editor. | Bram, Anthony D., editor.
Title: Psychoanalytic assessment applications for different settings /
edited by Jed A. Yalof and Anthony D. Bram.
Description: Abingdon, Oxon; New York, NY: Routledge, 2021. |
Includes bibliographical references and index. |
Identifiers: LCCN 2020032272 (print) | LCCN 2020032273 (ebook) |
ISBN 9780367649890 (hbk) | ISBN 9780367649876 (pbk) |
ISBN 9781003127291 (ebk)
Subjects: LCSH: Psychological tests. | Psychoanalysis. |
Clinical psychology.
Classification: LCC BF176 .P738 2021 (print) | LCC BF176 (ebook) |
DDC 150.28/7–dc23
LC record available at https://lccn.loc.gov/2020032272
LC ebook record available at https://lccn.loc.gov/2020032273

ISBN: 978-0-367-64989-0 (hbk)
ISBN: 978-0-367-64987-6 (pbk)
ISBN: 978-1-003-12729-1 (ebk)

Typeset in Bembo
by Deanta Global Publishing Services, Chennai, India

Jed A. Yalof

To my grandsons, Jonah and Julian, where the future resides.

Anthony D. Bram

In memory of Alice Bartlett, Barbara Jordan-Goss, Bill Leeds, and Irv Rosen. For their friendship and wisdom.

# Contents

# Acknowledgements

To Barbara, Brett, Jen Krikor, and my brother, Clay, who are the core of support – loving and values-centered. My experience at the Psychoanalytic Center of Philadelphia has given me access to the finest of analytic thinkers. The Society for Personality Assessment (SPA) has continued to support a psychoanalytic way of thinking about psychological testing for which I am most grateful. I have been lucky to have met analytically informed assessment colleagues through SPA. Along with my close friends, Jim Kleiger and Tony Bram, I have co-led the Psychoanalytic Association's annual "Assessment and the Analytic Identity" discussion group, which allows us to hold a place for psychological testing in mainstream psychoanalytic thought. Tony Bram has been a wonderful collaborator on this book and other ventures- a true HOFer among the pantheon of psychoanalytic assessors. The authors who contributed to this book were great to work with from start to finish. My work at Immaculata University has offered teaching, research, writing, student, and collegial engagements in the area of assessment that are hard to match. My colleagues, past and present, at the Austen Riggs Center, have opened up opportunities that add new meaning to psychoanalytic assessment applications in residential care: Particular thanks to Jeremy Ridenour, Kate Gallagher, Marina Bayeva, and Christina Biedermann. Last, to Jerry, an old friend, who read analytic theory to help himself through the toughest of times and who shared his knowledge with me during a crucial period in my professional development.

Jed A. Yalof

I am most grateful to Linda, Sophia, and Jack Bram and to my mother Vicki Bram for their love and support throughout this project and all of my endeavors. And to my late father S. Richard Bram, for teaching me how to write and for his encouragement to find my own way. I am also appreciative of the loving support offered by my sister Julie Goldfischer and the Helmig family. Thank you again to all of my mentors, teachers, and supervisors from the Menninger Clinic/Topeka, the Greater Kansas City Psychoanalytic Institute, St. Louis Psychoanalytic Institute, and Boston Psychoanalytic Society and Institute. As Johnny Pesky, Bobby Doerr, and Ted Williams had each other, so too am I fortunate to have had Jed Yalof as my teammate on this book and our many other professional collaborations. Finally, I am indebted to our fine lineup of authors for the time, effort, and expertise they devoted to their contributions.

Anthony D. Bram

# 1 Introduction

*Jed A. Yalof*

As psychoanalytic clinicians who specialize in psychological testing, we draw our inspiration from a legacy of psychologists (Lerner, 2007) who found a way to nurture and evolve professional identities that included their work as psychoanalysts and assessors. At the top of that list is Roy Schafer, whose many contributions to psychoanalytic psychology, psychoanalysis, and psychological testing continue to set the standard for how to comport an analytic attitude (1983) and think psychoanalytically across what is often the uneasy tension between psychoanalysis and psychological testing (Bram, Yalof, & Gottschalk, 2018). Schafer (1954) introduces his classic book *Psychoanalytic Interpretation in Rorschach Testing* with this statement

> No matter how helpful a clinical tool it may be, a psychological test cannot do its own thinking. What is accomplishes depends upon the thinking that guides its application. This guiding thought is psychological theory, whether explicit and systematized or implicit and unsystematized.
>
> (p. xi)

Schafer's statement brings into focus the two main aims of *Psychoanalytic Assessment Applications in Different Settings*. First, the book is decidedly psychoanalytic in its focus and unique in the sense that it is setting-specific. That is, our concern is with the application of a theoretical model across clinical settings and patients who are seen at that setting, rather than the way theory informs a particular test. A psychoanalytic theoretical approach to psychological testing includes such central concepts as defenses, reality testing, object relations, affect regulation, self-image, and interpersonal relations (Bram & Peebles, 2014). The interpretive process considers test variables, test content, response sequence, test behavior, and the relationship between patient and examiner (e.g., Berg, 1984; Schafer, 1954; Sugarman, 1981)[1]

Second, writing reports for multiple audiences while remaining true to a psychoanalytic mindset is not always easy. Consumers of psychological assessments want reports that are informative, applicable, and readable. Clinical settings that are not supportive of psychoanalytic ways of thinking and writing require the assessor's flexibility and adaptation to whatever the work culture expects. Schools, courts, medical, and primary care settings each require different styles of writing. Other settings, such as private practice or residential, might be more open to the use of overt psychoanalytic terminology, but that, too, depends on the extant culture of the workplace or preference of the referral source. Using theory is more often silent and implicit, rather than emboldened and vocal. There are a variety of psychoanalytic theories that inform a psychoanalytic approach to psychological testing (e.g., Yalof, 2017) and data points from which to draw (Sugarman & Kanner, 2000), but modalities must interface with focused applications (e.g., Acklin, 1992; Bram & Yalof, 2015; Cogan, Porcerelli, & Dromgoole, 2001; Kleiger, 1997; Schafer, 1967; Shectman & Smith, 1984; Smith, 1983; Yalof, 2020) in order to be useful. The assessor must convey an empathic and fair-minded tone when developing inferences and writing reports. Although there are several report writing strategies (e.g., Appelbaum, 1972; Bram & Peebles, 2014; Harty, 1986; Lerner, 1991; Schafer, 1948) that have a psychoanalytic bent, professional settings differ and require the assessor's versatility when thinking about how to use theory in a way that organizes an extensive array of data points (e.g., Bram, 2010; Meloy, 1992; Rothstein, Benjamin, & Eisenstadt, 1988; Yalof & Rosenstein, 2014). Again, this is not an easy task. Much like a psychoanalytic psychotherapy session, a psychoanalytically informed test report holds as its ideal a jargon-free, balanced, and understandable written intervention that is databased and responsive to the immediacy of clinical need (i.e., the referral question). It is the assessor's thinking that permits conceptual titration in a manner that fits the data and audience, including the patient.

To accomplish these two ends, we invited as chapter contributors a group of psychoanalyst-psychologists and psychoanalytically oriented psychologists who test, write reports, teach, supervise, and conduct evaluations in different settings, and have found a way to find a psychoanalytic voice in their assessment work. We made some decisions along the way that we thought would keep the reader's focus on the report itself. The test batteries used by different assessors are quite diverse and reflect the way each clinician made decisions and adaptations in response to patient, referral question, and setting. Chapters are written by senior-level psychologists with dedicated assessment practices and a history of contribution to the assessment literature. We decided that reproducing and presenting verbatim protocols for each test would be both cumbersome and a less efficient method of accomplishing our aims of allowing the reader to track the thinking of each psychologist and reflect on the data, which is parenthesized to support each inference. As such, we opted for the latter, and hope that the reader finds this approach instructive. One test that required special attention was the Rorschach; some authors used Exner's (CS; 2003) Comprehensive System, whereas others preferred the newer Rorschach Performance Assessment System (R-PAS; Meyer, Vigilione, Mihura, Erard, & Erdberg, 2011). We decided to prioritize the integrity of each method and each author's ability to interpret the method's data sensibly, while also recognizing differences (Bram & Yalof, 2018).

Chapters 2–9 each include a (a) brief introduction with literature review that orients the reader to the clinical setting, (b) referral and history, (c) rationale for test selection, (d) recommendations, (e) post-assessment reflections, (f) diagnoses, using two systems: The more traditional International Classification of Diseases (ICD-10; World Health Organization, 1992) system preferred by third-party payers, and *The Psychodynamic Diagnostic Manual* (PDM-2; Lingiardi & McWilliams, 2017) as a specific diagnostic model that captures various dimensions of psychological functioning in accord with a psychoanalytic viewpoint. Regarding the PDM-2, each chapter includes a three-axis diagnosis (personality, mental functioning, and symptoms) but did not require authors to report specific scores on the associated rating scales. Chapter10 differs in format because of its focus on teaching an approach to psychoanalytic formulation that can be applied to report writing.

The diversity of chapters will be of interest to practitioners whose psychoanalytic work covers different applications. Three chapters address the often-perplexing overlap of neurocognitive, academic achievement, and personality considerations with differential emphasis. In Chapter 3, Sharon Leak, presents a psychoanalytically sensitive portrayal of an adult woman's "equivocal" attention-deficit problems, neurocognitive compromise, and internal conflict. In Chapter 4, James Kleiger presents a case that integrates the psychological profile of an adolescent girl's struggle with specific learning disabilities, concurrent with very salient psychodynamic concerns. In Chapter, 8, Alan Schwartz and David York, working in a primary care facility in a hospital setting, present the evaluation of a medical student experiencing a mix of inattention, mood difficulties, and internal stress embedded within a conflict of ethnic cultures. They provide a culturally sensitive psychoanalytic synthesis of these problems.

Other chapters similarly address the application of psychodynamic principles but within very different settings. In Chapter 2, Anthony Bram, writing from the perspective of a private practitioner, uses a psychoanalytic approach when discussing the evaluation of a young man who suffered academic and emotional difficulties, including psychotic-like symptoms, associated with separating from his family and going to college. The test report is data-driven but theory-informed, attends to the patient-examiner relationship as a data source, and involves treatment-centered diagnosis. In Chapter 5, Jeremy Ridenour illustrates how his assessment of a young man with a history of trauma and psychotic symptoms demonstrates a fit between psychoanalytic assessment and a residential setting culture deeply immersed in psychoanalytic thinking. In Chapter 6, Diana Rosenstein applies psychoanalytic principles but in a custody assessment. In Chapter 7, Ali Khadivi focuses on the application of psychoanalytic assessment in a criminal case. In Chapter 9, Mark Waugh does the same but for a fitness-for-duty assessment. In Chapter 10, Christina Biedermann presents a case and model for teaching students to think psychoanalytically about assessment work.

Throughout the book, psychoanalytic concepts are woven skillfully within case illustrations. We invite the reader's psychoanalytic immersion in each chapter.

## Note

1 The terms "testing/psychological testing," "evaluation/psychological evaluation," and "assessment/psychological assessment" are used interchangeably throughout the book. Also, the terms "tester," "assessor," "evaluator," and "examiner" are used interchangeably throughout the book, as are "client" and "patient." The authors also do not make distinctions between the terms "psychoanalytic" and "psychodynamic."

## References

Acklin, M. L. (1992). Psychodiagnosis of personality structure: Psychotic personality organization. *Journal of Personality Assessment, 58*(3), 454–479.

Appelbaum, S. A. (1972). A method of reporting psychological test findings. *Bulletin of the Menninger Clinic, 36*(5), 535–545.

Berg, M. (1984). Expanding the parameters of psychological testing. *Bulletin of the Menninger Clinic, 48*(1), 10–24.

Bram, A. D. (2010). The relevance of the Rorschach and patient-examiner relationship in treatment planning and outcome assessment. *Journal of Personality Assessment, 92*(2), 91–115.

Bram, A. D., & Peebles, M. J. (2014). *Psychological testing that matters: Creating a road map to effective treatment.* Washington, DC: American Psychological Association Books.

Bram, A. D., & Yalof, J. (2015). Quantifying complexity: Personality assessment and its relationship with psychoanalysis. *Psychoanalytic Inquiry, 35*(Suppl. 1), 74–97. doi:10.108 0/07351690.2015.987595.

Bram, A. D., Yalof, J., & Gottschalk, K. (2018). Psychological testing and psychoanalysis: Fixable gap or great divide? *Journal of Projective Psychology & Mental Health. Journal, 25,* 166–172.

Cogan, R., Porcerelli, J. H., & Dromgoole, K. (2001). Psychodynamics of partner, stranger, and generally violent male college students. *Psychoanalytic Psychology, 18*(3), 515–533. doi:10.1037//0735-9735.18.3.515.

Exner, J. E. (2003). *The Rorschach: A comprehensive system: Basic foundations and principles of interpretation* (vol. 1, 4th ed.). New York: Wiley.

Harty, M. K. (1986). Action language in the psychological test report. *Bulletin of the Menninger Clinic, 50*(5), 456–463.

Kleiger, J. H. (1997). Rorschach shading responses: From a printer's error to an integrated psychoanalytic paradigm. *Journal of Personality Assessment, 69*(2), 342–364.

Lerner, P. (1991). *Psychoanalytic perspectives on the Rorschach.* Hillsdale, NJ: The Analytic Press.

Lerner, P. M. (2007). On preserving a legacy: Psychoanalysis and psychological testing. *Psychoanalytic Psychology, 24*(2), 208–230. doi:10.1207/s15327752jpa8503_03.

Lingiardi, V., & McWilliams, N. (Eds.) (2017). *Psychodynamic diagnostic manual* (2nd ed.). New York: Guilford.

Meloy, R. J. (1992). *Violent attachments.* New York: Aronson.

Meyer, G. J., Viglione, D. J., Mihura, J. L., Erard, R. E., & Erdberg, P. (2011). *Rorschach performance assessment system: Administration, coding, interpretation, and technical manual.* Toledo, OH: Rorschach Performance Assessment System, L.L.C.

Rothstein, A., Benjamin, L., Crosby, M., & Eisenstadt, K. (1988). *Learning disorders: An integration of neuropsychological and psychoanalytic considerations.* Madison, CT: International Universities Press.

Schafer, R. (1948). *Clinical application of psychological tests.* New York: International Universities Press.

Schafer, R. (1954). *Psychoanalytic interpretation in Rorschach testing.* New York: Grune & Stratton.

Schafer, R. (1967). *Projective testing and psychoanalysis.* New York: International Universities Press.

Schafer, R. (1983). *The analytic attitude.* New York: Routledge.

Shectman, F., & Smith, W. (1984). *Diagnostic understanding and treatment planning: The elusive connection.* New York: Wiley.

Smith, K. (1983). Object-relations concepts applied to the psychotic range of ego functioning: With special reference to the Rorschach test. *Bulletin of the Menninger Clinic, 47*(5), 417–439.

Sugarman, A. (1981). The diagnostic use of countertransference reactions in psychological testing. *Bulletin of the Menninger Clinic, 45*(6), 473–490.

Sugarman, A., & Kanner, K. (2000). The contribution of psychoanalytic theory to psychological testing. *Psychoanalytic Psychology, 17*(1), 3–23. doi:10.1037//0736-9735.17.1.3.

World Health Organization. (1992). *International statistical classification of diseases and related health problems* (10th Revision). Geneva: World Health Organization.

Yalof, J. (2017). Discussion of special issue articles "Rorschach case study: Multiple psychoanalytic models of Rorschach interpretation." *Rorschachiania, 38*(1), 71–82. doi:10.1027/1192-5604/a000088.

Yalof, J. (2020). When the assessor's limits are tested: Enactments and the assessment frame in psychological testing. *Journal of Personality Assessment, 102*(4), 573–583. doi: 10.1080/00223891.2019.1613241.

Yalof, J., & Rosenstein, D. (2014). Psychoanalytic interpretation of superego functioning following CS readministration procedures: Case illustration. *Journal of Personality Assessment, 96*(2), 192–203. doi:10.1080/00223891.2013.836528.

# 2 Psychoanalytic assessment in private practice

*Anthony D. Bram*

In this case presentation from my private practice, I aim to illustrate three didactic points that I believe to be central to psychoanalytic assessment. Specifically, I will demonstrate (a) a data-driven but theory-informed way of thinking and making inferences (Bram & Peebles, 2014); (b) the essential role of the patient-examiner relationship (Bram & Peebles, 2014; Schafer, 1954; Shectman & Harty, 1986) as a data source, including hypothesis-testing and other interventions around testing the limits (Klopfer, Ainsworth, & Klopfer, 1954); and (c) the concept of treatment-centered diagnosis including clarifying the underlying developmental disruption (Bram & Peebles, 2014; Peebles, 2012).

## Description of the private practice setting

I conduct psychological assessments with children, adolescents, and adults in my private practice. When setting up their private practices, psychologists in the United States decide whether to sign contracts with insurance companies, which for assessment can have implications involving the amount of direct time that can be spent with a patient and indirect time for collateral contacts and to score and interpret tests and write the report. For various reasons—flexibility, autonomy, ethical, and financial—I have opted to structure my practice outside of insurance contracts, so patients and families pay me directly, and at the end of evaluations I provide an itemized statement for them to submit to insurance for reimbursement if they have out-of-network benefits. Most of my assessment referrals come from psychiatrists and other mental health clinicians. When I receive referrals, I do a fair amount of preparatory work by phone and encrypted email—dialoguing with the referring clinician, family, or (if an adult) the patient—in an attempt to understand in depth the referral context and questions to be addressed. I also review previous evaluation reports and other documentation and ask the patient or family to complete detailed developmental history questionnaires. These efforts are in the spirit of the intensive outpatient evaluations conducted for many years at the Menninger Clinic in Topeka where I trained, in that assessments do not start from scratch and the patient and family are already known to a good extent when arriving for evaluation. This enables the focus of time with the patient to hone in immediately on alliance-building around the questions to be understood through the assessment rather than getting caught up in details of information-gathering and trying to piece together the context. Admittedly, this is a different way of working than many assessors in private practice and institutions, where the assessment sessions typically begin with extensive history-taking. Because of my emphasis on trying to engage patients in a process of using the test data as an opportunity to be curious, self-reflect, and puzzle with me about their own questions for the evaluation (Bram & Peebles, 2014), I consider this approach to be a variant of collaborative assessment (Fischer, 1994).

## Brief literature review of assessment applications in private practice

Dating back to the rise of clinical psychology in the United States during the first half of the twentieth century, the psychologist's primary clinical role involved assessment (Benjamin, 2005). The psychologist often served in this role as a member of a multidisciplinary team in institutional settings such as hospitals, universities, and the military. It had been rare for clinical psychologists to (a) be trained and allowed to function as psychotherapists or psychoanalysts, as this had been the purview of psychiatrists and (b) work as private practitioners. With the post-Second World War need for more treaters and the attendant expansion of graduate training in clinical psychology guided by the Boulder scientist-practitioner model (Shakow, Brotemarkle, Doll, Kinder, Moore, & Smith, 1945), increasingly psychologists began to be trained more to provide psychotherapy (Benjamin, 2005). To meet swelling mental health needs, psychologists began to migrate to private practice by the early 1960s (Albee, 1963) and, though many did so primarily offering psychotherapy, it is reasonable to surmise that many also brought their assessment skill-set to this setting. Recent research indicates that private practice is now the most common primary and secondary employment setting for health service providers in psychology (46% for each; Michalski, Mulvey, & Kohout, 2010), and among members of APA Division 12 (Society for Clinical Psychology) 58% engage regularly in assessment work. Unfortunately, there are not breakdowns of the percentage of private practitioners who engage in psychological assessment, let alone those who do so from a psychodynamic framework. Moreover, although for more than a half-century, psychodynamicallyoriented psychologists in private practice have been conducting and even writing about assessment, there really is not extant literature addressing the vicissitudes of practicing assessment *in this setting*. For example, elsewhere I have written about assessment cases in my private practice (Bram, 2010, 2015, 2018) but the didactic points at the core of those articles have not been specific to private practice but, rather applicable across settings. The same can be said for the writings of other psychodynamic assessors in private practice (e.g., Kleiger, 2017; Yalof & Rosenstein, 2014). This is in contrast with, say, the small but more cohesive body literature associated with psychodynamic assessment in hospital or residential settings (see Ridenour, this book).

Without a literature to draw on regarding specific psychodynamic assessment applications in solo private practice, what I can offer, based on 15-plus years of experience, is a sense of the kinds of referral questions that are likely to come the way of an assessor in this setting, and how I address them. Referral questions often involve trying to understand factors and conditions that will enhance or impede a patient's treatment engagement, be it in the context of current impasses (Bram, 2015) or beginning therapy with a backdrop of past treatment failures (Bram, 2010). Colleagues also refer when there are questions of analyzability (Bram & Yalof, 2015), disordered thinking (Kleiger, 2017), other diagnostic conundrums (Bram, 2018), and not uncommonly when a patient has had recent or past neuropsychological evaluations[1] but the patient is not well understood as a person and in terms of more nuanced treatment implications (Bram, 2013). It is worth noting, though, that such referral questions are relevant to assessors in other settings, such as group practices, agencies, hospitals, universities, among others.

## Case background

Joshua was a 19-year-old man who struggled academically and emotionally in his first semester of college in another state. He subsequently withdrew from school and returned home, where he continued to suffer symptoms of depression and anxiety. Back at home, he attended a local community college but again had difficulty getting to classes, and he frequently missed appointments with his psychiatrist. Adding to concerns were two brief episodes that had a paranoid delusional quality: Joshua had accused peers on his social media accounts of changing his posts—when the writings, photos, and sketches were clearly his own entries—in an effort to humiliate him. During these episodes, which were later learned to be associated with heavy marijuana use, his parents were also struck by Joshua's difficulty completing his thoughts. Although these symptoms abated some with reduction of his marijuana use, he continued to report feeling anxious, depressed, and distraught around his sense of failure and lack of direction in his life.

Joshua grew up mostly with his mother and stepfather, two older brothers and younger stepsister. At age 4, he suffered the tragic loss of his father, who was murdered as a bystander in an armed robbery. Developmentally, prior to this event, Joshua did not experience speech, motor, or cognitive delays, and was physically healthy. However, through his school years, Joshua had a history of difficulty getting along with peers and often preferred to be by himself. He had used marijuana regularly since age 16 but no other drugs or alcohol. His mother reported a biological family history of anxiety, depression, and schizophrenia.

Joshua attended private schools and was perceived by his parents to struggle with motivation and was not achieving, per parent report, to what they perceived to be his intellectual potential. A psychological evaluation in early adolescence estimated his intellectual functioning to be in the Very Superior range (99th percentile on an abbreviated intelligence test) but revealed weaknesses in his attention, executive functioning and working memory, and visual-tracking relative to his well-developed reasoning skills. That evaluation also highlighted Joshua's generalized anxiety. Since age 14, Joshua had been followed by a psychiatrist for therapy plus medication, targeting anxiety and attentional symptoms with antidepressant and stimulant medication. This was the same psychiatrist to whom Joshua returned after withdrawing from college.

In addition to concerns about Joshua's transient paranoid delusional symptoms and his inconsistent engagement in treatment, his psychiatrist was struck by Joshua's presenting with much more anxious preoccupation and guilt than had been typical over the years of their work together. When his psychiatrist contacted me to discuss the possibility of psychological assessment, she and I engaged in dialog that clarified that aims of the evaluation included better understanding (a) the presence, nature, and severity of disturbances in Joshua's thought processes that might account for the seemingly delusional beliefs, including to what extent the latter might reflect an emerging psychotic condition versus having been circumscribed to substance use, (b) reasons for Joshua's difficulties adjusting to and engaging in college, and (c) what modalities and intensity of treatment he requires. Joshua himself was agreeable to the recommendation for this evaluation, stating his hope that it will help him understand himself better, including his lack of motivation and what is necessary to be a "successful person."

Note that at the time of evaluation, Joshua's only psychotropic medication was an SSRI antidepressant. To get a clear read on the test data—especially on thought disorder indices on performance-based measures—I requested that he remain abstinent from marijuana for at least four weeks prior to the evaluation (which had been scheduled two months beforehand), and drug testing confirmed that he was able to do so.

## Rationale for the assessment battery

Addressing such clinically meaningful and complex referral questions required a multi-method assessment battery (Hopwood & Bornstein, 2014). This entailed self-report, performance-based, and collateral-report methods. Convergence and seeming incongruity among data from different types of methods facilitate weighing confidence in inferences and determining conditions under which they apply (Bram & Peebles, 2014). Given that the primary referral involved questions about thought disorder/psychosis, it was essential to include *performance-based* measures that allow in vivo assessment of reasoning and reality testing. Thus, there was no question that I would include the Rorschach, the gold-standard tool for assessment of thought disorder in clinical practice (Kleiger, 2017), which I administered, scored, and interpreted according to the Rorschach Performance Assessment System (R-PAS; Meyer, Viglione,

Mihura, Erard, & Erdberg, 2011). I also included the Thematic Apperception Test (TAT; Murray, 1943) because that also illuminates aspects of reasoning and reality testing (Bram & Peebles, 2014; Westen, 1991). To assess how Joshua's reasoning might vary under more structured, academic-like conditions—and also to better understand cognitive factors impacting his difficulties in college—I also included the Wechsler Adult Intelligence Scale-Fourth Edition (WAIS-IV; Wechsler, 2008; also see Bram, 2017). These performance-based measures would also be useful in assessing implicit capacities for emotional regulation and relatedness that bear on the second and third referral questions. Although, not a performance-based measure per se, as a psychodynamic assessor, I make use of the patient-examiner relationship as a data source in and of itself (Bram, 2010; Bram & Peebles, 2014; Schafer, 1954). Conceptualized as a "screen test for psychotherapy" (Shectman & Harty, 1986, p. 281), the patient-examiner relationship comprises the patient's attitude toward the assessor and the tests themselves, hypothesis-testing (including testing the limits, which turned out to be crucial in addressing referral questions for Joshua) interventions on the part of the assessor, and judicious use of the examiner's countertransference (Bram & Peebles, 2014).

In terms of *self-report* measures, I included (a) the Multiphasic Personality Inventory—2nd Edition (MMPI-2; Butcher, Dahlstrom, Graham, Tellegen, & Kaemmer, 1989) as a broadband measure to learn about Joshua's more conscious experience of unusual thinking and sensory-perceptual experiences, as well as his style of emotional regulation, his sense of self, and orientation to relationships; (b) the Beck Depression Inventory-II (BDI-II; A.T. Beck, Steer, & Brown, 1996) as a quick-to-administer and score screen of his mood and possible suicidal thinking, in case the latter needed more urgent attention; (c) the Prodromal Questionnaire-16 (PQ-16; Ising et al, 2012) for focused assessment of possible psychotic symptoms; (d) the Trauma History Questionnaire (THQ; Hooper, Stockton, Krupnick, & Green, 2011) and Impact of Events Scale-Revised (IES-R; J.G. Beck et al., 2008) to determine to what extent the tragic early loss of his father continues to impact his functioning; the Bipolar Spectrum Diagnostic Scale (BSDS; Ghaemi, Miller, Berv, Klugman, Rosenquist, & Pies, 2005) to help determine to what extent possible emotional dysregulation involves mania or hypomania; and (e) the Brief Fear of Negative Evaluation Scale (BFNES; Leary, 1983) and Social Phobia Scale (SPS; Mattick & Clarke, 1998) to clarify whether his reported history of eschewing interpersonal interaction is consistent with the fear of negative evaluation and avoidance associated with social anxiety. Although not originally included in the battery, as a result of what Joshua shared with me later in the evaluation (to be described below), I added the Social Media Disorders Scale (SMDS; van den Eijnden, Lemmens, & Valkenburg, 2016) to better clarify the nature, severity, and function of his avoidant behavior.

Finally, I employed the *collateral-report* method in the form of requesting that his mother complete a detailed developmental questionnaire This questionnaire was useful as it helped me determine whether Joshua might have suffered subtle neurodevelopmental delays—perhaps pointing to mild autism spectrum and/or nonverbal learning problems—that might help make sense of his long-standing social difficulties and thus would inform whether it was necessary to add other measures to further investigate these possibilities. Based on his mother's report, it did not seem these were likely diagnostic possibilities, so I decided not to include such measures.

## Summary of findings

I organize the findings around the three referral questions, involving (a) the presence, nature, and severity of disturbances in Joshua's thought processes and reality testing that might account for the seemingly delusional beliefs, (b) understanding psychological factors contributing to Joshua's difficulties functioning in college, and (c) implications for treatment. Note that I will elaborate further on treatment implications in the "Implications and Recommendations" section later in this chapter.

## Referral question #1: Presence, nature, and severity of disturbances in thought processes and reality testing

So here the referral question involved whether Joshua's recent symptoms might be indicative of emerging schizophrenic-spectrum or other psychotic illness as opposed to a brief, substance-induced psychosis. As always, to make sense of the data and make sound inferences and weight with appropriate levels of confidence, I relied on the principles of repetition and convergence of data and aimed to systematically reconcile seemingly incongruous findings through thinking conceptually (Bram & Peebles, 2014). Neither Joshua's s self-report on the MMPI-2 (which was valid; e.g., Lie [L] T = 43, Correction [K] T = 51) nor the Prodromal Questionnaire-16 (PQ-16) pointed in the direction of severe thought disorder or psychosis. Joshua's MMPI-2 profile included a code-type 78, but this was driven by his extreme social withdrawal (Psychoticism T = 59, Introversion T = 92, Psychotic Symptomatology [BIZ$_1$] T = 44, Persecutory Ideas [Pa$_1$] T = 52, Social Alienation [Sc$_1$] T = 76). His score on the PQ-16 Questionnaire was below the threshold for psychosis risk: He endorsed four of the 16 items, whereas six is the research-based threshold. The items that he endorsed on the PQ-16 reflected anhedonia, social anxiety, distractibility by distant sounds, and thoughts being so strong that he can almost hear them; he did not endorse items specific to perceptual abnormalities and delusional thoughts. Moreover, in response to follow-up inquiry, he showed insight that he understood that it was he, not his peers, who had posted on his social media accounts, and that his previous beliefs were likely related to his excessive marijuana use at the time.

Seemingly consistent with his self-reports, Joshua's responses to the performance-based WAIS-IV, Rorschach, and TAT did not point to major impairments in his capacities for logical reasoning and accurate reality testing.

His responses to the Verbal Comprehension subtests of the WAIS-IV were sophisticated, well-articulated, and easy to follow, with the following subtest and scaled scores (SS) noted as follows: Similarities SS = 17; Vocabulary SS = 18; Information SS = 15; and Comprehension SS = 15. His Verbal Comprehension Index (VCI = 141, 99.7th percentile; see Bram, 2017) was well above average. His TAT stories were coherent, tied to the stimuli, and did not involve perceptual distortions. Similarly, his Rorschach profile (here SS = standard score) on the R-PAS did not show significant vulnerabilities to lapses in reasoning (WSumCog SS = 91, SevCog Raw = 0) or reality testing (FQ-% SS = 110; FQo% SS = 113). In addition, when I followed up his three FQ- responses using Rothschild-Yakar et al.'s (2015) testing-the-limits methodology (self-rating on a seven-point scale "To what extent would others see what you saw in this area of the blot?"), Joshua demonstrated insight that others would likely not see what he did on those cards. Nevertheless, although the amalgam of performance-based data appeared to be converging strongly with Joshua's self-report suggesting no disordered thinking/emerging psychosis, there was a seeming incongruity in the data that raised a concern for me that I needed to address before feeling confident about drawing this conclusion. The incongruity was as follows: Joshua was clearly extremely bright and verbal (WAIS-IV General Abilities Index [GAI] = 133, 97th percentile; VCI = 141, 99th percentile), but his R-PAS profile showed his Complexity score and associated variables to be surprisingly low (SS = 85; F% SS = 118; Blend Raw = 0) indicating that his approach to the Rorschach was rather constricted. This pattern struck me, even before I computed the R-PAS scores.

As this constriction was clearly not the result of cognitive limitations, it was a reasonable hypothesis that it served a self-protective function for Joshua. Perhaps through his constricted orientation to the task, Joshua was able to keep a lid on more bizarre perceptions and reasoning that might become evident should he allow himself to be more spontaneous and elaborative? Thus, I thought that it would be crucial to test the limits to see if he might be more vulnerable to such perceptual-cognitive disturbances under different conditions.

To test this hypothesis in the patient-examiner relationship, I relied on Appelbaum's (1959) *altered-atmosphere* procedure (see also Bram & Peebles, 2014). Conducted after the formal Rorschach administration, the altered atmosphere is more relaxed and less test-like: "The patient is invited to glance through the cards again in an altered atmosphere more favorable to informality, spontaneity, and initiative … . He may respond differently, providing information that cannot be obtained with the standardized administration" (p. 179). Appelbaum offered a gist of how he actually did this:

> Directly following the usual test administration, I … discard some of the paraphernalia of the testing situation, implying by my behavior that the test is over. While putting down my pen, shuffling response sheets together, leaning back in the chair, adopting a more conversational tone, I hand all the cards back to the patient and suggest that he go through the cards again

to see whether he might see something else, something perhaps he did not notice before.

(p. 179)

So with Joshua, after the standardized R-PAS administration, I adopted this more casual stance and asked him to "just flip" through the cards one more time and let me know if he saw something new or whether there was anything that he saw before that he did not say. As he reviewed the cards, I returned to my seat but did not lift my pen and stayed silent. Intermittently, he shook his head and looked distressed but did not comment. After all ten cards, he shook his head again and looked up at me sheepishly and anxiously. I asked, "Anything?" "Yeah," Joshua said. Hesitation and then "A lot of dicks ... and stuff like that." I nodded and asked in a gentle, supportive tone if he might show me which cards, where he saw it, and what made it look like that. He pointed to Card III D26 "dicks on the people" (FQo), Card IV D1 "big dick" (FQu), and Card VIII D2 he anxiously struggled to say the word but eventually mumbled, "female genitalia" (FQu). Clarification of these new responses revealed that each of them involved pure Form, and none of his verbalizations was consistent with any cognitive (thought disorder) scores. In terms of the original intent of the testing-the-limits intervention, now I had more confidence in the diagnostic inference that the data did not suggest a major thought disorder/incipient psychotic illness and that the previous episodes were likely substance induced. I will have more to say below, however, about how this testing-the-limits interaction continued in a way that contributed meaningfully to address the second referral question.

Before concluding this summary of findings related to this first referral question, it is crucial to highlight that for the psychodynamic assessor (and hopefully other evaluators as well), questions about disordered thinking and psychosis are not binary ones. That is to say, even if overall findings do not point to a primary psychotic condition, we aim to elucidate *conditions under which* a person might be prone to lapses in—and recovery of—reasoning and reality testing. Such clarification will have implications for supporting adaptive functioning and optimizing engagement in treatment (Bram & Peebles, 2014). To make such conditions-under-which inferences, we examine particular ego functions (or psychological capacities; in this case, reasoning and reality testing) as they vary across and within tests or methods. For Joshua, across-test comparisons revealed that the only lapses he exhibited in reasoning (DV1 Raw = 2, DR1 Raw = 1; two responses that were confusing to follow, though not meriting a formal R-PAS cognitive score) and reality testing (FQ- Raw = 3, FQ-% SS = 110) were on the Rorschach. *This contributed to an inference that Joshua was more vulnerable to slipping in these ego functions under conditions of being more on his own with less support, guidance, and feedback from others* (i.e., conditions of less external structure, analogous to the conditions of the Rorschach; see Bram & Peebles, 2014 and Bram, 2017).

Within-test comparisons—in this case, applying the strategy of configurational analysis (Bram & Peebles, 2014; Schafer, 1954; Weiner, 1998)—involved examining Joshua's individual Rorschach responses that garnered FQ- and/or cognitive scores (or other non-scored confused communications) to ascertain patterns of when such lapses are more likely. For Joshua, two of his three mild cognitive scores (reflecting a loss of precision in language [DV1] and focus [tangential DR1]) occurred on chromatic cards; and of his two confused responses that did not meet criteria for an R-PAS cognitive score, one was on a chromatic card, and the other was in association with a response coded for morbid (MOR) and oral-dependent language (ODL). All three of his FQ- responses were on the fully chromatic cards, two of which also were associated with affect-laden thematic scores (MOR, ODL). Taken together, *I made the additional inference that Joshua's reasoning and reality testing were more likely to be vulnerable under conditions of greater emotional stirring* (akin to the chromatic characteristics of the particular Rorschach cards and the evoked emotional themes).

### Referral question #2: Psychological factors contributing to difficulties functioning in college

A useful way for psychodynamic assessors to conceptualize psychological factors driving manifest symptoms and behaviors involves Peebles' (2012) notion of *underlying developmental disruption (UDD)* (see also Bram & Peebles, 2014). Briefly, we can understand a person's overt symptoms in terms of any combination of the following non-mutually exclusive models of UDD: (a) structural weakness (or ego deficit, i.e., insufficient maturation of psychological capacities), (b) maladaptive character patterns (i.e., rigid, automatic, outside awareness, and ego-syntonic patterns of sense of self, self-protection, thinking, and relating), (c) trauma (i.e., when external events have interfered with one's sense of self and experience of others, and have overwhelmed one's capacities to self-regulate and process information), and/or (d) internal conflict (i.e., unintegrated, competing goals, wishes, motivations, feelings, or aspects of the self). Each model is associated with a different set of treatment implications (Bram & Peebles, 2014; Peebles, 2012). In Joshua's evaluation, the data pointed toward underlying (a) structural weaknesses, (b) trauma, and (c) maladaptive character patterns that contributed to his unsuccessful efforts to function in college. Below, I will review the data that led to these formulations.

#### Structural weaknesses as UDD

Joshua suffered from (a) a profound weakness in his capacity for emotional regulation, manifested in symptoms of severe depression (BDI-II score = 44, severe range; MMPI-2 Scale 2 [Depression] T = 93) and anxiety (MMPI-2 Scale 7 [Psychasthenia] T = 109) that rendered him unable to attend class and complete his schoolwork, (b) uneven cognitive functioning that made it difficult to translate his impressive knowledge-base and verbal capabilities into effective output; and (c) the above-described vulnerability for his logical reasoning and accurate reality testing to lapse when he is more on his own to face unfamiliar and less structured situations, as is the case when one leaves home to go away to college.

*Emotional regulation*

Joshua's underdevelopment in emotional regulation involved strong self-protective efforts to constrict his acknowledgment and expression of what he is feeling (Rorschach F% SS = 118; 5 of his 22 Rorschach responses were noted for his likely being impacted by shading or color but not articulating those determinants;[2] MMPI-2 Repression [R] scale T = 72) and to distance from and avoid situations that are apt to stir him up (Rorschach R8910% SS = 84). His self-reports on the BFNES and SPS further underscored the pervasiveness of his avoidance of social situations that are apt to evoke his intense self-consciousness and fears of negative evaluation. This pattern was another factor contributing to his pattern of avoidance of attending class and subsequent isolation when he has attempted college.

An additional aspect of his difficulty with emotional regulation became clarified as part of aforementioned "altered atmosphere" intervention in the patient-examiner relationship. Recall that when asked for additional responses following standardized Rorschach administration, Joshua offered three responses, all of which involved sexual organs. I inquired whether these were brand new responses or percepts he saw the first time but chose not to report. Joshua responded that he had seen them the first time but did not acknowledge them because he was ashamed. I encouraged Joshua to tell me more about his shame about these responses, and he shared that he had been embarrassed to tell his therapist and me that he spent much of his time alone engaged with online pornography, some of which was quite violent. On the SMDS, referable to his online pornography use, he endorsed eight of nine items, suggesting an addiction-like quality. Joshua added that what troubled him most is that he and his long-distance partner had enacted some of these violent, sadomasochistic sexual fantasies in their phone sex. Tearfully, Joshua shared that this contributed to immense guilt and shame (corroborating and clarifying what his psychiatrist had observed and wondered about), both of which further fueled his depression and massive avoidance. Similar to his past heavy marijuana use, I understood one function of his engagement in pornography to be a maladaptive but desperate means of self-soothing that serves his efforts at emotional escape. The combination of his severe emotional distress and such efforts to avoid and escape contributed to Joshua's having little room for him to focus to engage in the academic and social tasks of college.

Although Joshua's challenges with emotional regulation were considerable, the preponderance of data did not point to these being consistent with characteristics of a bipolar-spectrum condition. His self-report on the MMPI-2 did not indicate the kind of grandiosity or psychomotor acceleration associated with mania (Scale 9 [Mania] T = 43; Psychomotor Acceleration [Ma$_2$] T = 53; Ego Inflation [Ma$_4$] T = 43]), and on the BSDS he indicated that the prototypical profile of mania did not fit him well. Further convergent evidence was found on the Rorschach where he did not demonstrate the type of silly/jocular/fanciful style of reasoning (e.g., FAB = 0, INC = 0) that is often associated with bipolar conditions.

### Uneven cognitive functioning

Generally consistent with findings when he was 13, the data here underscored that the more mechanical skills needed to learn and perform in school (WAIS-IV Working Memory Index [WMI] = 108, 70th percentile; Processing Speed Index [PSI] = 84, 14th percentile, Low Average) were not as well developed as his sophisticated verbal capacities and nonverbal reasoning capacities (General Abilities Index [GAI] = 133, 99th percentile, Very Superior range; Verbal Comprehension Index = 141, 99.7th percentile, Very Superior; Perceptual Reasoning Index [PRI] = 119, 90th percentile, High Average).[3] These findings, especially his slow visual-motor processing speed, suggested that Joshua was apt to know so much more than his output would suggest.[4] One can imagine just how frustrating and even demoralizing it could feel for Joshua to be so bright but have output be so time-consuming and laborious. This has likely played a central role in his history of academic underachievement and challenges to being a productive college student.

### Lapses in logical reasoning and reality testing

As detailed above in the context of the first referral question, Joshua's capacities to reason logically and perceive situations accurately are vulnerable to deterioration under conditions of (a) being more on his own with less external structure and (b) greater emotional stirring. Separating from home and family to attend college in a distant geographic area created such conditions for Joshua, rendering him unable to adequately access these crucial ego functions in the service of making an adaptive adjustment to the social, emotional, and academic demands associated with a major life transition.

### Trauma as UDD

Although Joshua was initially adamant that the early tragic loss of his father was far in the past and thus had little bearing on his current emotional and relational difficulties, the evaluation findings were compelling that this traumatic loss was continuing to exert an impact on him. His self-report on the MMPI-2 pointed generally in this direction (HK scale T = 93), but in response to an interview based on the IES, Joshua acknowledged the extent to which he continues to think about his father, has intrusive thoughts and images of his father's murder, and how hard he works to try to distract himself from and avoid thinking about it. He also shared that it is difficult for him to watch television shows and movies involving themes of police and violent crime. Moreover, Joshua was surprised and dismayed when in response to my encouraging him to reflect on his TAT stories (a patient-examiner testing-the-limits strategy; see Bram & Peebles, 2014) he noticed that they "were mostly about crime and death." When we reviewed his stories, indeed nearly half contained such themes: A woman calling 911 as her home is burglarized (Card 5), rageful and/or vengeful murder (Card 3BM, Line Drawing card)[5], and mourning the death of a spouse (Card 15). I encouraged him to consider the personal meaning of such responses, but after some thought, he was not sure. I then wondered with him (a trial interpretation within the patient-examiner relationship) to what extent these themes embedded in his TAT narratives might possibly be a manifestation of his implicit/unconscious preoccupation and interpersonal outlook colored by the early traumatic loss of his father. Joshua responded that this made sense intellectually, but he reiterated his earlier remark that it was still difficult to accept that the murder of his father had any ongoing impact on him all these years later. This was consistent with his reflection on his set of responses to the IES: Almost apologetically, Joshua expressed that "I feel that I'm making a bigger deal about it than it is." But he also wondered what his life would be like, specifically whether he would be struggling as he is now to launch as an adult, had he grown up with his father. Although trauma as UDD is a broader construct than and is thus not isomorphic with post-traumatic stress disorder (PTSD) according to the *Diagnostic and Statistical Manual, Fifth Edition* (DSM-5; American Psychiatric Association, 2013)/*International Classifications of Diseases and Related Health Problems, 10th Revision* (ICD-10, World Health Organization, 1992; refer to Armstrong, 2011 and Bram & Peebles, 2014), I conceptualized both as applicable to Joshua.

### Maladaptive character patterns as UDD

Joshua's maladaptive sense of himself and styles of emotional self-protection and relating with others were sufficiently ingrained, rigid, automatic, and ego-syntonic to be considered characterological (MMPI-2 code-type 782 suggesting chronic maladjustment). Specifically, his maladaptive character patterns revolved around his (a) profound self-criticism and associated deep-rooted sense of inadequacy, damage, and shame, (b) predominant reliance on emotional and interpersonal avoidance, and (c) relational orientation marked by guardedness and mistrust.

### Self-criticism, inadequacy, and shame

Testing underscored that Joshua's depression was driven by an implicit view of himself as "messed up" and damaged (R-PAS MOR raw = 3 of 22 responses, SS = 118), consistent with his more conscious experience of himself as inadequate, worthless, and a failure (MMPI-2 Code-type 782, Low Self-Esteem [LSE] T = 91; specific BDI-II items). Joshua was harshly self-critical, self-blaming, and laden with guilt (MMPI-2 Self-Alienation [Pd5] scale T = 87). Joshua's massive guilt is entwined with his difficulties developing a healthy, satisfying, and safe attitude toward sexuality (MMPI-2 endorsed three of six critical items around Sexual Concern and Deviation; patient-examiner data emerging from altered atmosphere). As described earlier, he hesitantly but courageously shared with me that his immersive exposure to pornography has impacted his sexual practices in a way that has frightened him and intensified his expectations of being deserving of punishment. Additionally, Joshua consistently overlooked and underestimated his considerable strengths. During the evaluation, this was most evident during the administration of the WAIS-IV when (a) there was often doubt inflected in his voice even when offering correct responses and (b) he expressed discouragement with his performance when he had actually scored close to or above the 99th percentile. He was pleasantly surprised when I offered feedback (another patient-examiner intervention) on his stellar performance, and we discussed ways that his underestimating misappraisals of his capacities interfere with his confidence and persistence in his efforts to complete schoolwork; that is, he is more apt to give up if he *believes* himself to be unsuccessful, even if that may not be true. I hypothesized that Joshua's difficulties accurately self-assessing his capacities and performance were related to his uneven cognitive functioning: It is often confusing for people with such extreme cognitive variability (and confusing for their parents and teachers) to know what level of expectation is appropriate for which kinds of tasks. There is a tendency to expect that if a person is good at one kind of cognitive task, they will be equally good at another, and falling short of such expectations must be the result of lack of effort. Cumulatively, such experiences can contribute to a core sense of oneself as ineffective, helpless, lazy, and no good.

*Avoidant style*

I also understood Joshua's emotional and interpersonal avoidance to reach characterological proportions because of its extremity and pervasiveness and the fact that it had become a default solution to most problems in his life. Joshua acknowledged that were it not for his parents' concerns and encouragement to seek this evaluation and consider treatment options, he would be inclined to keep to himself, stay in his apartment, smoke "a lot of pot," "watch porn," and try not to think about his inability to attend school or work. Despite the entrenched and accepted nature of Joshua's avoidant style of coping, his aforementioned distress about his use of pornography—and ability to share it with me—was a hopeful sign of his potential for therapeutic accessibility and malleability (i.e., at least this aspect was becoming more ego-dystonic).

*Guardedness and mistrust*

Joshua's Rorschach and TAT responses highlight that he had not internalized much of a sense that relationships are the source of meaningful help, connection, and problem-solving. For example, on the Rorschach, he had only a single response scored for Cooperation (COP) and Mutuality of Autonomy Health (MAH; Card II "people high-fiving"), but that was immediately followed by a response on the same card of "blood stain" (coded Morbid [MOR]) suggesting an implicit expectation that even seemingly benign interpersonal contact can suddenly result in injury. Although this was only a single sequence in his Rorschach and there were not converging themes in his other Rorschach and TAT responses, it is possible to wonder whether this sequence hints at the kind of violent, sadomasochistic themes to which he has been drawn through pornography. What was more apparent was that Joshua's TAT stories were notable for the absence of representation of sustained, comforting, or helping relationships. His being on guard for potential mistreatment and harsh judgment was evident on both performance-based (R-PAS complexity adjusted Vigilance Composite [V-Comp] SS = 119) and self-report measures (elevated BFNES score). As part of the ongoing process of feedback during the evaluation, when I discussed these findings with him, Joshua acknowledged how difficult it is for him to ask for help because of his anticipation of criticism and judgment and that, because these expectations are so embedded, typically it does not even occur to him that he might ask for it. He shared that while away at college and struggling, he did think of seeking help from the student counseling center but ultimately felt too ashamed to reach out to them. It is important to note that Joshua's shying away from people is *not* the result of an inherent lack of interest in people (R-PAS H = 3, SS = 106, M = 5 SS = 109). In fact, there was evidence not only that he is interested in people but that he also has strong implicit longings to be taken care of and nurtured (R-PAS ODL% SS = 114). These data provide a window in the internal bind he is— longing for connection and care but expecting it to be inaccessible or fraught with risk (MMPI-2 782 code-type).

## Referral question #3: Implications for treatment

Although I will elaborate later in the "Implications and Recommendations" section about the modalities and intensity of treatment necessary for Joshua, here I present some psychological strengths that stood out as relevant to his treatment and prognosis. My sense has been that as psychodynamicallyoriented assessors, we are wont to pay short shrift to our patient's strengths and how those can be accessed in treatment. First, it would be important that treaters recognize and consider ways of capitalizing on Joshua's considerable intellectual and verbal gifts (as noted above, WAIS-IV GAI and VCI at or above the 99th percentile; Similarities SS = 17), pointing to his potential to make use of insight-oriented and psychoeducational interventions.[6] Also a notable strength was that despite being avoidant of and fearful of his feelings (as detailed above), Joshua actually possessed a fairly well-developed emotional vocabulary. On the TAT, his narratives were marked by an ability to appreciate and articulate a nuanced range of emotions (e.g., from "happy" and "scared" to "exasperated," "remorse," "rage," and "betrayed") for his characters. This suggested a potential to apply such language *to himself in real time* in a way that will enable him to better contain, contextualize, and convey his internal experience in treatment. Another strength boding well prognostically was that Joshua displayed a burgeoning curiosity about his emotional life. In particular, when encouraged to reflect on test responses[7] suggestive of anger [AGC Complexity Adjusted SS = 110, e.g., Card I "angry face," Card IV "Godzilla"; TAT stories involving rageful characters], he expressed: "I never used to admit I was angry. I'd just be passive-aggressive. Now I realize I'm angry but don't know why. I need to work to understand that." This was a meaningful shift in what he was able to acknowledge and share because the MMPI-2, which he had completed just days earlier, indicated that he was less likely to view and present himself as angry (Aggressiveness [AGGR] T = 33, Irritability [$ANG_2$] T = 51). That he was receptive and thoughtful to my earlier interpretation linking his TAT stories about "crime and death" to the ongoing impact of the loss of his father was also a hopeful sign of his ability to make use of more expressive psychoanalytic interventions.

### ICD-10 and PDM-2 diagnoses

Though the primary aim of evaluations that I conduct is typically not a taxonomic diagnosis (ICD-10 or DSM-5), it was possible to arrive at such diagnoses that did offer some broad-strokes guidance for pharmacotherapy and other aspects of treatment. These include:

F32.2 Major Depressive Disorder, Severe, without Psychotic Features
F43.12 Post-Traumatic Stress Disorder
F12.150 Cannabis Use Disorder with Delusions, moderate-to-severe, in remission
F40.10 Social Anxiety Disorder
F63.9 Impulse Disorder, Unspecified (referable to pornography use)
F60.6 Avoidant Personality Disorder

From the vantage point of the *Psychodynamic Diagnostic Manual, Second Edition* (PDM-2; Lingiari & McWilliams, 2017), the following diagnoses were applicable to Joshua:

**Level of Personality Organization**: Borderline
**Personality Syndromes (P Axis)**: Anxious-avoidant and phobic
**Mental Functioning (M Axis)**: Significant defects in basic mental functions
**Symptom Patterns (S Axis)**: Major Depressive Disorder, Cannabis Use
    Disorder with Delusions (in remission), Post-Traumatic Stress Disorder,
    Social Anxiety Disorder, Unspecified Impulse Disorder

As I have written elsewhere (Bram, 2013; Bram & Peebles, 2014), I believe that psychological testing is most conducive to what Peebles (2012) referred to as *treatment-centered diagnosis*. This diagnostic understanding includes, among other things, a conceptualization of the UDD, along with implications for therapeutic alliance. I detailed the treatment-centered diagnosis in the "Summary of Findings" section above. Essentially, this involved Joshua's structural weaknesses (emotional regulation, uneven cognitive functioning, and reasoning and reality testing), psychological sequelae of trauma referable to the tragic early loss of his father, and maladaptive character patterns (centering around avoidance, shame, and mistrust), the latter of which has interfered with his ability to seek and accept help.

## Implications and recommendations

Based on these findings, I concluded that Joshua would benefit from a long-term, multi-modal, stepwise treatment plan. Given the severity of Joshua's depression and anxiety alongside proneness to avoidance that makes consistent access to outpatient treatment and other supports so challenging, residential treatment would be essential to gain therapeutic traction. An optimal residential program for Joshua would be geared specifically for young adults and their developmental needs, offer an integration of skill-building, relational and pharmacological interventions, and offer services to treat people with difficulties around substance use/addictions. It is worth underscoring here that a good psychodynamic understanding can link to interventions that are not necessarily psychoanalytic in technique. Thus, in terms of skill-building, group interventions applying dialectical behavior therapy (DBT) could help strengthen his capacities for emotional regulation; and cognitive-behavioral therapy (CBT; e.g., cognitive restructuring, exposure, and assertiveness/socials skills training) can more specifically target his longstanding, pronounced social anxiety and assist him to appraise himself in more realistic, positive ways. Because of his mistrust, shame, and disinclination to accept help, it would be important for treaters in the program to recognize that his engagement and collaboration would not be given from the outset and would need to be an aim in and of itself and thus take time to cultivate.

The new understanding involving the profound roles of shame, trauma, sexual preoccupations, and characterological factors indicated that there was more than just a need for skill-building in the residential setting. Specifically, these revelations illuminated the additional need for a more relationally based, expressive treatment to provide a safe, private space to help better understand and process, among other things, the impact of trauma, his sexual longings, and associated object relations paradigms. Aforementioned strengths in his intelligence, verbal ability (including the ability to think abstractly), emotional vocabulary, and burgeoning curiosity and reflectiveness would serve him well in this more traditional psychotherapeutic work. Moreover, my testing-the-limits interventions and Joshua's responses to them allowed me to explicate the following considerations for his therapist and other treaters to hold in mind—the importance of (a) appreciating that there is likely more going on under the surface for Joshua than is immediately apparent, (b) attunement to the role of shame in limiting discussion of important themes, and (c) consideration of potential ways of loosening some of the formality of the therapeutic atmosphere (akin to the "altered atmosphere" intervention) in a way that might make him less apt to feel judged. Among other things, the latter might include the therapist's speaking in a less formal, more casual manner, refraining from taking in-session notes, and not adhering rigidly to a predetermined treatment protocol.

Following at least several months in a residential program, the next step would likely be a partial/day hospital program where Joshua could continue the skill-building group work and (depending on the location) resume individual psychotherapy with his outpatient therapist, and receive support around maintaining sobriety (essential as marijuana serves his massive efforts at avoidance and risks reactivating psychotic symptoms). The transition to a partial hospital program would need to involve assisting him to establish a living situation that would mitigate against isolation and to allow him to demonstrate an ability to access outpatient services.

The subsequent transition to intensive outpatient would involve meeting with his therapist multiple times a week, attending groups to be identified and prioritized based on his needs at the time, working part-time, and gradually returning to college (i.e., beginning with a course or two at a time). Depending on his ability to follow through on treatment recommendations independently, the need for a case manager could be considered. It would be essential that Joshua's return to school be scaffolded by regular meetings with an executive function coach/tutor who can assist him to organize and problem-solve assignments and to whom he would feel accountable. Along similar lines, he would benefit from support to proactively contact the disability services on campus to facilitate communication with his instructors. It is hoped by this time, though, that with intensive treatment under his belt, Joshua would be more confident and capable of seeking out help and advocating for himself at school and elsewhere.

I concluded my test report on this hopeful note,

> Although a challenging road of treatment is ahead, Joshua's significant strengths—notably his intellectual and verbal gifts, not to mention, the curiosity and courage he exhibited during the evaluation—and the supportiveness of his family, there is good reason for hope that with some time he can complete college and gradually become the successful person he wishes to be.

## Feedback

In this kind of collaborative psychoanalytic assessment, feedback is not just an endpoint of the evaluation, but it is a *dynamic process* embedded in the patient-examiner relationship throughout (Berg, 1985; Bram & Peebles, 2014).

Feedback is aimed at encouraging curiosity, reflectiveness, and self-understanding as well as testing hypotheses as part of the psychotherapeutic "screen test" (Shectman & Harty, 1986, p. 281). With Joshua, recall that feedback included (a) informing him of his impressive showing on WAIS-IV subtests, which opened a discussion of his self-critical misappraisals of his performance and how that impedes him in school and (b) encouraging him to consider the meaning of his TAT stories and/or Rorschach responses, leading to recognition of his anger and the ongoing traumatic impact of his early loss. Notice that in these examples, feedback was *not* a unidirectional, static moment of my telling Joshua about the test findings and his merely being a passive receptable of this information.

Following the testing itself and completing the writeup the following week, I met with Joshua, and we read through my report in detail. Typically, I write reports to be accessible to the patient, family, referring clinician, and other treaters. We met for 90 minutes, and because the feedback had been ongoing throughout the assessment, there were no major surprises for him in the findings. He was ambivalent, though, about his parents' seeing the part of the report involving his revelation of his pornography use, but ultimately he agreed—in the interest of "trying to be more open about my struggles and what I need"—for us to leave it in for them to see. Regarding my recommendation for residential treatment, which we had not discussed during testing sessions, I anticipated his reaction so in the report tagged the following to this recommendation:

> It is crucial to emphasize that the thought of a residential treatment in general is likely to be highly anxiety-provoking for Joshua, as it would be an immediate confrontation of his social anxiety and mistrust without being readily able to avoid. Thus, it will take some time for him to consider this recommendation and then to acclimate to a program and to develop trusting relationships with individual treaters.

As expected, his initial response to the idea of residential treatment was negative, and he tried to make a case for continuing as an outpatient. I believe that my including the aforementioned caveat in the report helped Joshua recognize that his hesitation was entwined with the difficulties that had him feeling so stuck in his life. After my subsequent feedback session with his parents (he had consented to my sharing the report and meeting with them), they clearly saw the need for residential treatment, worked to secure the financial resources, and had a series of conversations with Joshua that eventuated in his reluctant willingness to enter such a program. Of course, I also shared the report with and had a follow-up phone call with Joshua's psychiatrist, and she was appreciative of the thoroughness of the evaluation, the ruling out of a currently emerging psychotic illness, the enhanced understanding of Joshua's guilt, and the recognition of his urgent need for a more intensive level of care. She was able to assist Joshua's family consider different options for residential treatment.

## Assessor reflections

Two related points stood out to me when reflecting back on this evaluation. First, my work with Joshua underscored the essentiality of optimizing use of the patient-examiner relationship. I learned so much more about Joshua and how he might respond to different therapeutic interventions—and he learned so much more about himself—than I/we would have otherwise as a result of our engaging around the data in real time. Second, this assessment reminded me of how important it is to conduct assessments with an attitude of curiosity, puzzlement about seeming incongruities, and openness to surprise. Recall that it was my effort to grapple with the incongruity between Joshua's low R-PAS Complexity score and his Very Superior WAIS-IV GAI that led to my "altered atmosphere" intervention, which facilitated Joshua's opening up about his immense shame, the source of it, and how it was related to his pervasive avoidance. This is an attitude that will likely serve assessors well regardless of the setting in which they work.

## Notes

1 In my geographic area around a major city in the northeast of the United States., neuropsychological evaluations have become very common and are now often the default first-line assessment referral made by mental health clinicians. In my view, neuropsychologists who can integrate sophisticated personality assessment are in short supply (c.f., Yalof, 2006, for an illustration of how this integration might occur).

2 In the Rapaport tradition (Rapaport, Gill, and Schafer, 1968; also see Lerner, 1998); I am referring to what Mary Jo Peebles and I have called "determinant qualifiers" (Bram & Peebles, 2014). This can involve noting when color or shading determinant likely impacted a patient's response but it is avoided or denied when clarifying determinants. For example, I noted a "C avoid" for Joshua's Card III response "butterfly" to the red D3 location when he articulated only Form as a determinant when it was likely that the color had something to do with his generating this response.

3 The differences between his lower PSI and his VCI, PRI, WMI were not only statistically significant but clinically significant (i.e., exceedingly rare; Base Rates respectively were 1.0%, 1.1%, and 6.7%). Note too that although his WMI was in the Average range, it was significantly lower than his Very Superior VCI, both statistically and clinically (Base Rate = 0.8%).

4 Because his earlier evaluation made use of an abbreviated intelligence test that did not assess processing speed, it was not clear to what extent Joshua's depression might have exacerbated what was already slower processing speed.

5 This was Card 10 from TAT Series B (Bram & Peebles, 2014; Morgan, 2003), which was part of the set used at the Menninger Clinic in Topeka and that I continue to use.

6 Psychoeducational and other interventions would also need to take into account his more modest working memory and significantly slowed visual-motor processing speed.

7 Encouragement to reflect on the meaning of one's test responses is another patient-examiner testing-of-limits intervention (see Bram & Peebles, 2014).

## References

Albee, G. W. (1963). American psychology in the sixties. *American Psychologist, 18*(2), 90–95.
American Psychiatric Association (2013). *Diagnostic and statistical manual* (5th ed.). Washington, DC: American Psychiatric Press.

Appelbaum, S. A. (1959). The effect of altered psychological atmosphere on Rorschach responses: A new supplementary procedure. *Bulletin of the Menninger Clinic, 23*, 179–189.

Armstrong, J. (2011). *Trauma is more than PTSD: Preview of APA's trauma clinical assessment guidelines*. Paper presented at the Society for Personality Assessment. Boston, MA.

Beck, A. T., Steer, R. A., & Brown, G. K. (1996). *Beck depression inventory-II*. San Antonio, TX: The Psychological Corporation.

Beck, J. G., Grant, D. M., Read, J. M., Clapp, J. D., Coffey, S. F., Miller, L. M., & Palyo, S. A. (2008). The impact of event scale–revised: Psychometric properties in a sample of motor vehicle accident survivors. *Journal of Anxiety Disorders, 22*(2), 187–198.

Benjamin, L. T. (2005). A history of clinical psychology as a profession in America (and a glimpse into its future). *Annual Review of Clinical Psychology, 1*(1), 1–30.

Berg, M. (1985). The feedback process in diagnostic psychological testing. *Bulletin of the Menninger Clinic, 49*(1), 52–69.

Bram, A. (2018). Understanding a therapeutic impasse: Use of R-PAS in a multi-method assessment of alliance dynamics and underlying developmental disruption. In J. Mihura & G. Meyer (Eds.), *Applications of the Rorschach performance assessment system* (pp. 119–137). New York: Guilford.

Bram, A. D. (2010). The relevance of the Rorschach and patient-examiner relationship in treatment planning and outcome assessment. *Journal of Personality Assessment, 92*(2), 91–115.

Bram, A. D. (2013). Psychological testing and treatment implications: We can say more. *Journal of Personality Assessment, 95*(4), 319–331.

Bram, A. D. (2015). To resume a stalled psychotherapy? Psychological testing to understand an impasse and reevaluate treatment options. *Journal of Personality Assessment, 97*(3), 241–250.

Bram, A. D. (2017). Reviving and refining psychodynamic interpretation of the Wechsler intelligence tests: The verbal comprehension subtests. *Journal of Personality Assessment, 99*(3), 324–333.

Bram, A. D., & Peebles, M. J. (2014). *Psychological testing that matters: Creating a road map for effective treatment*. Washington, DC: American Psychological Association.

Bram, A. D., & Yalof, J. (2015). Quantifying complexity: Personality assessment and its relationship with psychoanalysis. *Psychoanalytic Inquiry, 35*(Suppl. 1), 74–97.

Butcher, J. N., Dahlstrom, W. G., Graham, J. R., Tellegen, A., & Kaemmer, B. (1989). *Minnesota multiphasic personality inventory-2 (MMPI-2): Manual for administration and scoring*. Minneapolis, MN: University of Minnesota Press.

Fischer, C. T. (1994). *Individualizing psychological assessment: A collaborative and therapeutic approach*. New York: Routledge.

Ghaemi, S. N., Miller, C. J., Berv, D. A., Klugman, J., Rosenquist, K. J., & Pies, R. W. (2005). Sensitivity and specificity of a new bipolar spectrum diagnostic scale. *Journal of Affective Disorders, 84*(2–3), 273–277.

Hooper, L., Stockton, P., Krupnick, J., & Green, B. (2011). Development, use, and psychometric properties of the Trauma history questionnaire. *Journal of Loss and Trauma, 16*(3), 258–283.

Hopwood, C. J., & Bornstein, R. F. (Eds.) (2014). *Multimethod clinical assessment*. New York: Guilford.

Ising, H. K., Veling, W., Loewy, R. L., Rietveld, M. W., Rietdijk, J., Sara Dragt, K., … van der Gaag, M. (2012). The validity of the 16-Item version of the prodromal questionnaire (PQ-16) to screen for ultra high risk of developing psychosis in the general help-seeking population. *Schizophrenia Bulletin, 38*(6), 1288–1296.

Kleiger, J. H. (2017). *Rorschach assessment of psychotic phenomena.* New York: Routledge.

Klopfer, B., Ainsworth, M. D., Klopfer, W. G., & Holt, R. R. (1954). *Developments in the Rorschach technique* (vol. 1). San Diego, CA: Harcourt Brace Jovanovich.

Leary, M. R. (1983). A brief version of the fear of negative evaluation scale. *Personality and Social Psychology Bulletin, 9*(3), 371–376.

Lerner, P. (1998). *Psychoanalytic perspectives on the Rorschach.* Hillsdale, NJ: The Analytic Press.

Lingiardi, V., & McWilliams, N. (Eds.) (2017). *Psychodynamic diagnostic manual* (2nd ed.). New York: Guilford.

Mattick, R. P., & Clarke, J. C. (1998). Development and validation of measures of social phobia scrutiny fear and social interaction anxiety. *Behaviour Research and Therapy, 36*(4), 455–470.

Meyer, G. J., Viglione, D. J., Mihura, J. L., Erard, R. E., & Erdberg, P. (2011). *Rorschach performance assessment System: Administration, coding, interpretation, and technical manual.* Toledo, OH: Rorschach Performance Assessment System, L.L.C.

Michalski, D., Mulvey, T., & Kohout, J. (2010). *2008: APA survey of psychology health service providers.* APA Center for Workforce Studies. Downloaded 7/11/19 from https://www.apa.org/workforce/publications/08-hsp/?tab=1.

Morgan, W. G. (2003). Origin and history of the "Series B" and "Series C" TAT pictures. *Journal of Personality Assessment, 81*, 133–148. doi:10.1207/S15327752JPA8102_05.

Murray, H. (1943). *Thematic apperception test manual.* Cambridge, MA: Harvard University Press.

Peebles, M. J. (2012). *Beginnings: The art and science of planning psychotherapy* (2nd ed.). New York: Routledge.

Rapaport, D., Gill, M., & Schafer, R. (1968). *Diagnostic psychological testing* (rev. ed.). New York: International Universities Press.

Ridenour, J. M. (this volume). Psychodynamic psychological testing in residential and hospital-based settings. In J. Yalof & A. D. Bram (Eds.), *Psychodynamic psychological testing in different settings.* New York: Routledge.

Rothschild-Yakar, L., Lacoua, & Koren, D. (2015). *Validation of a new Rorschach-based method to assess insight into problems in thought and perception: A population-based study among adolescents with and without attenuated psychosis symptoms.* Paper presented at the annual meeting of the Society for Personality Assessment, Brooklyn, NY.

Schafer, R. (1954). *Psychoanalytic interpretation of Rorschach testing.* New York: Grune & Stratton.

Shakow, D. (Chairman), Brotemarkle, R. A., Doll, E. A., Kinder, E. F., Moore, B. V., & Smith, S. (1945). Graduate internship training in psychology. Report by the subcommittee on graduate internship training to the committee on graduate and professional training of the American psychological association and the American association for applied psychology. *Journal of Consulting Psychology, 9*, 243–266.

Shectman, F., & Harty, M. K. (1986). Treatment implications of object relationships as they unfold during the diagnostic interaction. In M. Kissen (Ed.), *Assessing object relations phenomena* (pp. 279–303). Madison, CT: International Universities Press.

van den Eijnden, R. J. J. M., Lemmens, J. S., & Valkenburg, P. M. (2016). The social media disorders scale. *Computers in Human Behavior, 61*, 478–487.

Wechsler, D. (2008). Wechsler *adult intelligence scale-fourth edition* (WAIS-IV). San Antonio, TX: The Psychological Corporation.

Weiner, I. B. (1998). *Principles of Rorschach interpretation.* Mahwah, NJ: Lawrence Erlbaum.

Westen, D. (1991). Clinical assessment of object relations using the TAT. *Journal of Personality Assessment, 56*(1), 56–74.

World Health Organization. (1992). *International statistical classification of diseases and related health problems* (10th Revision). Geneva: World Health Organization.

Yalof, J., & Rosenstein, D. (2014). Psychoanalytic interpretation of superego functioning following CS readministration procedures: Case illustration. *Journal of Personality Assessment, 96*(2), 192–203.

# 3   Through a psychoanalytic lens

## A sharpened view of neuropsychological assessment

*Sharon Leak*

Each referral for psychological assessment embodies unique individuals and circumstances: There is the referring clinician or institution, the psychologist carrying out the assessment, and the "audience" who will receive the report. There is the explicit referral question that has been posed, alongside a possible implicit or unformulated query, goal, or agenda. And there is the setting in which the psychologist meets with the individual, and possibly others connected with the assessment, to carry out the clinical interview and administer a carefully selected set of measures.

Bringing a psychoanalytic mindset to such an encounter enriches the assessment experience for all parties involved—and enhances its diagnostic utility. This occurs in perhaps uniquely unexpected ways when a neuropsychological question precipitates the referral (Leak, 2019). In this chapter, I bring together intertwining threads of individuals and circumstances in the setting of an increasingly frequent neuropsychological assessment query, one that is posed across the age span for children, adolescents, and adults: Does this person have an attention–deficit disorder (ADHD; American Psychiatric Association, 2013)? By moving beyond the strictly "neuropsychological" when carrying out an ostensibly neurocognitive evaluation, it becomes possible to appreciate the value of applying a psychoanalytic mindset to all aspects and stages of the assessment process.

## Description of setting and brief literature review

As a clinical psychologist who works in private practice with children, adolescents, and adults, I carry out all assessments in the physical space of my office; this is my current "setting" but not the only one in which I've ever worked. Further, there is a broader backdrop, or setting, to consider. Whether responding to a request for psychological evaluation from the physical vantage point of my office, a school, or an inpatient unit, two related questions have remained pertinent: Who will be listening to me as I talk about my findings and who will be reading my report? In the setting of a neuropsychological inquiry related to ADHD, from whichever physical space it originates, I am expected to translate neurocognitive data into a language that communicates a patient's strengths and vulnerabilities; further, for psychological testing to "matter" to the individual and to those who will take up the findings, I must connect results to an individual's daily functioning and proposed interventions (Bram & Peebles, 2014).

What is *less* expected in the realm of neuropsychology, but often welcomed after initial puzzlement or skepticism, is bringing a psychoanalytic mindset to the assessment process. Whether the psychological evaluation confirms that ADHD is a primary contributor to a patient's challenges, or is intertwined with other issues that carry equal weight, or is more apparent than real, psychoanalytic principles must play a central role in testing that aims to understand the patient, first and foremost, as a person (Bornstein, 2010; Bram & Yalof, 2015; Leak & Hayden, 2015; Meersand, 2011; Yalof, 2006). Psychoanalytic thinking is especially unexpected in the setting of a neuropsychological inquiry for ADHD, where one finds an amplification of the pervasive problem of relying heavily on self-report measures (Bornstein, 2001) and "widespread and uncritical use" of impressionistic, subjective rating scales that "may be more a measure of the discomfort of the parent or teacher than of the disability of the child" (Carey, 2002).

Psychologists who move beyond a descriptive approach—who instead carry out in-depth assessments—face the challenge of translating psychoanalytic insights about intertwined neurocognitive and personality data into a language that is at once accurate and understandable to their audience. In my practice, I am typically preparing the report not only with the referring clinician, school, or agency in mind, but also with a plan to give a copy of the report to the patient (or, in the case of children and adolescents, to the parents). In the setting of sharing such neuropsychological data, I have found several ways to maintain the integrity of the test findings, while also respecting patient confidentiality and the potentially deep impact on patients of learning their test results.

### Editing or amending the comprehensive report

For virtually all psychological assessments, I prepare two reports. First, I create a comprehensive report that includes background information, clinical observations, test scores, analysis and interpretation of the data, and my clinical formulation and recommendations. Then, I edit or amend the report to best serve the patient and the audience. At one end of the report-writing spectrum, when the patient or family will be sharing the written report with those who are less psychologically sophisticated or have less stringent safeguards around confidentiality (for example, schools, including colleges, and some medical professionals), I edit the report to remove or diffuse sensitive background information and clinical diagnoses. I might change my detailed description of a multigenerational history of dyslexia, ADHD, and bipolar disorder in the patient's family to a simple statement: "A history of learning and emotional challenges in the extended family is pertinent to the current assessment." I then give patients (or parents) copies of both reports, allowing them to share whichever report they choose with other parties.

At the other end of the report-writing spectrum, when I am writing for referring clinicians who will use the test results to inform continuing therapeutic work with adult patients, I amend the report: I expand upon the potential benefits or pitfalls of integrating medication with psychotherapy, transference/countertransference dynamics, and other issues pertinent to an ongoing treatment. Knowing that these subtler clinical issues will *not* be included in the patient's report, I explain my procedure to patients at the outset: I will write a comprehensive report for them, with a clinical addendum included in the therapist's copy; I obtain the patient's written consent. At the end of the evaluation, I discuss the findings in a feedback session with the patient. I then forward copies of both reports to the therapist, with the understanding that the patient will arrange to read the comprehensive report in the therapist's waiting room just before a therapy session, or in the session itself; this allows the patient to absorb the written material in a protected setting, and then choose to keep the report or leave it with the therapist.

The experience of reading a clinical document about oneself has the potential to be disorganizing, no matter how sensitively information is conveyed. Indeed, it was after a patient's deeply troubling response some years ago that I developed my current practice of disseminating the written report to adult patients via a collaborative session with the referring therapist: In the feedback session, a young woman had responded to my explanation of her attention problems with reflective comments, conveying a sense of feeling understood and better able to understand herself. I had no qualms about giving her the written report, and she left with it in hand. Shortly after leaving my office, however, upon reading in the background information that her openly provocative behavior embarrassed her parents and brother—information that she herself had conveyed to me without evident concern—she experienced a moment of deep despair and cut herself so severely that she required inpatient hospitalization. Having learned that it is not possible to know how information from a report will be taken in, I now take care to arrange for the patient to read the material within the protected environment of the therapeutic relationship.

Indeed, in the setting of neuropsychological assessments that focus on determining the potential contribution of attention or learning problems to presenting concerns (and true in the case just described), I have found a shifting tide in recent years: Patients can be disappointed to find that they do *not* have ADHD or a learning disability. They may react negatively to test findings, either immediately or at a later point in time, when their presenting complaints of an apparently neurocognitive nature are discovered to be the result of a mood or anxiety disorder or tied to the patient's personality structure. A similar reaction may occur when apparent underachievement is *not* found to be the result of ADHD or a learning disability, but rather is a function of having average intelligence that does not equip one with the intellectual resources to perform well in a highly competitive setting. For some patients, an emotional or personality disorder feels more damning and less amenable to concrete intervention: How does one proceed in the absence of a "legitimate" claim to stimulant medication or support services? However, for others, there is a deep interest in grappling with the alternative psychodynamic conceptualization that the assessment illuminates; catalyzing this interest is but one goal of such assessments.

### The language of neurocognitive vulnerabilities and psychoanalytic thinking

As I speak to patients and write reports, I try to avoid unnecessary clinical jargon, instead aiming for language that will capture both the subjective experience of the patient and another's observations. At times, this involves "translating" problematic behaviors into less shaming words—phrasing that aligns with the patient's inner experience but also acknowledges the observer's perspective. Or, when a clinical term (such as a formal diagnosis) is warranted, I redefine it in the language of everyday experience. So, for a patient with ADHD who is observed to make frequent "careless errors," I talk about vulnerabilities in selective attention that make it challenging to remain attuned to details that others process quickly and automatically. Or for a patient who becomes "paranoid" when asked to carry out certain tasks, I describe the area of neurocognitive vulnerability (for example, weak reading fluency) that leaves the patient feeling exposed and shamed if asked to read aloud—and "suspicious" of the intentions of those who demand public performance. These subjective descriptions resonate with the patient, validate the observer's perspective, and alert all involved to the need for interventions or accommodations that address the underlying issue without blaming or shaming (Leak & Hayden, 2015).

Similarly, because narcissistic disorders are readily intertwined with ADHD or give rise to symptoms that mimic attention problems (Leak, 2019; Morrell, 1998), I explain the personality disorder from within to minimize feelings of shame: "Diagnostically, the clinical history and test data are consistent with a narcissistic character structure that sets the stage for fluctuating anxious and depressive states, and a fragile sense of self; attention, concentration, and memory can become compromised in this context." I continue,

> It is critical to note that narcissism as a clinical term captures something important and different from the pejorative use of the word by the lay person, where "narcissistic" conveys the image of a boastful, self-centered, and demanding person. The clinical term captures instead the difficulty maintaining an image of oneself as lovable, desirable, and capable in the absence of external affection, admiration, and support.

And to capture aspects of a particular male patient's presentation, I add,

> One sees a sensitivity to the reactions of others, a consciously self-effacing manner, and vulnerability to feeling shame and humiliation. Although a quiet and at times unanchored belief in his talents lies beneath his surface

inhibition, he lacks the confidence rooted in a true integration of strengths and limitations

A detailed clinical vignette will illustrate the value of applying psychoanalytic thinking to a neuropsychological evaluation where the referral question focused on determining whether ADHD was contributing to the patient's challenges. As noted earlier, all aspects and stages of the testing process are enriched when a psychoanalytic mindset shapes the assessment.

## Case background

### Referring concerns

Ms. T, a 48-year-old newly divorced mother of three adolescents, was referred for psychological evaluation shortly after initiating psychotherapy with an experienced male psychiatrist and adult psychoanalyst. Ms. T had entered treatment to disentangle her long history of learning and emotional challenges. During her school years, she struggled across all academic domains, finding math especially difficult. As she moved from childhood into adolescence and adulthood, she had problems with everyday aspects of attention, concentration, and memory: Ms. T described losing focus during conversations, "drifting" while reading books, poorly recalling what she had talked about with others, failing to retrieve names or words when "on the spot," and "blanking out" in the face of cognitively challenging tasks. Most recently, her already high level of anxiety had reached new heights, exacerbating preexisting challenges while also disorganizing and paralyzing her attempts to initiate and complete critical tasks.

Ms. T decided to enter psychotherapy when her curiosity and concern were piqued by a friend's comment: "You look like *you* have ADD," said this woman, whose son had just been diagnosed with attention problems. After several sessions, Ms. T's psychiatrist agreed that she met some descriptive criteria for the disorder, but his psychoanalytic training alerted him to other possibilities. The dyad decided to seek a formal assessment. At the most general level, therapist and patient sought to identify the relative contributions of neurocognitive and emotional factors. More specific questions touched on the past, present, and future: What made it so difficult for Ms. T to learn as a child? What caused her mind to "go blank" in the middle of conversations? Did intrapsychic conflicts play a role in her uneven attention and memory? Would Ms. T benefit from a medication trial? Did the findings suggest types of work that she should avoid or seek out?

### Childhood

Ms. T grew up as the oldest of three children and only girl in a troubled but intact family. Her father was a businessman who preferred the pleasures of domestic life to his career; in the evenings, he served as a protective buffer against her mother, a domineering primary caregiver whose intellect might have been better channeled into a professional life. Ms. T experienced her mother as a frightening force—unaffectionate and unsentimental, critical and complaining. And, when the family moved from their bustling city neighborhood to a rural community as Ms. T was preparing to enter school, her mother became physically abusive to her daughter in this isolated setting. Her mother, to her credit, recognized that this behavior was arising from her own misery and a repetition of her troubled childhood. She sought play therapy for Ms. T that ultimately protected them both from the physical expressions of the mother's anger, but the frightening emotional climate remained largely unchanged. Ms. T felt free—as if a burden of guilt had lifted and that she could become an adult—only when her mother died when Ms. T was in her 30's.

Ms. T's mother told her daughter of suffering from severe morning sickness while pregnant with her, but she shared no other information about the pregnancy or delivery. Nor did she share memories of her daughter's infancy and early childhood, leaving me with only the minimal history of prenatal and early childhood development that Ms. T herself could recall. Unfortunately, I did not have access to additional information about her mother's pregnancy or delivery; nor did Ms. T have collateral information, such as baby books documenting early developmental milestones or school records of behavior or academics, to corroborate her recollections. I could not determine, for example, whether there were challenges in motor development that are often present for those with ADHD (Bird, 2002) or the delayed speech and insensitivity to rhyme that are typical of individuals with dyslexia (Shaywitz, 2003).

Ms. T recalled enjoying good physical health as a child and adult, with no history of hospitalization (apart from childbirth), serious illness, head trauma, or seizures. Her challenges, as she recalled, became evident upon entering school. Ms. T remembered herself as a timid, well-behaved student who was creative and artistic but weak at academics. She experienced herself as a slow reader and poor speller, although she gradually discovered books and enjoyed reading despite her uneven focus. Math was her nemesis: She especially had difficulty learning multiplication tables, relying instead on serial addition. Only when asked about her performance in visually based math did Ms. T recall that she more easily learned long division, fractions, and percentages; she later avoided advanced math courses, never taking algebra or geometry.

### Adulthood

Upon graduating from high school, Ms. T entered a two-year arts program that allowed her to pursue her interest in photography. She met her future husband in this context, marrying him at the urging of others who considered him a "good match" for her, rather than because she fell in love or shared his values. Her three children, with whom she reported good relationships, made the marriage worthwhile; but when she no longer felt valued by their father, she decided to pursue a divorce. At the time of the evaluation, she had established a comfortable dating life and was beginning to pursue freelance work based on her talent in photography.

### Clinical observations and structure of the assessment

Ms. T presented for evaluation as an artfully attired, impeccably groomed woman who tentatively disclosed her anxiety about being tested at the initial clinical interview—her worry that her inadequacies would be painfully exposed: She would be relieved to have an explanation of her learning challenges in the form of an ADHD or dyslexia diagnosis, but she would also feel a great deal of shame. Ms. T revealed, too, that she had "fled" several prior psychotherapy relationships after only a few sessions, when she began to doubt that the therapists were attuned to her issues, including a need for clear boundaries. She was not yet experiencing a need to flee her current treatment and hoped that the testing would allow her to prevent another abrupt departure.

I heard in our initial interview session the explicit questions that Ms. T hoped the assessment would answer, as well as her implicit plea to be valued—to be considered a person of worth despite any neurocognitive or emotional challenges, without having her separate identity appropriated or violated. Indeed, at a deeper, less formulated level, when she asked me in a deferential tone how we—she, her therapist, and I as her assessor—would proceed if my findings did not fit with her subjective sense of what was wrong, I heard her asking whether her questions could be answered and dependency needs satisfied without having to relinquish her independent thinking. She visibly relaxed when I told her that her own input would be vital in determining how to intervene. Ms. T's tentative tone and disclosures facilitated our discussion of her wishes and fears, setting the stage for a collaborative assessment process. Following the one-hour interview session, she completed seven hours of formal testing across three sessions, spending an additional hour filling out a self-report personality measure in my waiting room; she returned a month later for a feedback session. Several months after reading the test report with her therapist, Ms. T sought a follow-up session, hoping that revisiting the results could shed light on "a testing question" that had come to mind.

Ms. T's presentation evolved over the course of the assessment. Throughout cognitive testing, her anxiety was palpable, but her defensive strategies shifted from moment to moment and across time. Initially, her affect was constricted, and her mood was controlled carefully. Her body appeared tensely coiled, but without restlessness or a reduced level of energy. Her speech was paced carefully, and her thought processes were logical and coherent. This controlled presentation was interrupted by momentary bursts of anxious despair and "blanking out," most often when she felt impending failure was inevitable based on test instructions or practice items. However, as we made our way through the intelligence, achievement, and neuropsychological measures (see "Rationale for Battery"), Ms. T's affect broadened, her body relaxed, and she began to respond more flexibly to areas of challenge: She openly expressed her fear and shame (with occasional tears), conveyed genuine humor amidst her anxious laughter, and shared moments of insight ("I think sometimes it's my fear that I'll be awful at something—more than the test itself!—that determines how I actually perform"). Time and again, Ms. T proved able to reflect on her experience and sense of self, although she varied in her ability to access her observing ego at the moment of challenge.

As we shifted into the realm of the ambiguous-demand performance-based measures, Ms. T became yet more openly collaborative and able to share what the tests evoked in her, whether it was her pleasure narrating certain stories, or her shame about early memories, or her felt restraint in responding to inkblots. While remaining focused on the tasks, she could step back to reflect on her experience and communications. Her broad vocabulary and articulate expression of ideas were most evident here. Even at moments of affective challenge, she was able to express her confusion or distress while channeling her conflicts into the projective material.

## Rationale for battery

Given the multifaceted referral question, I chose a comprehensive assessment battery. Ms. T's presentation and clinical history suggested that I should privilege neither neurocognitive nor personality aspects of the assessment. I heard in her experience of school-based learning the possibility of ADHD, dyslexia, and/or dyscalculia. I also wondered about the resilience of her personality structure, given the trauma of early physical abuse and emotional neglect, and her very high level of anxiety. Ms. T was at a crossroads in her life and was in treatment with a sophisticated clinician; both were in a position to make productive use of textured findings, so I wanted to be comprehensive while respecting the limits of our time and her financial resources.

For all neuropsychological assessments of ADHD, I select measures in a step-wise fashion. I begin with the age-appropriate Wechsler scale, which for Ms. T was the Wechsler Adult Intelligence Scale—4th Edition (WAIS-IV; Wechsler, 2008). The WAIS-IV not only allows one to assess a patient's overall intellectual resources but also provides beginning data regarding ADHD. One often finds stronger higher-order cognitive capabilities in the profiles of individuals with ADHD (measured by the WAIS-IV Verbal Comprehension and Perceptual Reasoning domains) and less developed lower-level automatic functions that facilitate complex problem-solving—lesser cognitive proficiency (measured by the Working Memory and Processing Speed domains). Further, one can scrutinize the score profiles and qualitative findings for other data: Is the Information subtest low relative to other verbal scores, reflecting the impact of attention problems on school-based learning? Does the patient's verbiage, recall of digits, or out-of-order steps when mentally solving arithmetic problems reflect the sequential processing weaknesses that typify ADHD? Are there features of the patient's score profile or response process that suggest alternative hypotheses (such as anxiety) to explain attention problems?

Next, if an explicit part of the referral question asks whether the patient has a specific learning disability (most often dyslexia), or if there are aspects of a patient's history or clinical presentation that raise this question, such as delayed language development, trouble learning to read, characteristic mis-spellings on my registration forms, word retrieval difficulties or semantic/ phonological substitutions in conversation, I include an achievement measure and a structured writing sample. Without any of these indicators, I administer the structured writing sample alongside the intelligence test, using it as a screening measure.

For Ms. T, I included in her test battery an achievement measure (the Woodcock-Johnson IV Tests of Achievement; WJ-IV; Schrank, Mather, & McGrew, 2014) and the writing sample. Ms. T and her therapist had raised the question of dyslexia *and* Ms. T described math as her "nemesis." The latter might suggest either a specific learning disability in math *or* ADHD, which disproportionately affects math learning (Capodieci & Martinussen, 2017; Tosto, Momi, Asherson, & Malki, 2015). The choice to include an achievement measure was bolstered by the absence of information about Ms. T's early developmental milestones and extended family history, her report of difficulty learning across all academic domains, and her experience of word-retrieval difficulties (a feature of expressive language that often occurs with dyslexia). Also, her therapist had wondered about how Ms. T's academic competencies might bear on her new, independent career ventures. At the same time, I noted that her spelling was correct on registration forms and her only observed difficulty with accurate word retrieval came during our initial phone contact when Ms. T said that her problems with focus, organization, and task initiation had been "exasperated" (exacerbated) recently by anxiety, a word substitution as easily explained by a conflict-driven slip of the tongue as by a phonological confusion.

As I moved to the next step in selecting test measures, I already had administered and scored the WAIS-IV and WJ-IV from the first session, allowing me to determine that Ms. T did *not* have a specific learning disability. I was then able to limit neuropsychological measures to those assessing key features of ADHD: attention, memory, and executive functions. I chose a range of evaluator-administered measures: The Trail Making Test (Reitan, 1986), Stroop Color and Word Test (Golden & Freshwater, 2002), Conners' Continuous Performance Test—Second Edition (CPT-II; Conners & Staff, 2002), Wide Range Assessment of Memory and Learning— 2nd Edition (WRAML2; Sheslow & Adams, 2003), and Wisconsin Card Sorting Test—Computer Version 4 (WCST-CV4; Heaton, Chelune, Talley, Kay, & Curtiss, 1993). I also included the Brown ADD Scales to obtain Ms. T's subjective rating of ADHD symptoms (Brown, 1996).

To gain insight into Ms. T's personality structure and intertwined neuro-cognitive and emotional functioning, I added personality measures. I administered the Early Memories Test (Mayman, 1968), Animal Preference Task (APT; Tuber, 2012), Thematic Apperception Test (TAT; Murray, 1943), and

Rorschach (Exner, 1993). Due to time constraints, I did not include a drawing series (Hammer, 1958)—of interest given Ms. T's artistic talents—as she told a number of long TAT stories that filled our allotted time. She also completed the Personality Assessment Inventory (PAI; Morey, 1991) in my waiting room on a separate occasion. For both neuropsychological and personality domains, I always include self-report and evaluator-administered measures as companion pieces to better understand and integrate the patient's subjective experience with formal test results (Bram & Peebles, 2014; Bornstein, 2002; Leak, 2019; Leak & Hayden, 2015).

## Summary of findings

In reviewing findings from formal testing, I find it helpful to move from the most to the least structured measures, highlighting key aspects of score profiles alongside qualitative features of the response process. For Ms. T, we should be keeping in mind the central referral question: Does this patient have an attention-deficit disorder that either is a primary contributor to her challenges or is intertwined with other issues that carry equal weight?

### Intelligence testing

On the WAIS-IV, Ms. T demonstrated above-average verbal capabilities and exceptional perceptual reasoning skills, alongside weaker working memory and processing speed (Verbal Comprehension Index = 107, 68th percentile; Perceptual Reasoning Index = 127, 96th percentile; Working Memory Index = 83, 13th percentile; Processing Speed Index = 105, 63rd percentile). Her subtest score profile was noteworthy: Whereas on perceptually based sub-tests Ms. T earned uniformly high scores of 14 and 15, on verbal subtests she earned scores of 13 and 12 on Similarities and Vocabulary, respectively, but a significantly lower score of 9 on Information. Although within the broadly average range, this latter score underscored her weaker retention of material typically learned during the school years. This lower score, alongside her weak working memory and less robust processing speed, constituted typical areas of compromise in those with ADHD (Wechsler, Raiford, & Holdnack, 2014). However, at this preliminary stage of analysis, one should also ask whether Ms. T's cognitive profile reflected instead—or in addition—a repressive emphasis: Was her mode of cognition consistent with Shapiro's (1999) hysterical style and might she defensively avoid a deeper seeking of knowledge because of unconscious fantasies stimulated by the discovery process (Rapaport, Gill, and Schafer, 1968)?

Indeed, one must consider the intertwining of neurocognitive weaknesses with anxiety to appreciate Ms. T's difficulty fully demonstrating her capabilities. On the Information subtest, she had particular difficulty with numbers and locations, appearing flustered and widening her eyes in disbelief that she could be expected to know such material. Similarly, on the Digit Span subtest, where she earned a subtest score of 9, she had an adequate span of apprehension (Digits Forward = 6); but when she had to recruit true working memory skills on the Backward and Sequencing trials, although she ultimately recalled up to five digits, there was marked intra-test variability due to lapses in attention and missequencing of digits. Anxiety clearly played a role in exacerbating her working memory challenges, as conveyed through her comments, physiological arousal, and affect: "My hands are sweating!" she remarked upon completing practice items for the Backward trial, and "Gone!" she announced when she could not retrieve even a single digit for several items on the Sequencing trial. Similarly, on the Arithmetic subtest, Ms. T earned a subtest score of 5, becoming overtly distressed as she disclaimed her ability to solve math problems in her head: "I can only do it with paper and pencil," she said dispiritedly. Indeed, her average scores on later math achievement tests assessing conceptual and computational thinking, alongside her below-average math fluency, suggested that anxiety exacerbated problems with rote memory.

### Neuropsychological testing

Ms. T's uneven WAIS-IV performance hinted at the ADHD assessed through formal neuropsychological measures: Her relatively weaker long-term memory for school-based information suggested that attentional weaknesses had intruded on learning for many years. Further, she had a weak working memory, her processing speed was mildly slowed, and together these measures of cognitive efficiency were significantly weaker than her higher-order verbal comprehension and perceptual reasoning capabilities. Given this disparity, Ms. T's intellectual potential was better captured by her General Ability Index of 121 (92nd percentile) than by her Full Scale IQ of 109 (73rd percentile). However, an anxious response to "not knowing" played a role in the reduced concentration of this bright woman, triggering a flight from active ideation characteristic of the global, impressionistic cognitive style described by Shapiro (1999). Spotty retrieval of what she *did* know and uneven deployment of skills she *did* possess seemed to dominate the clinical picture. Therefore, while the WAIS-IV suggested problems with aspects of attention and memory, there is a difference between conditions with a neurodevelopmental basis (i.e., *true* ADHD) and those due to conflict or other considerations. Further testing clarified this distinction.

The intertwining of Ms. T's cognitive style, anxiety, and neurocognitive weaknesses was highlighted on tests explicitly designed to measure aspects of attention, memory, and executive functions. Here, the initial test instructions or her first glimpse of a test could potentially set off a downward spiral: Fearful that her weaknesses would be exposed, she became unable to think and was at risk of creating a self-fulfilling prophecy. It was during this phase of the assessment, as she completed a wide range of neuropsychological measures, that her waxing and waning anxiety prompted her earlier noted insight: "I think sometimes it's my fear that I'll be awful at something—more than the test itself!—that determines how I actually perform."

On brief tests of alternating and divided attention, Ms. T's performance was variable. On the Trail Making Test, her comfort with the format ("Oh, like dot-to-dots!") allowed her to move forward with a cautious ease. She earned scores that were fully within normal limits on both Trails A and B—simple and complex attention—but made a sequencing error on Trail A. Although she completed the remainder of the test without error following the standard evaluator prompt, she worked with visibly greater caution on Trails B to ensure accuracy.

On the Stroop Test, Ms. T responded with unusual affective intensity from the outset. Upon looking at the list of color words and listening to my instructions explaining that this was a test of "how fast you can read the words," she placed her right arm over the second and third columns of words as she took in the full set of directives. She explained that the page of words was "too visually overwhelming—too busy." For word, color, and color-word trials, she used this approach to limit her visual field, pointing with her left hand and shifting her arm to the right as she moved from one column to the next. Her resultant word and color scores were significantly below the mean (T = 36 and T = 33, mean T = 50, SD = 10), rendering color-word and interference scores meaningless (T = 46 and T = 50). Not only do scores on word and color trials that are more than one standard deviation below the mean invalidate interference scores (Golden & Freshwater, 2002), but Ms. T's approach spoke more to her cognitive rigidity in response to feeling affectively overwhelmed than to any specific neurocognitive interpretation.

On the Conners' CPT-II, Ms. T settled in comfortably, even asserting herself by adjusting the computer screen of the laptop to improve her line of vision before moving from the practice trial to the test proper. Throughout this 15-minute test, where she was asked to click the mouse in response to all letters except *X*, she remained calm and visibly focused on the screen. However, her score profile told a different story, highlighting problems with sustained attention and adjusting to changes in the tempo of the stimuli presented (Hit SE Block Change = 66, Hit RT ISI Change = 61, Hit SE ISI Change = 65; mean T = 50, SD = 10). Central to her profile was Ms. T's difficulty regulating varying levels of stimulation or arousal—a core deficit for those with ADHD: Although *overall* accuracy and consistency of responding declined across time, Ms. T's accuracy improved across time when ISI = 1" instances were calculated (an optimal level of stimulation); she became significantly slower and more erratic when the ISI slowed to (a non-optimal) 2" or 4." Her score profile, which indicated poor vigilance and inconsistent attention, alongside within-normal-limits scores on indices assessing impulsive responding, highlighted inattentive features of ADHD.

On the WRAML2, the intertwining of an impressionistic cognitive style, anxiety, and neurocognitive weaknesses again came to the fore. From the outset, Ms. T expressed disbelief that she was expected to recall either stories read aloud to her or a 16-word list repeated across four trials. Indeed, she was at her worst on verbal subtests, which required an internal focus. This was true whether the task assessed memory for stories, typically stronger in those with attention problems as the inherent narrative structure facilitates encoding and retrieval, or if the tasks assessed typically weaker rote memory and working memory (Story Memory: Immediate Recall = 8, Delayed Recall = 9, Recognition = 6; Verbal Learning: Immediate Recall = 6, Delayed Recall = 5, Recognition = 6; Verbal Working Memory = 7; mean subtest score = 10, SD = 3).

And yet despite declaring "my brain is a vacuum," Ms. T demonstrated typical primacy and recency effects, as well as a sharp uptick in her performance on Story Memory and Verbal Learning once her anxiety subsided. Of interest with respect to conflict-driven intrusions was Ms. T's virtual "blanking out" of the first story read to her, which told of a mother-daughter outing. Perhaps anxiety associated with this first WRAML2 subtest was intensified by an unconscious shutting out of (not remembering) the abusive relationship with her own mother. When comparing her recall on both stories (which have a comparable number of items), Ms. T's immediate recall was doubled on the second story and her delayed recall was nearly tripled. Nevertheless, her poor recognition scores indicated that she was unsuccessfully encoding or organizing information to facilitate remembering. In addition to the evident cluster of neurocognitive weaknesses, Ms. T's performance here also raised the possibility of trauma-induced overstimulation and a failure to encode.

Ms. T's performance was better, although still weak relative to her intellectual potential, when subtests did not provoke an anxious reaction upon initially confronting the task. She earned average scores on visual and auditory subtests assessing her passive span of apprehension (Finger Windows = 9, Number-Letter = 10), despite intra-test variability due to frequent sequencing errors. If there was a visual-kinesthetic element, which allowed Ms. T to "do" something—and maintain an outward focus—this lessened her anxiety. So, when she briefly viewed abstract designs before drawing them from memory or replicated number/number-letter sequences by pointing to a visual array, Ms. T performed capably (Design Memory = 9, Symbolic Working Memory = 12). She did, however, have a vulnerability to proactive interference that outwardly captured the anxious "scrambling" of information that she experienced internally. Ms. T's total memory score (General Memory Index = 87, 19th percentile) gave credence to her memory complaints, but this single score masked her relative visual-kinesthetic strengths, as well as her intensely fearful reaction to turning her thinking inward to problem-solve.

On the Wisconsin Card Sorting Test, Ms. T was faced with a complex problem-solving task assessing her inferential reasoning and ability to respond to feedback, while continually monitoring her response process. Yet, the hands-on nature of this test and its visual stimuli allowed her to settle into her seat in front of the laptop with evident comfort—thus allowing subtle weaknesses in her executive functions to stand apart from her anxiety. In matching a single card on the computer screen to one of four key cards, she easily discerned the underlying concepts guiding the match process (standard score =

100, 50 percentile) and did not perseverate when shifting from one category to the next (perseverative responses = 110, 75 percentile; perseverative errors = 109, 73 percentile). However, although she was organized in her approach, she failed to maintain set in two instances. She immediately recognized that she had drifted from the category guiding her match process and was relatively untroubled by these lapses (uttering a quiet, matter-of-fact "oh, shoot"). However, it took several more responses for Ms. T to regroup and reorient herself to the category that preceded her lapse. Thus, one could see on the WCST both the lapses in attention and the weakness in self-monitoring that often characterize ADHD.

On the Brown ADD Scales, Ms. T's responses to the 40-item descriptive measure yielded significant elevations on all five indices (Organizing & Activating to Work: T = 68, Sustaining Attention & Concentration: T = 75, Sustaining Energy & Effort: T = 88, Managing Affective Interference: T = 77, Utilizing Working Memory & Accessing Recall: T = 82; mean T = 50, SD = 10). The score profile captured the intensity of Ms. T's subjective concerns and was consistent with impressions from neuropsychological and personality measures: She described significant difficulty manipulating immediately available information or accessing data from long-term memory storage; and the overwhelming feeling states generated by her sense of failure derailed her ability to persevere and remain focused. However, she also reported somewhat stronger organizational skills and a contained approach—areas of strength that likely had served her well unless affective intrusions became intolerable. Unsurprisingly, her total score (T = 83) placed her in the "ADD highly probable" range.

### Achievement testing

Before turning to the personality measures, it is instructive to briefly review the results of achievement testing, as the WJ-IV findings illustrated how ADHD can affect academic functioning even in the absence of a specific learning disability. Although score profiles and qualitative features of Ms. T's performance contraindicated a specific learning disability, she had difficulty recognizing her academic strengths given intrusions on her learning from weak attention, concentration, memory, and executive functions—weaknesses intensified by her cognitive style and anxiety. Reading and written language capabilities were not fully commensurate with intelligence, with reading and writing fluency representing her lowest (but still average) scores. However, profile and qualitative analyses indicated Ms. T's firm mastery of sound-symbol relationships, good sight-word recognition and reading comprehension, and a strong command of the mechanics of writing; in fact, her spelling was good, in contrast to her statement during the clinical interview that she was a poor speller. She wrote with a creative flair but occasional lapses in punctuation. "Underachievement" and lesser academic fluency alongside intact basic and higher-order language-based academic skills, with a vulnerability to lapses in punctuation: These are typical findings for individuals with ADHD, especially for older adults who have shied away from academic fields and avocations after completing high school.

Nor did Ms. T's math skills, which yielded standard scores for conceptual and calculation abilities in the mid-90s and fluency in mid-80s, suggest a specific learning disability. Instead, results indicated the characteristically disproportionate impact of ADHD on this subject area: Math scores were one or more standard deviations below Ms. T's Full Scale IQ of 109, and these scores were weak relative to reading and written language scores. Her errors centered on the weak retrieval of multiplication facts and a tendency to missequence steps in the problem-solving process—both of which were exacerbated by her anxiety; yet, she demonstrated a solid number sense and accurate math reasoning. For Ms. T, math deficits reflected neurocognitive weaknesses in rote memory and sequential processing that were intensified by her retreat from active, effortful thinking, including her choice in high school to decline enrollment in higher-level math courses. In the context of once again considering the impact of a global, impressionistic cognitive style on learning and daily functioning, it is fitting to turn to findings from personality measures.

### Personality testing

Ms. T's conscious description of concerns, as captured by the single self-report measure in the personality domain, dovetailed nicely with the deeper layers of functioning illuminated by the ambiguous-demand performance-based measures. The PAI yielded a valid and internally consistent profile, one without significant elevations on overall scales assessing psychopathology. However, there were mild to moderate elevations on critical subscales: Anxiety: Cognitive $T = 61$ and Affective $T = 62$; Anxiety-Related Disorders: Phobias $T = 62$; Depression: Cognitive $T = 64$; Paranoia: Hypervigilance $T = 69$; Schizophrenia: Social Detachment $T = 64$ and Thought Disorder $T = 70$; Borderline: Identity Problems $T = 65$ (mean = 50, SD = 10). Further, among critical items endorsed were two that acknowledged "sometimes" reliving or being troubled by memories of a bad experience. When considered together, these findings captured not only the disruptions in thinking that prompted Ms. T to seek treatment, but also suggested that a less integrated sense of self (identity), distrust of others, and weaknesses in affective regulation were aspects of her personality structure that prompted a subtle withdrawal from the social world.

The ambiguous-demand performance-based measures enriched and deepened understanding of the PAI results, highlighting a constellation of underdeveloped psychological capacities and a restricted range of defensive strategies that Ms. T had developed to cope with areas of challenge. A vulnerability to affective dysregulation was perhaps the most prominent structural weakness, closely related to a limited capacity to trust in others—her conflict around finding reliable, yearned-for guidance and comfort, while also maintaining a safe interpersonal distance. These twin areas of psychological vulnerability were fertile ground for a defensive style aimed at self-protection: Ms. T avoided, constricted, and repressed emotions to keep her affective experience at a tolerable level and to feel competent and in control; she turned to externalization and projection when feeling more threatened. If interpersonal expectations and situational demands remained clear and logical, her reasoning and reality testing remained fundamentally intact. When affectively overwhelmed, however, she became vulnerable to misperceiving situations or the motivations of others, attributing to them a hostile intent that could precipitate her distancing and ultimate flight. Ms. T's defensive style served the important function of allowing her to experience herself as capable, in control, and safe; but this protective style also limited her, occurring at a cost to her artistic expression, spontaneity, intelligent "thinking" and effective problem-solving, and negotiation of deeper, more satisfying interpersonal relationships. Analyses of the content, sequence, and formal scores of the personality tests added yet another layer of understanding to impressions gleaned from the clinical interview and cognitive measures.

### Affect regulation

The data indicated that Ms. T's emotional constriction and consequent vulnerability to moments of affective flooding had roots in fear of overstimulation both from outside and inside: Might she be exposed as inadequate by unmanageable task demands or have her separate sense of self threatened by others' traumatic impingement? Or would she simply become overwhelmed by the anxiety evoked by her own wishes and fears?

Ms. T's repeated emotional dysregulation on the intelligence and neuropsychological testing, as described in the review of earlier data, captured her flood of anxiety when confronted by tasks' demands that left her feeling exposed as inadequate. More prominent on the less structured personality measures were a fear of traumatic impingement by others and the anxiety stimulated by her inner wishes and fears. Ms. T's earliest memory was of her mother swinging at her, as she (then a 5-year-old child) tried to hide in the corner. The detail that stood out most clearly, she reported, was "my arms and hands in front of my face, protecting myself." When asked if this memory often came to mind, Ms. T's reply captured both a frequent response to trauma and her own entrenched defensive strategy: "No, I push it away." One finds in this memory a template of the conflict and aggression—even adaptive aspects—that must be disavowed as part of her own personality. On the APT, where Ms. T was asked for preferred and non-preferred animals, she elaborated on this theme: "I'd never want to be something aggressive, like a lion or tiger; it's not my personality. It just seems an intense life: killing something viciously, ripping it apart—aah! The leadership part of that doesn't appeal to me either."

On the TAT, there also was evidence of Ms. T's propensity to constrict affect to protect herself from overwhelming feelings. Her 6-minute response to Card 1, a card described by Murray (1943, p. 21) as a young boy "contemplating a violin which rests on the table in front of him" (the first of 13 cards that I administered) occurred only after I offered the standard prompt in response to her terse description: "This is the first time this boy has ever seen this type of instrument. He's studying it in an attempt to comprehend what it is and what to do with it. My story is that short." Prompted to elaborate, Ms. T ultimately told a richly emotional story with hints of sublimated sexual discovery, narrating a boy's unfolding curiosity and creativity under the tutelage of a trusted mentor—perhaps capturing positive aspects of her assessment experience and optimism regarding her future psychotherapy (but hinting at the potential for an erotic transference). She continued in this relaxed manner until her body subtly tightened upon being handed the fifth card administered, Card 13MF, with its more explicit pull for sexual and aggressive themes: "A young man is standing with downcast head buried in his arm. Behind him is the figure of a woman lying in bed" (Murray, 1943, p. 23). She externalized her uncomfortable reaction in an opening remark: "Hmm, they're all trying to be depressing. ... All right, I'm trying to twist this not to be so depressing." She did not succeed.

Without apparent awareness, Ms. T shifted from the third-person perspective of her prior stories to a first-person perspective, telling a brief, disjointed story. For the remaining TAT stories, she maintained the first-person perspective and shifted from her earlier 4- to 6-minute narrations to stories of approximately 2 1/2 minutes. Her subsequent stories centered on anxiety-driven, depressively toned, unresolved conflicts. For Card 13MF, she identified with the man in the story, whose "terrible marriage" was not improving despite his great efforts. As she moved to quickly conclude the story, Ms. T adopted a light tone to distance herself from feelings of betrayal, abandonment, and helplessness: With her leg beginning to jiggle, she said, "I'm going to be soap-opera-ish: She's had an affair with my best friend. Now I've got no one to turn to. I imagine her with him and it breaks my heart. I don't know what to do next."

Ms. T conveyed further nuances of her affective life on the Rorschach, but before turning to analysis of her brief protocol, I would like to clarify my (hybrid) administration procedure. It has been noted that the Rorschach is less a "test" and more a variety of "systems" (Exner, 1969) or "methods" (Tuber, 2012), and seasoned assessors often have had training in several systems. Indeed, I was introduced to the Rorschach in graduate school using the system of Rapaport, Gill, and Schafer (1968), added aspects of Klopfer's approach to my understanding of content and sequence analysis (Klopfer, B., Ainsworth, Klopfer, W.G., & Holt, 1954) during my internship and fellowship, and shifted to Exner's Comprehensive System (CS; 1993) in my postgraduate years. It was this latter system that I used for Ms. T's administration. Upon more recently shifting to routine use of the Rorschach Performance Assessment System (R-PAS; Meyer, Viglione, Mihura, Erard, & Erdberg, 2011), I scored and analyzed her protocol using the R-PAS.

Having found clinically useful information in non-standard Rorschach administrations and "invalid" protocols with too few responses (R), I agree with Brickman and Lerner (1992) that assessors should neither discard such data nor re-administer the test, but should learn instead to feel comfortable "in not being bound to scoring systems or standard administration procedures at all costs" (p. 183). It can be more useful both clinically and pragmatically to introduce a parameter that enhances the information that *is* available; at the same time, formal scores from a measure must be interpreted cautiously under such conditions (Leak, 2019). Such is the case for Ms. T, whose administration included certain non-standard procedures that I will describe.

When during the Response Phase of the CS administration, Ms. T began to offer only a single response after the first card, I turned back to my earlier training in the Rapaport, Gill, and Schafer system: I prompted with "anything else?" and waited for 90 seconds" before moving on. Despite this procedure (but without the R-PAS explicit prompt to give "two responses ... or maybe three, to each card"; Meyer et al., 2011, p. 8), Ms. T responded quickly to each card but then could "see" nothing more, for a total R = 11. To enrich my understanding of her inner life, I further tested the limits, inviting her to elaborate on implied object relationships by inquiring "as if?" in response to human movement (M) responses (Mayman, 1977), as well as in response to animal movement (FM) responses (Bram & Peebles, 2014). For example, when she offered "two cartoon women facing each other" in response to Card VII, her elaboration following the "as if?" prompt during the Inquiry allowed her to add "imitating each other, being silly, having fun"—which conveyed a playful and cooperative relational tone.

As I turn back to analyses of Ms. T's affective life as seen through the content, sequence, and formal R-PAS scoring of her protocol, it will be important to keep it mind that these R-PAS norms were based on a different mode of administration, as well as a significant deviation from "the optimal range of R from 18 to 27" (Meyer et al., 2011, p. 411). Because R is significantly correlated with so many variables, perhaps most notably Complexity, which reflects "the sophistication of Location, Space, and Object Qualities; and the density of Determinants and Contents" (Meyer et al., 2011, p. 349), all of Ms. T's reported scores were Complexity Adjusted; this alternative scoring is used when an individual's Complexity Standard Score is less than 85 (or greater than 115). Thus, it is applicable to Ms. T, whose response profile generated a standard score of 73. Keeping in mind these cautions regarding a non-standard administration and an "invalid" protocol, it becomes possible to consider the still-rich yield of data.

Perhaps most striking for Ms. T in the affective realm was evidence of her dysregulation despite efforts to constrict. She began on Card I with a response sequence that captured her caution in allowing others to know her thoughts and feelings, with the breakthrough of frightening (for her) content heightening a subsequent self-protective constriction. She first saw "a mask of a fox" and then "a devil." Following both the Response and Inquiry phases, she was asked to identify the cards she liked best and least: Ms. T said she liked Card I the least "because it had a demonic look to it." It was after providing two responses to the first card that she pulled back, offering only a single response for each of the remaining nine cards.

For Ms. T, her R = 11 attested to constriction, while also bringing to the fore her global, impressionistic cognitive style. Her W% SS (Standard Score) = 130 (98th percentile), captured her "big picture" approach to problem-solving, which proved fertile ground for affective lability as she simultaneously failed to access what she knew and attempted to shut out what she wished to avoid. Additionally, affective dysregulation despite attempts to minimize, avoid, and repress her experience emerged in her F% SS = 72 (3rd percentile), and (CF+C)/SumC% SS = 113 (81st percentile).

### Experience of self and other

Ms. T's affective dysregulation was entwined with her distrust of others. Given early childhood experiences with a mother who was at once overbearing *and* detached with regard to her daughter's deeper dependency needs, it was unsurprising to find Ms. T's fears of being controlled, dismissed, or abandoned. Yearnings for nurturance and intimacy easily precipitated a defensive distancing to protect against the unconscious fantasy of overstimulation, impingement, or disappointment when the need for closeness was aroused.

In viewing the entire assessment through a psychoanalytic lens, it was interesting to observe that Ms. T's fear of being controlled interpersonally first emerged not on the personality tests, but via "projective" analysis of her Wechsler scale (Allison, 1978), most notably the WAIS-IV Similarities subtest. Having earned full credit for each of her responses prior to item #15, Ms. T's preoccupations began to intrude as she negotiated abstract, person-centered concepts. Sometimes, she spoiled a response that began well; other times, she eked out a 1-point response. On item #15, her previously succinct responses yielded to struggles to locate the right words: I can't think of the words I want to put to this; I view them both as opposites … someone else is in control of both." For #17, she started out by equivocating on the relationship between different types of people and then spoiled the response in a very concrete way before recovering with a better answer that still fell short of full credit. For #18, she got stuck on themes of interpersonal "power" and "control" when a more abstract response would have been better.

On the APT, Ms. T's strong affectional needs and yearning for nurturance came to the fore as she described her preferred animals; in her associative sequence, there also was a shift from openly voiced desires for comfort, to a flight from impingement, and then an image that allowed her to be protected from the world *and* with others. "Maybe a rabbit," she said for her first animal, explaining during the inquiry phase that

> it just seems like a soft, comfortable, cozy life. There doesn't seem to be a lot of conflict. I mean, obviously there are your enemies—you'd have to hop away fast—but I visualize the den as a safe place where you'd be with family.

Her second animal was "a cat—that softness again" and, perhaps as she considered having her affectional needs satisfied, she added a note of independence and curiosity—albeit from the safety of above: "being able to leap on to things, look down on what's going on in the world—be exploring." And her third animal: "a dog—laying around and being taken care of."

These responses capture something similar to Texture (T) responses on the Rorschach. Ms. T's single T occurred on Card II, her third response—and thus the one that followed her earlier noted second response of "a devil" on Card I. She looked at Card II for only 2" before saying, "A guinea pig. That's coming from the color, mostly. Yeah. I see fur, the pink nose, pink eyes, fur spots, and little ears" (pointing out a face). During the inquiry, she explained, "They're just kind of hanging out, looking at me." In response to my "as if" inquiry, she replied, "I don't see any emotion here—just curiosity, I guess." I queried "fur" and she stroked the blot with a single finger, telling me that "the streaks make it look like fur."

Careful scrutiny of the content, sequence of verbiage, and formal R-PAS scoring of this third response given by Ms. T (W, Ad, FQo, Mp, CF, T, INC1, PH, Pr) revealed a passive, cautiously watchful stance that might have emerged when an upsurge of aggression (from the prior devil response) precipitated a desire for comfort *and* the careful guarding of interpersonal boundaries; the conflict resulted in mild affective dysregulation and subtle lapses in logic. A similar longing for—and fear of—close interpersonal relationships was conveyed by scores that merited scrutiny given her constricted protocol: Ms. T demonstrated an interest in people (SumH SS = 106, 65th percentile), a strong need for mirroring validation of her experiences (r SS = 122, 93rd percentile), and a capacity for cooperative relationships juxtaposed with preoccupations about aggressive intentions or actions—plus the potential to distort these impulses, whether they emanated from inside or outside (COP SS = 111, 78th percentile; AGM SS = 121, 92nd percentile; M- SS = 123, 94th percentile).

*Reasoning and reality testing*

Assessment findings revealed neither severe nor pervasive weaknesses in Ms. T's ability to think logically and to accurately perceive situations. However, as noted earlier, she was at her best—with clear reasoning and accurate perception accented by elements of playfulness, creativity, and curiosity—when demands felt in line with her strengths *and* the expectations were clear and predictable. It is when the intensity or complexity of the situation increased, and she felt exposed, impinged upon, or threatened—whether by external demands or an upsurge in her own impulses—that one saw a blurring of internal and external experiences and perceptions. Her reasoning and reality testing momentarily deteriorated, and she became vulnerable to feeling deliberately shamed or threatened, when others might have felt merely challenged or invited into a problem-solving dialog.

Final samples of raw data illuminated Ms. T's reasoning and reality testing, and the manner in which her resilience came to the fore or was challenged. On the TAT, Ms. T told a story to Card 5, where a "middle-aged woman is standing on the threshold of a half-opened door looking into a room" (Murray, 1943, p. 21). This card yields "an unusually high … percentage of stories with neutral emotional tone," both according to older norms (Holt, 1978, p. 90) and in my ongoing experience with the TAT. For this patient, however, it elicited a deeply sad story about a heated argument that occurred when a mother rejected her daughter's Mother's Day offering. Ms. T then moved to Card 12F, a typically more challenging card (Holt, 1978, p. 104): "The portrait of a young woman. A weird old woman with a shawl over her head is grimacing in the background" (Murray, 1943, p. 22). However, the patient told her story with genuine pleasure:

> Ok! My name is Andre and I think I'm a wonderful painter; I love to paint portraits. This portrait is of myself and my grandmother. I wanted to show her as the mischievous lady that she is: my grandmother *loves* to play tricks, especially on me, because I tend to be very serious. And it makes me feel very special that she pays such attention to me. I really think I've captured both of our personalities in this portrait.

This story represented a rare exception in the sequence of depressively toned narratives that Ms. T told after shifting to the first-person point of view. To accomplish this, she invoked an area of personal strength (art), with perhaps a hint of omnipotence; a perceptual distortion (seeing the younger figure as a male—rare in the past but perhaps less so in the current socio-cultural climate); "trickery" that was taken up playfully but nevertheless hinted at the patient's interpersonally suspicious nature; and an extra generational boundary. After infusing a "neutral" card with considerable conflict and aggression, this result was more adaptive than problematic.

On the Rorschach, there were the most vivid moments illustrating Ms. T's vulnerability to misinterpretation or distortion. Although her WSumCog and Level 2 Cog were not able to be meaningfully interpreted given a constricted verbal sample due to low R, her significantly elevated FQ-% SS = 143 (>99th percentile), assumed greater importance given her efforts to constrict. Qualitatively, her response to Card X captured the waxing and waning of perceptual accuracy and reasoning—the latter comparable to earlier examples from the WAIS-IV Similarities. She began with a slight variation on the popular crab (D1 location area), but she added human activity (FAB1): "My first thought was crabs: just crabs marching along a rock." During the Inquiry, she explained, "They're blue, with a great claw" (D12 location area and AGC; the rock is D9 location area). Her hand gesture as she mimed the "great claw" also conveyed a hint of aggression, suggesting that it was the affect and ideation stirred by this percept that led to a subsequent deterioration in perceptual accuracy. She continued during the Response Phase, "I also see these yellow and orange ones (D15 location area); I guess they're crabs, too. And up here are the smaller gray guys (D8 location area). So, in all, there are six crabs."

Within this generally adequate response, one codes down to a FQ—based on the poor form quality of the crabs at D15 location area. Further, in conjunction with other test data, one can speculate on a constellation of features that hinted at moments of destabilization: when Ms. T's playful quality became artificial (akin to her "I'm going to be soap-opera-ish" on the TAT), occurred in the context of aggressive content, and was accompanied by a shift from more sophisticated language to subtly childlike phrasing ("just crabs marching along a rock" and "here are the smaller gray guys"), she seemed to be struggling to contain or express disturbing thoughts and feelings. This nuanced analysis informs therapeutic recommendations: being able to identify such moments in treatment would allow one to intervene optimally with Ms. T, whose affective regulation and caution about interpersonal closeness are central areas of vulnerability.

## Integrated formulation

Ms. T was a bright and sensitive woman whose intelligence, creativity, effective problem-solving, and interpersonal relationships were undermined by ADHD, predominantly inattentive presentation, and a personality structure organized at the lower end of the neurotic spectrum (Waldron, Gordon, & Gazzillo, 2017): anxious-avoidant/phobic, hysteric-histrionic, and dependent personality features were most prominent. Her vulnerability to affective dysregulation was heightened by intertwined neurocognitive and personality-related structural weaknesses, including a global, impressionistic cognitive style. She easily became flooded by feelings that were experienced as intolerable, shutting down her thinking and leaving her feeling exposed as inadequate. Certain at such moments that she was incapable of finding a solution on her own, Ms. T also was reluctant to turn to others for help. She yearned for a comforting guidance to strengthen her capabilities and support her curiosity—intellectual and otherwise, but she feared that instead she might be judged, or have her subjective experience misunderstood, or her independent thinking appropriated or dismissed.

Ms. T was vulnerable to becoming overwhelmed both from the outside and the inside. Whether she was struggling with cognitive demands that were exacerbated by her ADHD and the flight from active ideation typifying a global, impressionistic cognitive style, or she was warding off impingements that threatened her independence and separate sense of self, or she was attempting to shut out frightening impulses that arose from within, Ms. T relied on a constellation of defenses that was at once protective and limiting. Her defensive style was marked by avoidance, constriction, and repression; when momentarily destabilized, she might shift to externalization and projection.

Ms. T's habitual mode of coping likely developed in the context of a shy, sensitive temperament that was intensified by early physical abuse and, at the very least, an emotionally insensitive home atmosphere. Then, as she entered school, Ms. T did not have the advantage of finding pleasure in her developing intellectual and academic competencies, as learning challenges related to ADHD undermined her performance and confidence in herself. Deprived of the pleasures of more fully investing in school, especially given her judgments of herself as inferior to her classmates, Ms. T's separation from her parents (perhaps especially her mother) likely was further hindered. Optimistically, at the time of her assessment, Ms. T was attempting *not* to take flight from treatment; instead, she was preparing to explore alternative ways of managing her anxiety, hoping to better understand herself so that she could expand her creative potential and engage more deeply with others.

Within the descriptive framework of the *International statistical classification of diseases and related health problems* (10th Revision)(ICD-10); World Health Organization, 1992-5), the following diagnoses best captured Ms. T's clinical issues:

## ICD-10 diagnosis

F90.0 Attention-Deficit/Hyperactivity Disorder, Predominantly inattentive presentation
F41.1 Generalized Anxiety Disorder
F60.89 Other Specified Personality Disorder (mixed personality features)

From the vantage point of the *Psychodynamic Diagnostic Manual, Second Edition* (PDM-2; Lingiardi & McWilliams, 2017), the following diagnoses were applicable to Ms. T:

## PDM diagnosis

**Level of Personality Organization**: Neurotic
**Personality Syndromes (P Axis)**:    Anxious-avoidant/phobic, hysteric-histrionic, dependent
**Mental Functioning (M Axis)**:       Moderate impairments in basic mental functions
**Symptom Patterns (S Axis)**:         Anxiety; deficits in attention, concentration, and memory

## Recommendations

The findings indicated that a key therapeutic aim was to help Ms. T develop and expand her emotional repertoire—to increase her affect tolerance and expression, as well as her trust in closeness and comfort. She needed help discovering that she had options available to reduce the intensity of her feelings and manage them more effectively, whether through the power of her own mind (her intellect, her creativity, and potentially soothing internal objects) or through her actions in the interpersonal and material worlds. Ms. T's strong self-observing capacity—a psychological-mindedness that was serving her more often in after-the-fact analyses than during moments of acute distress—already had alerted her to some of the costs of her constricted, mistrustful, and avoidant defensive style. She came to the assessment with an expressed wish *not* to flee her current psychotherapy as she had fled earlier treatments, and she wanted to identify ways of coping that would facilitate her reintegration into the professional world. Her curiosity about characteristic ways of coping in the past and her interest in future goals set the stage for presenting recommendations that she could hear from her vantage point.

Ms. T would benefit from long-term psychodynamic psychotherapy or psychoanalysis, providing her with a protected space to tell her story, over time, and observe how current dilemmas, her past, and the here and now of the therapeutic relationship converged to illuminate her central dynamics. The treatment should be carefully paced, scrupulously observing boundaries, and respecting the patient's tentative style of disclosing. She was in the fortunate position of working with a well-trained psychoanalyst who was attuned to increasing the frequency of sessions only as Ms. T developed increased trust within the therapeutic relationship.

The patient and her therapist—a psychiatrist—should discuss the potential benefits of a medication trial to address Ms. T's ADHD. Medication could attenuate neurocognitive aspects of her vulnerability to feeling so easily disorganized and, in her mind, exposed to the world as inadequate. Because medication (typically a stimulant) is most beneficial in ameliorating problems with immediate and sustained focus, as well as with rote and working memory (identified areas of challenge for Ms. T), she might benefit from such a trial.

It would be important to recognize and discuss from the outset that medication does not by itself improve executive functions; rather, it sets the stage for a readiness to develop effective and consistent strategies. Further, anxiety and structural weaknesses related to personality style (including weak ego functions) often contribute in important ways to problems with attention, concentration, memory, and executive functions (as was the case for Ms. T); at a given moment in time, these issues can be indistinguishable from neurocognitively based symptoms.

Regardless of the relative contributions of neurocognitive and emotional factors, it is not uncommon for a patient to obtain only partial benefit from a medication intervention. It is critical to keep this issue in mind, as otherwise there is the potential for the patient and clinician to become caught up in a search for the "perfect" medication regimen. Exploring a range of medications or dosage levels is not strictly contraindicated, but perhaps especially when a patient has had a partial response to medication and a new area of vulnerability arises, one should pause: there is the potential to be derailed from intrapsychic conflicts that contribute far more potently than neurocognitive deficits. In my experience, there are frequent instances—even among sophisticated clinicians and patients—when continual changes to a medication regimen are defensive, ultimately undermining the treatment. Potential benefits of psychotherapy and hard-won pragmatic changes in habitual routines fail to come to the fore in this context.

A final recommendation focused on facilitating Ms. T's return to the professional world of photography, where she had been taking tentative steps to establish a freelance business. Given test results that indicated visual-analytic strengths and a tactile-kinesthetic style of learning, a career in this area appeared to be a good match for her capabilities. In moving ahead with her business ventures, Ms. T could enhance the quality of her work through pragmatic steps, simultaneously reducing her anxiety about a loss of focus and memory lapses, all while continuing to work through conflict-driven aspects of these issues in therapy.

First, when Ms. T experienced doubts about her talents or ability to learn new skills, she might call to mind objective results from the assessment to remind her of areas of strength. Turning inward to access prior discussions of her capabilities—whether from formal testing, from the therapy process, or from conversations with significant individuals in her life—would allow her to internalize affirmation of her talents and compassion for areas of challenge. Second, attention and memory problems intensify under time pressure, so Ms. T could make a practice of scheduling commitments with generous time frames to allow for mishaps, without disrupting her punctuality or production deadlines. Third, Ms. T could create materials to serve as her professional calling card, while also supporting her memory. For example, she might prepare a portfolio of photo options, with a price list for typical events, venues, and packages. Because math felt so daunting, she could include a notation stating that other options could be arranged upon request, with pricing provided after consideration of time and material demands (ensuring that she would not be pressured to "produce" on the spot). For any profession, it can be necessary to find ways to offset or transform areas of challenge, so Ms. T's materials and practices would not need to be offered with apology. Rather, they would represent her capacity to draw on areas of talent while also bolstering areas of weakness, sculpting her professional offerings and reputation.

## Feedback

Ms. T returned for a feedback session a month after testing was completed, with her response to this final phase of the assessment lending weight to treatment recommendations. I typically begin feedback sessions by asking patients what was uppermost on their minds as they were making the trip to my office that day, and in response to this question Ms. T acknowledged her anxiety that she would discover something was "terribly wrong" *and* her hope that she might learn something about herself that would help her move forward. As I slowly summarized the results over the next 45 minutes, pausing at key junctures to ensure that she could ask questions and was understanding me, Ms. T visibly relaxed. In the final quarter of this hour-long session, I asked her to tell me what she had heard—what fit (or did not fit) with her own experience, what was puzzling or surprising, and how she was feeling about the assessment as a whole.

Ms. T voiced surprise and pleasure in hearing that she had strong visual-analytic skills—"There are actual scores that say I'm well above average in this area that's right at the heart of what I want to do with my life!"—and a mixture of sadness and relief to discover that ADHD explained some of her problems with attention and memory. She then reflected on information about her emotional dysregulation and ambivalence about closeness, commenting,

> That must be why I've tried therapy so many times but then kept having to run away from it. I'd get scared by something that was happening and I just wouldn't go back. Maybe this time I can talk to my therapist if something scares me.

We were to return to this comment when Ms. T called me several months later to request a follow-up session to discuss "a testing question" prompted by the assessment results. She explained that she and her therapist had read the report together in her next therapy session; she then took the report home, re-reading it several times. Recently, she had thought of a question that she hoped I could answer, but she preferred to discuss it in person. I agreed to her request, anticipating that there was something in the test data that she wanted to better understand.

In this follow-up session, Ms. T first thanked me again for all of my hard work and said how helpful she had found the testing process, even though it was often painful. She continued, noting that she had begun to wonder if the good testing relationship we had established might mean that we could work well together in therapy. As I confronted this unexpected turn of events, I struggled to find a way to work with the new material in a way that honored what we had together learned about Ms. T. I asked her to tell me about what might be unfolding in her ongoing therapy that was prompting this request. She explained, with a hint of embarrassment as she mimed her complaint, that her therapist gestured in a particular way when he was making a point, and that she was finding this "weird" and "off-putting." I was struck by an aggressive edge to her gesture—a kind of visual hyperbole, given that I know my colleague well enough to be familiar with this (to me) benign gesture. I wondered if, for the patient, he had become the abusive mother in the transference, and I was being recruited as the father who would buffer the patient from trauma. (And, in writing about this moment, I found myself thinking of the crab with the "great claw" that destabilized the patient's thinking on Card X of the Rorschach).

Neither wanting to create a narcissistic injury nor wanting to take on the interpretive role of the therapist, I stayed in the role of the assessor: I told Ms. T that I was remembering her closing comments in our feedback session—how she hoped that if something scared her in her current therapy experience, she could find a way to talk about it. She looked genuinely startled. She reflected for a moment before asking me, "Do you think I could do that?" In this phrasing I heard two meanings: "Do you think I'm capable of talking about my anxiety rather than fleeing again?" And, "Do you think it's safe to speak openly with my therapist?" I met her gaze, and with a sincere belief in both her and my colleague's capabilities, I calmly replied, "Yes, I do."

I learned from her therapist at a later time that Ms. T did indeed become able to speak more openly in a treatment that lasted for three years at an unchanged frequency. Additionally, she was involved in a satisfying romantic relationship and had made strides in her career, learning to take a stand with people in the business world and with her brothers when discussing care for their aging father. At the same time, the test results gave her permission to ask for help without feeling stupid. Further, she became able to consider both neurocognitive and psychodynamic contributions to her attention and memory problems after stimulant medication provided partial benefit. Indeed, her therapist said the recommendation that medication not be repeatedly changed was one of the most helpful suggestions, as it allowed him to gently remind the patient of conflictual issues that were coming to the fore when she would ask to change or increase her medication in response to unclear thinking. Together, they could discuss how medication was not the complete solution and explore what issues were arising that kept Ms. T from using her sharp mind.

Unfortunately, the treatment ended abruptly (but perhaps unsurprisingly) when a sudden, unexpected insurance change meant that Ms. T could no longer pay her therapist's full fee. He was quite willing to lower the fee substantially to make payment manageable, but the patient felt unable to accept this offer and fled the treatment. It seems likely that she could not tolerate the level of dependency that she would feel in accepting this offer, but the therapist let her know in a follow-up phone call that he would welcome her return in the future, leaving the door open.

## Assessor reflections

This assessment proved to be an enriching experience. Emotionally, I felt rewarded by the opportunity to make meaningful contact with Ms. T, a woman who was taking risks to know herself better at a critical crossroads in her life. Intellectually, I felt challenged by a diagnostic "puzzle" that inquired into the possibility of ADHD, a specific learning disability, anxiety, and personality issues—all of which are of interest to me, especially in their frequently intertwined presentation. Professionally, I felt gratified that my initial optimism was justified—that I had carried out this comprehensive assessment for a colleague who could (and did) make use of the complete test report. Learning that he had not fallen prey to colluding with the patient in the search for a "perfect" medication regimen, and that my cautionary note about this had proven helpful to him in reorienting the therapeutic dyad to Ms. T's conflictual issues, affirmed for me the value of viewing neuropsychological assessments through a psychoanalytic lens.

It was this psychoanalytic lens that guided my thinking during key moments of challenge. Given Ms. T's early, tentative disclosures regarding her anxiety about being tested and her history of fleeing multiple treatments, I wanted to be sensitive to her potential for emotional dysregulation and her need for boundaries, but also to her implicit plea to be seen—and judged—as capable. I knew, too, that within my busy professional schedule, I had little flexibility to extend the number of hours I was allotting to the assessment, or to change appointments once the testing schedule was set in place. With an awareness of how easily I could be drawn into offering something "extra" to this vulnerable and likable patient (Yalof, 2020), I proceeded thoughtfully.

My challenge was to consider the pragmatic and the clinical as two sides of the same coin, allowing them to work together—rather than in opposition—toward the aims of the assessment. Holding in mind both the limits of time and the need to observe Ms. T's own capacities, I neither solicited nor closed off her emotional responses to test measures as they emerged; nor did I step in to comfort her or modulate moments of distress, other than to empathically listen and judiciously respond to her perceptive offerings. In this manner, we were able to maintain a steady, productive pace. I noted to myself that Ms. T was punctual and attended all appointments as scheduled. With my (reluctant) choice to forgo the projective drawing series (unbeknownst to the patient), we completed the assessment in the original time allotted.

A final challenge arose when Ms. T wondered in the later follow-up session if she and I could make the transition from the assessment relationship to working together in therapy. At that moment, a psychoanalytic mindset was invaluable in organizing my thoughts and experiences as they came to mind. I have come to know that the testing experience can be a powerful one, often allowing the patient to idealize the assessor; this was not the first time I had encountered such a request. Although it is my policy not to take into treatment a patient who is in therapy with another clinician at the time of the testing, I was not guided in this clinical moment by my policy; indeed, it seemed barely pertinent to the issue at hand.

Rather, uppermost in my mind were Ms. T's repeated episodes of fleeing treatment, her earlier expressed hope that testing would allow her to prevent another abrupt departure, and the phrasing of her request when she called for the follow-up session with me: she had "a testing question" that she thought I could help her answer. Considered through the volume of test data, I heard Ms. T asking me once again—albeit at a less conscious level and with heightened anxiety about the therapeutic relationship—to help her not flee treatment. By listening to her phrasing ("Do you think I could do that?"), I could join her at the preconscious level, at once affirming her newfound capability to talk directly about what troubles her *and* that her therapist would neither withdraw nor retaliate in response. Ms. T could ask for help and move forward independently in this final exchange of a psychoanalytically guided assessment.

## References

Allison, J. (1978). Clinical contributions of the Wechsler adult intelligence scale. In B. Wolman (Ed.), *Clinical diagnosis of mental disorders* (pp. 355–392). New York: Plenum Press.

American Psychiatric Association. (2013). *Diagnostic and statistical manual of mental disorders* (5th ed.). Washington, DC: American Psychiatric Publishing.

Bird, H. R. (2002). The diagnostic classification, epidemiology, and cross-cultural validity of ADHD. In P. S. Jensen & J. R. Cooper (Eds.), *Attention deficit hyperactivity disorder: State of the science-best practices* (pp. 1–16). Kingston, NJ: Civic Research Institute.

Bornstein, R. F. (2001). Has psychology become the science of questionnaires? A survey of research outcome measures at the close of the 20th century. *General Psychologist, 36*, 36–40.

Bornstein, R. F. (2002). A process dissociation approach to objective-projective test score interrelationships. *Journal of Personality Assessment, 78*(1), 47–68.

Bornstein, R. F. (2010). Psychoanalytic theory as a unifying framework for 21st century personality assessment. *Psychoanalytic Psychology, 27*(2), 133–152.

Bram, A. D., & Peebles, M. J. (2014). *Psychological testing that matters: Creating a road map for effective treatment.* Washington, DC: American Psychological Association Books.

Bram, A. D., & Yalof, J. (2015). Quantifying complexity: Personality assessment and its relationship with psychoanalysis. *Psychoanalytic Inquiry, 35*(Suppl. 1), 74–97. doi:10.108 0/07351690.2015.987595.

Brickman, A. S., & Lerner, H. D. (1992). Barren Rorschachs: A conceptual approach. *Journal of Personality Assessment, 59*(1), 176–184.

Brown, T. E. (1996). *Brown attention-deficit disorder scales: For adolescents and adults.* San Antonio, TX: PsychCorp/Pearson.

Capodieci, A., & Martinussen, R. (2017). Math error types and correlates in adolescents with and without attention deficit hyperactivity disorder. *Frontiers in Psychology, 8*, 1801. https://doi:10.3389/fpsy.g.2017.01801.

Carey, W. B. (2002). Is ADHD a valid disorder? In P. S. Jensen & J. R. Cooper (Eds.), *Attention deficit hyperactivity disorder: State of the science-best practices* (pp. 3–10). Kingston, NJ: Civic Research Institute.

Conners, C. K., & Staff, M. H. S. (2002). *Conners' continuous performance test II.* North Tonawanda, NY: Multi-Health Systems.

Exner, J. E. (1969). *The Rorschach systems.* New York: Grune & Stratton.

Exner, J. E. (1993). *The Rorschach comprehensive system: Basic foundations* (vol. 1, 3rd ed.). New York: Wiley.

Golden, C. J., & Freshwater, S. M. (2002). *Stroop color and word test: Revised examiner's manual.* Wood Dale, IL: Stoelting.

Hammer, E. F. (1958). *The clinical application of projective drawings.* Springfield, IL: Charles C. Thomas.

Heaton, R. K., Chelune, G. J., Talley, J. L., Kay, G. G., & Curtiss, G. (1993). *Wisconsin card sorting test manual.* Lutz, FL: Psychological Assessment Resources.

Holt, R. (1978). *Methods in clinical psychology: Projective assessment* (vol. 1). New York: Plenum Press.

Klopfer, B., Ainsworth, M. D., Klopfer, W. G., & Holt, R. R. (1954). *Developments in the Rorschach technique: Technique and theory* (vol. 1). Yonkers-on-Hudson, NY: World Book Co.

Leak, S. (2019). Bringing a psychoanalytic mindset to neuropsychological testing: From parameters and testing the limits to the "something more." *Psychoanalytic Psychology, 36*(1), 44–52. doi:10.1037/pap0000167.

Leak, S., & Hayden, S. (2015). *Shame and guilt in dyslexia and attention-deficit disorder: An integration of neurocognitive and psychodynamic perspectives.* Unpublished manuscript.

Lingiardi, V., & McWilliams, N. (Eds.) (2017). *Psychodynamic diagnostic manual* (2nd ed.). New York: Guildford Press.

Mayman, M. (1968). Early memories and character structure. *Journal of Projective Techniques and Personality Assessment, 32*(4), 303–316.

Mayman, M. (1977). A multidimensional view of the Rorschach movement response. In M. A. Rickers-Ovsiankina (Ed.), *Rorschach psychology* (2nd ed., pp. 229–250). Huntington, NY: Krieger Publishing.

Meersand, P. (2011). Psychological testing and the analytically trained child psychologist. *Psychoanalytic Psychology, 28*(1), 117–131.

Meyer, G. J., Viglione, D. J., Mihura, J. L., Erard, R. E., & Erdberg, P. (2011). *Rorschach performance assessment system: Administration, coding, interpretation, and technical manual.* Toledo, OH: Rorschach Performance Assessment System.

Morey, L. C. (1991). *Personality assessment inventory.* Odessa, FL : PAR.

Morrel, A. (1998). Attention deficit disorder and its relationship to narcissistic pathology. In P. Beren (Ed.), *Narcissistic disorders in children and adolescents: Diagnosis and treatment.* Northvale, NJ: Jason Aronson.

Murray, H. A. (1943). *Thematic apperception test.* Cambridge, MA: Harvard University Press.

Rapaport, D., Gill, M., & Schafer, R. (1968). *Diagnostic psychological testing* (rev. ed.). New York: International Universities Press.

Reitan, R. M. (1986). *Trail making test: Manual for administration and scoring.* Tucson, AZ: Reitan Neuropsychological Laboratory.

Schrank, F. A., Mather, N., & McGrew, K. S. (2014). *Woodcock-Johnson IV tests of achievement.* Rolling Meadows, IL: Riverside.

Shapiro, D. (1999). *Neurotic styles.* New York: Basic Books.

Shaywitz, S. (2003). *Overcoming dyslexia: A new and complete science-based program for reading problems at any level.* New York: Vintage Books.

Sheslow, D., & Adams, W. (2003). *WRAML2: Wide range assessment of memory and learning* (2nd ed.). Lutz, FL: PAR.

Tosto, M. G., Momi, S. K., Asherson, P., & Malki, K. (2015). A systematic review of attention deficit hyperactivity disorder (ADHD) and mathematical ability: Current findings and future implications. *Biomed Central, 13,* 204. https://doi:10.1186/s12916-015-0414-4.

Tuber, S. (2012). *Understanding personality through projective testing.* New York: Jason Aronson.

Waldron, S., Gordon, R. M., & Gazzillo, F. (2017). Assessment within the PDM-2 framework. In V. Lingiardi & N. McWilliams (Eds.), *Psychodynamic diagnostic manual* (2nd ed.). New York: Guildford Press.

Wechsler, D. (2008). *Wechsler adult intelligence scale—fourth edition (WAIS-IV).* San Antonio, TX: Pearson.

Wechsler, D., Raiford, S. E., & Holdnack, J. A. (2014). *Wechsler intelligence scale for children—fifth edition (WISC-V).* Bloomington, MD: Pearson.

World Health Organization. (1992). *International statistical classification of diseases and related health problems* (10th Revision). Geneva: World Health Organization.

Yalof, J. (2006). Case illustration of a boy with nonverbal learning disorder and Asperger's features: Neuropsychological and personality assessment. *Journal of Personality Assessment, 87*(1), 15–34.

Yalof, J. (2020). When the assessor's limits are tested: Enactments and the assessment frame in psychological testing. *Journal of Personality Assessment, 102*(4), 573–583. doi: 10.1080/00223891.2019.1613241.

# 4   A psychoanalytic approach to psychoeducational evaluations

*James H. Kleiger*

A father's voicemail message sounded quite routine. "My 13-year-old daughter, Joelle, has learning disabilities and needs an updated psychoeducational evaluation." Nothing out of the ordinary about this request, right? However, I was intrigued by the next part of the message. "Oh, and by the way, she's gotten herself in quite a pickle with her school." In this case, the "pickle" consisted of highly provocative behavior, which, although nonviolent, precipitated a maelstrom of concern at home, in the school community, and with the local sheriff's department, which threatened to contact the FBI. A legitimate request for a psychoeducational evaluation was the calling card for parent, school, and local law enforcement concern about acute risks associated with this child's behavioral and psychological functioning. The school instructed Joelle's parents that they would suspend Joelle until she had completed a psychological evaluation to ensure that she was not at risk for committing an act of violence on school grounds.

When I think of Joelle, I am reminded of the importance of conducting a balanced assessment, which provides sufficient breadth and depth to understand the multiple factors that can contribute to impediments in learning and performance in school. Too often, assessors truncate the vision or scope of our evaluations, over-focusing on neurocognitive deficits and learning impairments, while sacrificing a thorough assessment of the person with the disability. Or, conversely, as in cases like Joelle's where the behavioral disruption was so provocative as to draw all the attention, we often overlook the myriad meanings associated with or the multiple functions served by the student's cognitive and behavioral symptoms. To restrict our focus only on "learning disabilities" or "disruptive behavior" shortchanges the child by limiting our understanding to surface-level observables. Joelle's tale teaches us that every learning and behavioral problem may be understood in a broader dynamic way, which can open up previously unforeseen avenues of treatment.

## Description of setting

As an independent psychoanalyst practitioner, I conduct comprehensive psychological, neurocognitive, and educational assessments in an outpatient setting. As was the case with Joelle, students are frequently referred by their therapists, who voice concerns about their patient's psychosocial and behavioral functioning. I encourage referring clinicians to formulate specific assessment questions to help guide the evaluation. When parents call, they typically list their concerns about their child's psychosocial and behavioral functioning, along with pressing questions about learning and school performance. Public school Educational Management Teams (EMTs) are another constituent of a comprehensive evaluation and focus chiefly on cognitive and educational concerns, and with students like Joelle, disruptive behavior and its associated risks. The freedom of independent practice allows me to conduct thorough evaluations that establish a baseline for the child's educational strengths and weaknesses and explore cognitive, emotional, and psychodynamic causal pathways that manifest as impediments to learning and performance.

## Brief literature review

Standards for psychoeducational evaluations specify that the scope of assessment should determine relative contributions of difficulties in cognitive functioning, psychosocial development, and adaptive behavior to specific problems in learning (Stetson & Stetson, 2001). Although inclusions of psychological and behavioral measures are critical to performing a comprehensive psychological assessment, Rothstein and colleagues (Rothstein, Benjamin, Crosby, & Eisenstadt, 1995) noted that psychological and neuropsychological explanations are rarely integrated. Instead, assessors frequently focus more on neuropsychological explanations with secondary, sometimes perfunctory, sections addressing the child's psychosocial functioning. Rothstein and colleagues recommended that evaluations attempt to highlight the psychological complexities and nuances of learning disorders and highlighted the way in which learning disorders covary with, and infuse, psychological conflicts and behavioral problems. This was the type of reasoning that informed my understanding of the complicating background factors underlying Joelle's referral for a comprehensive and psychodynamically-informed psychoeducational assessment.

## Case background

Several years prior to the evaluation, Joelle's parents had separated. Her mother moved out and rented a nearby apartment. The older of two sisters, Joelle divided her week living between parents' homes. Although she did not speak much about her family break-up, her therapist said she had talked about missing her mother.

Joelle had a neuropsychological evaluation when she was seven years old. Diagnosed with attention deficit hyperactivity disorder (ADHD), combined presentation (American Psychiatric Association, 2013) and multiple specific learning disabilities, she had an Individualized Educational Plan (IEP; Wright & Wright, 2015) that specified a range of special educational services and accommodations. Initially, she had been prescribed Concerta to treat her inattentiveness and hyperactivity; however, this medication was discontinued in the sixth grade because her parents did not see much improvement in her symptoms. With high school a few years away, Joelle's parents had questions about whether she might benefit from a smaller and more specialized educational setting, and if they should reconsider medication.

Joelle's therapist of two years referred her for this evaluation. A psychologist who specializes in working with adolescents, Dr. P. had concerns about Joelle's provocative behavior that had sent shockwaves through the school community. Previously diagnosed with specific learning disorders with impairments in reading, writing, and math, Joelle came to the attention of school authorities after parents of classmates reported that she had sent sexually explicit and racially insensitive cartoons and video clips from her older cousin's YouTube account. Parents in her small community had been sensitized to violence in the school system and were attuned to anomalous behavior, which might signal a child at risk. In the six months prior to the incident, Joelle had been "obsessively" (a word that she used) searching the internet for highly provocative cartoons, which were designed to shock and amuse viewers with their dark and socially inappropriate and offensive content.

Early in her treatment, Dr. P. had concerns about Joelle's reports of hearing voices; but he determined that these were personified manifestations of her "conscience." Joelle seemed to maintain an awareness that the "voices" were a part of her own mind, as opposed to disembodied or alien sources attempting to communicate with her. Dr. P. also noted some signs and symptoms of depression and anxiety.

Together with parents, the referring psychologist posed several questions: (a) How do we understand Joelle's "pickle"? What might lie behind her ostensibly poor judgment? Does her behavior present concerns for the school? (b) How severe are her learning deficits and what are the implications and recommendations for an educational plan?

When I met Joelle in the waiting room with her parents, I was struck by her small size and impish appearance. She assumed a casual posture, seated between two worried-looking parents. I introduced myself to the parents, while Joelle eyed me with apparent interest. She shook my hand firmly and flashed a grin as she accompanied me into my office.

She wore shorts and pink tennis shoes, without laces. Each shoe was adorned with memes written by different colored markers. Her closely cropped auburn hair sprouted a single pigtail from the top of her head. She had large brown eyes and an easy smile. Joelle's voice was high-pitched. Her affect was flexible, and she seemed in little emotional distress. She appeared to enjoy the 1:1 interview time, as she responded to questions with elaborate answers. However, as I would find out later, her engaging and cooperative style shifted when we began performance testing. At this shift, Joelle exhibited a disinterest, accompanied by a foot-dragging compliance on many testing procedures. During our second appointment she sat in the lobby, waiting for me to notice the purple and pink streaks in her hair.

Joelle spoke openly about her collection of YouTube cartoons and videos, which had gotten her in so much trouble. She said she thought it was "kind of funny and kind of not." Joelle explained that many of the offensive cartoons were "funny because they are so bad!" She thought most of her peers thought they were funny too, as they often laughed, rolled their eyes, or responded, "Dude, that is so sick!" Joelle explained that her greatest mistake was emailing these to her peers. From there, things got out of hand. "Some kids' parents checked their email. Then they called the principal, who suspended me that day. Next thing I knew, the deputies were knocking at my door, telling me I might go to jail. My mom totally lost it!"

Joelle described how badly she felt watching her mother break down into tears when the deputies knocked at their door. When asked her purpose of amassing such a large collection of downloaded cartoons, memes, and video clips, Joelle said that she had set an arbitrary goal of "getting 100 of them." Beyond this, she offered no other explanation about her underlying intent. With this incident behind her, Joelle said that it had been a big mistake and that she is still suffering the consequences. She claimed that "I made a big mistake and had a lapse of judgment and now I got to live with it."

## Rationale for battery

With appropriate standards of practice and aspirational principles in mind, I widen the scope of my usual testing batteries when evaluating complex problems affecting a youngster's educational status to include equal attention to (1) cognitive functioning (intellectual abilities, oral language, memory and learning, attention and executive functioning), (2) academic proficiency (basic skills, fluency, and complex problem solving), and (3) psychosocial and emotional functioning. Regarding the last of these, assessment of personality issues must extend beyond self-report or parent and teacher observations. Although it is critical to know what the patient can tell us about herself and how key adults observe the child across settings, we also want to understand what the individual *cannot* tell us. For this reason, it is imperative to employ a set of implicit measures that provide an assessment of personality resources or ego functions that contribute to an understanding of structural aspects of personality functioning, including management of affects and impulses, organization of thinking and reality testing, and the patient's experience of herself and others. Additionally, beyond static descriptions of symptoms and personality organization, we are particularly interested in ascertaining unconscious motivation, possible areas of conflict, and ways in which the patient's symptoms, whether they are behavioral or neurocognitive in nature, can be deployed as compromises when the individual is in conflict.

As part of a comprehensive evaluation, I solicit collateral information, such as a developmental history questionnaire, previous evaluation reports, school records (progress reports and IEP). I conduct separate interviews with parents and child and ask parent and teacher to complete rating scales, the BASC-3 (Reynolds & Kamphaus, 2015), and the BRIEF-2 (Goia, Isquith, Guy, & Kenworthy, 2015). Given the breadth and depth of my examination focus, I utilized a flexible, domain-centered, multi-method approach and included the following empirically based instruments in my evaluation of Joelle:

*Neurocognitive*: Wechsler Intelligence Scale for Children, Fifth Edition (WISC-V; Wechsler, 2014); Woodcock-Johnson Tests of Oral Language, Fourth Edition (WJOL-IV; Schrank, Mather, & McGrew, 2014a); Rey Complex Figure Test and Recognition Trial (RCFT; Meyers & Meyers, 1995); Delis-Kaplan Executive Functioning System (D-KEFS; Delis, Kaplan, & Kramer, 2001); Test of Memory & Learning, Second Edition (TOMAL-2; Reynolds & Voress, 2007); Integrated Visual-Auditory Continuous Performance Test, Second Edition (IVA-2; BrainTrain, 2017).
*Academic Proficiency*: Woodcock-Johnson Tests of Academic Achievement, Fourth Edition (WJA-IV; Shrank, Mather, & McGrew, 2014a); Wechsler Individual Achievement Test, Third Edition, Essay Composition (WIAT-III; Wechsler 2009).
*Parent and Teacher Rating Scales*: Behavioral Assessment System for Children, Third Edition (BASC-3; Reynolds & Kamphaus, 2015), Parent & Teacher forms and Behavioral Rating Inventory of Executive Functions, Second Edition (BRIEF-2; Goia et al., 2015), Parent, Teacher, & Self-report forms.
*Psychological and Emotional*: Personality Assessment Inventory, Adolescent (PAI-A; Morey, 1991); Rorschach-Performance Assessment System (R-PAS; Meyer, Viglione, Mihura, Erard, & Erdberg, 2011; Thematic Apperception Test (TAT; Murray, 1943).

## Summary of findings

A bit of a diamond in the rough, Joelle was a colorful, articulate, impish, and charming girl, who presented with a myriad of processing, learning, perfor-mance, emotional, and behavioral challenges. Some of her difficulties were more apparent than others, having been present and well documented for many years. Of primary importance was the extent of Joelle's internal struggles that could have been easily overlooked by focusing only on her ADHD, learn-ing challenges, or more recent high-profile behavioral incidents. Although her processing, learning, and behavioral issues merited a great deal of attention, the evaluation offered an opportunity, not only to review her functioning across multiple cognitive, learning, and psychosocial domains, but also to understand Joelle's difficulties and provocative behavior in a more integrative fashion. As such, her functional difficulties could be discussed in terms of: (a) her highly variable cognitive abilities, which ranged from superior to well below aver-age, with particular deficits in processing speed, attentional, and executive functions, (b) her long-standing learning challenges, which continued to manifest as deficits in academic fluency and dysgraphia, with relative weaknesses in reading comprehension and math computation, and (c) her marked psychological turmoil, consisting of severe masked depression, marked by irritability, anxiety, low self-esteem, difficulties regulating her emotions, thoughts, and behavior. Finally, it was important to view Joelle's provocative behavior through an integrative prism, by understanding her neurodevelopmental vulnerabilities from a psychodynamic perspective, with particular attention to underlying motivational factors and possible psychological functions that her self-defeating behavior might have served.

## Cognitive functioning

Joelle's neurocognitive vulnerabilities included (a) marked variability in her functioning, (b) extremely slow visual processing speed, word retrieval, and production, (c) dysgraphia, and (d) significant impairment in focusing, sustained attention, inhibition, working memory, planning, and organization.

### Cognitive variability

Joelle demonstrated uneven scores on intellectual measures with a dramatic discrepancy between her WISC-V Verbal Comprehension Index (VCI SS = 120, 91st percentile, Very High range) and Processing Speed Index (PSI SS = 72, 3rd percentile, Very Low range). The discrepancy between her VCI and PSI was 48 points! Joelle's remaining Index scores were average range on the Visual-Spatial Index (VSI SS = 105) and Fluid Reasoning Index (FRI SS = 106).

Core VCI subtests showed that Joelle had an impressive fund of verbal knowledge (Vocabulary = 15) and strong verbal reasoning abilities (Similarities = 13). Strikingly, fewer than 0.5% of subjects in the WISC-V standardization sample had inter-Index discrepancies of this magnitude. She also scored surprisingly high on the Working Memory Index (WMI SS = 122, Very High), a composite of auditory processing, mental manipulation of information, and short-term memory. However, despite strengths on auditory-verbal tasks, Joelle's speed for scanning and discriminating visual information quickly and accurately was quite impaired.

There were also significant discrepancies between language clusters on the WJOL-IV. For example, Joelle's average oral language expression (Oral Expression = 109, 73rd percentile) and comprehension abilities (Listening Comprehension = 100, 50th percentile) were markedly superior to her normatively weak fluency for retrieving and generating words from semantic memory (Speed of Lexical Access = 80, 9th percentile). This meant that, under time pressure, Joelle was slower than most children in retrieving known information from her long-term memory (and in generating words to fit specified categories). The dramatic disparity between her slow lexical processing speed and average expressive/receptive language mirrored the gap that was found between her WISC-V VCI and PSI. Thus, Joelle's processing speed and fluency deficits were present on measures of both intellectual functioning and oral language. Despite having verbal intellectual capacities higher than 90% of her peers, Joelle's verbal agility and fluency were weaker than 90% of her peers. Thus, although she knew a great deal and reasoned effectively with words, she was painfully slow in retrieving and producing information she stored in long-term memory. Practically speaking, verbal interactions with Joelle might lead others to assume that she should be able to complete simple tasks, retrieve, and generate information quickly. However, sadly, this was not the case.

*Inattention and impulsivity*

In addition to marked cognitive variability, extremely slow visual processing speed and word retrieval fluency, there was evidence of significant impairment in Joelle's sustained attention and impulse control. She had difficulty staying focused on visual stimuli on a test of sustained attention, in which she needed to remain alert to auditory and visual signals on a computer screen (IVA-2 Combined Sustained Attention Quotient = 62, Extremely Impaired range). Joelle had trouble sustaining her focus when the signals were scarce; in other words, when there was not a lot of visual or auditory stimulation. However, she also showed a distinct tendency to over-react to inappropriate visual stimuli, or visual targets, which were off-task (IVA-2, Full Scale Response Control Quotient = 70, Moderately Impaired). When it was time for her to ignore distracting, off-task stimuli, Joelle had significant difficulty shifting her attention and inhibiting her responses to these, incorrect, off-task targets. This neuropsychological deficit might have some relevance to her habit of collecting offensive videos and memes. Not only was she hyper-focused on these inappropriate, off-task distractions on her computer, but Joelle may also have had difficulty tuning them out and controlling her responses to them. They may have been highly distracting and pulled her away from the material on which she was supposed to be focusing. Thus, YouTube videos and cartoons might have had an emotionally charged, "irresistible" stimulus pull, that she had difficulty ignoring.

Although there was not much evidence of overt hyperactivity, there were indications of more subtle, fine-motor hyperactivity and restlessness (IVA-2 Fine-Motor Hyperactivity Quotient = 86, Mildly Impaired). During testing, Joelle had difficulty sitting still. She fidgeted, wiggled, shifted her position in the chair, and got up to pace around the office.

*Executive dysfunction*

Finally, there was considerable evidence, from both performance testing and parent/teacher rating scales of conspicuous deficits in executive regulation of her behavior, as well as in her executive organization, self-monitoring, and working memory (Elevations on BRIEF-2 Parent and Teacher Global Executive Composite exceeded T scores of 72 and were clinically significant). Joelle also demonstrated difficulties in testing tasks designed to assess aspects of executive functioning. Sometimes, the structured nature of assessment tasks helps individuals perform adequately in a quiet, controlled, 1:1 context. This was not the case for Joelle, who had as much difficulty on many of these tasks as she had apparently demonstrated in her day-to-day setting. She had difficulties in a complex figure-copying task designed to assess visual–motor integration, planning, and organization (RCFT). Joelle copied the complex figure in an arbitrary manner that lacked an apparent strategy for analyzing the figure, synthesizing, organizing, and reassembling the component parts to reconstruct the whole figure. Her willy-nilly approach to this task provided a window into how she might typically deal with similar kinds of complex and unstructured assignments. Thus, a convergence of findings from parent and teacher rating scales, on the one hand, and the performance testing, on the other, strengthened the conclusion that Joelle's poorly developed executive functions were a major factor limiting her performance in school. Finally, parents and teacher ratings of her mental flexibility suggested that Joelle had difficulty shifting cognitive sets and reorienting her attention when it was appropriate to move on (Elevations on both Parent and Teacher BRIEF-2 Shift scales exceeded T scores of 70, all falling within the clinically significant range). She also had enormous difficulty on a cognitive set-shifting task requiring her to divide her attention and move back and forth between two instructional sets (D-KEFS Trail Making Test, Number–Letter Switching, 1, <1st percentile). Thus, there was impressive evidence that Joelle had a propensity for becoming stuck. Not only might she have had problems screening out distracting, off-task stimuli, but she may also have been susceptible to becoming cognitively and emotionally stuck and unable to shift attentional sets.

### Learning and performance problems

Given these cognitive liabilities, it was easy to extrapolate to Joelle's problems in the classroom. Joelle was previously diagnosed with learning disabilities. Learning disabilities are based on underlying neuropsychological deficits, which keep an individual from learning to presumed potential. In contrast, performance difficulties reflect a broader range of interferences, stemming from deficits in attention and executive functions, loss of motivation, emotional, and other psychosocial difficulties, which regardless of whether the individual has a learning disability, collectively affect her performance in school. Joelle struggled both with learning and performance-based challenges.

Evidence of the learning disabilities, documented in a previous neuropsychological testing report, continued to be present in her current testing. Joelle's principal deficits were apparent in her labored academic fluency (WJA-IV Academic Fluency Cluster SS = 72, 3rd percentile, Low range). Her basic skill level placed her within the Average range (WJA-IV Academic Skills Cluster

SS = 95, 37th percentile, Average). This was the case on composites of Basic Reading Skills (SS = 103, 58th percentile, Average) and Basic Writing Skills (99, 48th percentile, Average). These skills were still below her WISC-V VCI baseline of 120, but they were likely to have been influenced by her processing speed deficits rather than by conceptual deficits. Thus, there was no evidence of a language-based learning disability, characterized by phonetic or orthographic dyslexia.

Joelle's score on a composite of academic problem solving was even higher (Academic Applications SS = 107, 68th percentile, Average). Here, she demonstrated an ability to deploy her core reading, math, and spelling skills to working successfully on applied academic tasks (e.g., reading comprehension, sentence writing, and math word problems), which far outstripped her labored pace of accessing and processing academic facts. Similar to the disparities found in her cognitive-intellectual assessment (i.e., WISC-V, VCI significantly higher than WISC-V, PSI), there was a similar gap between average-level knowledge and skills, on the one hand, and normatively weak academic fluency, on the other.

There were two exceptions to this average skill/knowledge versus impaired fluency gap in her achievement profile. First, Joelle scored below average on a composite of math calculation and fluency (Math Calculation Skills SS = 73, percentile, Low range). However, her score on this composite was primarily a product of extremely slow fluency for basic math facts (Math Facts Fluency, 62nd percentile, Very Low range). In contrast, her score on an untimed calculation subtest bordered between Low Average and Average (SS = 89, 21st percentile). Thus, although her basic computations skills were modest to begin with, her exceedingly slow math fluency was her most significant problem. Interestingly, despite her normatively slow fluency and automaticity for simple math facts and her relatively weak computational skills, Joelle achieved her best score on a measure of applied math, in solved word problems that required analysis and application of correct computational steps. Her above-average score on this measure suggested a potential that might be masked by her extremely slow pace of math work and her weak calculation skills (Applied Problems SS = 115, 85th percentile, High Average). The second exception in her achievement profile was evident in her performance on a compositional writing task. Joelle demonstrated marked difficulties when she was asked to write an essay (WIAT-III, Essay Composition subtest). Although she had scored within the Average range on a structured, single-sentence writing subtest (WJA-IV Writing Samples SS = 99, 48th percentile), she labored unsuccessfully on a less structured essay-writing task. Joelle held her pencil with an immature 4-point grip and spent half of the allotted time staring at her blank page. When she began writing, she formed her letters slowly, often ignoring the spacing between words. Her handwriting was not completely legible. An overall score on the Essay Composition subtest was below average (SS = 86, 18th percentile). Her component scores on measures of word production (Word Count) and written organization (Text Organization & Theme Development) fell below the 20th percentile.

In summary, the results of the cognitive and educational assessment high-lighted the marked variability in Joelle's abilities. A verbally bright girl with average language-based cognitive and academic skills, she was encumbered by extremely slow processing speed, retrieval fluency, along with deficits in executive and attentional functions. Thus, although she was knowledgeable, articulate, and capable of abstract thinking, her learning and school perfor-mance were hindered by deficits in processing speed, sustained attention, cog-nitive flexibility, planning, and organization.

### Psychological functioning

Joelle's behavioral challenges and her erratic, often marginal academic per-formance might overshadow the extent of her internal emotional distress, the intensity of her impulses, and poorly regulated emotions, thoughts, and fanta-sies. In addition to feeling worse than others might imagine, the issue of affect and impulse regulation was of paramount importance. Impulse control had long been an issue. However, what made regulation a problem, was, in part, the strength of the impulses and affects that impinged upon her. Joelle appeared to harbor intense internal pressure that she had difficulty ignoring, neutraliz-ing, articulating, or understanding. As noted above, her obsessive collecting of offensive videos, memes, and cartoons may have had an "irresistible" stimulus pull, that she had trouble screening out or shifting from.

Those around her might not have readily picked up on the level of her internal distress. The distress signals she sent may not have been the usual ones. More specifically, although parents acknowledged "mild" problems with anxiety, obsessional thinking, low self-esteem, and withdrawal, the testing revealed a much greater level of emotional turbulence and distress than others might have been aware of. Certainly, the presence of underlying depressive or anxious distress had not been noticed and reported by her teachers. I suspect that her behavioral and performance challenges had consumed all of the oxy-gen and required more immediate attention. Furthermore, Joelle's analytical thinking, her sense of social injustice, and her playful demeanor, affect, and humor did not directly communicate emotional perturbation or internal chaos. Nonetheless, the psychological testing was quite consistent regarding her strug-gle with painful, dark, and tormenting feelings.

On private self-report measures (PAI-A, which she completed on her own), Joelle also complained of severe underlying depression (T = 86), character-ized by feelings of inadequacy, worthlessness, embittered pessimism, boredom, irritability, discouragement, and a loss of pleasure. Her innately slow process-ing speed and compromised attentional and executive functions may have been further eroded by her depression. Depression zapped her energy and limits her interests and motivation. She also complained of not feeling well and described a general physical malaise. Her mother reported a long-standing sleep disturbance, which matched Joelle's acknowledged problems sleeping, along with a lack of pep and appetite. In addition to her sense of boredom and her difficulties deploying her attention toward things that held little interest, Joelle gravitated towards distractions as forms of entertainment and self-stimulation, which momentarily deflected her attention from her underlying malaise and despair.

Mixed in with her depression was a significant amount of fearfulness and hostility, which did not appear to be manifest in direct, overt expressions of terror or aggression toward others. Nonetheless, she seemed to experience significant pressure emanating from fearful, aggressive thoughts and fantasies (R-PAS PPD SS=134, AGC SS = 124, AGM SS > 150). While she may not have expressed these through combative or violent behavior, Joelle may have found other avenues of expression. One of these involved directing angry, hostile feelings toward herself. For example, Dr. P. described aggressive fantasies, which he thought had previously played a role in the hostile voices she used to hear. According to her therapist, Joelle initially denied anger at her parents' divorce, and mother's moving out, in particular. For much of her time in therapy, she was unable to talk productively about her feelings. However, when her therapist capitalized on her ability to form conceptual connections and linked her warded off anger to the voices, she was able to let the voices fade away. Another form of self-directed aggression involved Joelle's self-loathing and risk for self-harm. Her father bolstered this concern by noting that she often talked about how she hated herself. When we talked directly about these issues, Joelle acknowledged suicidal thoughts but said that she did not want to die. Finally, her search for dark, frightening, and aggressively tinged videos, cartoons, and memes may have provided another outlet for her anger. The aggression and hostility conveyed through some of these images provoked concerns about her potential for violence, which ultimately led to a major disruption in her life. Once again, her preoccupation with sharing and disseminating such provocative material may have served both a way to discharge the aggressive pressure she was feeling inside, and, at the same time, distract herself and others from the turmoil she felt.

Concerns about what lay behind Joelle's collecting and sharing her memes prompted some questions about whether these behaviors reflected underlying psychotic tendencies. If the question was whether Joelle was actively psychotic, then the answer was clearly, no. Although she had a history of hearing voices, she processed these in therapy and maintained that these symptoms no longer occurred. Beyond a past history of hearing voices, there were no clear-cut symptoms of an underlying psychosis. On psychological measures, there was no evidence of disorganized or illogical thinking. Occasional instances of immature reasoning were mild.

Nonetheless, Joelle may have had difficulties controlling what she thought about and when to filter, disengage, and ignore. She could easily become caught up with (and have difficulty shifting from) her darkly aggressive and morbid ideas, especially when responding to unstructured stimuli, which required impromptu decisions and judgment. Ineffective filtering was a key issue. When left on her own to interpret complex and ambiguous situations, Joelle had difficulty sticking with just the facts without embellishing her perceptions and impressions with emotionally tinged, often-dark and aggressive, personal associations. She tended to lose objectivity and interpreted events in a highly personalized and impressionistic manner. Furthermore, she gravitated toward abstract concepts, which at times, became lost in vague and emotionally laden references. Other, less apparent, challenges in her psychological functioning included Joelle's subtle grandiosity and alertness to signs of potential dangers in the environment. Despite having a deeper sense of inadequacy and worthlessness, Joelle exuded a breezy confidence to most with whom she had casual contact. She occasionally came across as sure of herself, seemingly unencumbered by what others might think. She eschewed conformity and embraced unconventionality and individualism. Although her intelligence, abstract thinking, and desire to be different, at times, led to creative outcomes, at other times, Joelle strived to be different just for the sake of being different. When trying so hard to be unique, Joelle may tend to miss what is more common, obvious, and appropriate. Although most likely a friendly and colorful figure among her peers, she was also cynical and mistrusting of others. She tended to expect the worst from people, which she conveyed through a cynical, satirical viewpoint. Thus, it was no surprise that she had been a fan of the French satirical magazine *Charlie Abdo*. Despite any reported potential for displaying kindness and social concern, she may not have thought deeply about others' feelings or experiences. The offensiveness of some videos and cartoons reflected not only extremely poor judgment but a striking lapse of empathy.

### Integrated formulation

Joelle's recent behavioral problems could be understood by weaving together the strands of cognitive and psychological perspectives. From a neurocognitive perspective, her fascination with collecting memes reflected both her attraction to off-task visual stimuli and her difficulty filtering, controlling, and shifting her attention. As described above, there was almost an irresistible quality to the videos and cartoons Joelle pursued. Furthermore, offensive memes may have allowed her to externalize and express the darkness, chaos, fear, and hostility that she struggles with inside. In addition, this behavior attracted a lot of attention, some positive reactions from peers, and some highly negative responses from authority figures. Regarding the latter, Joelle's cartoons may have become a voice for her rebellious urges to shock and to flout authority, and as a way of provocatively pushing the envelope and testing limits. Again, all of this kept the focus outside of herself. By igniting a storm of controversy around her, Joelle did not have to be left alone with her own dark and frightening feelings. Her actions drew attention; she got a reaction from peers and unwanted attention from authority figures. However, the main battlefront was between her and others, perhaps allowing a respite from the more pressing turmoil within.

Finally, although more speculatively, some of Joelle's struggles and efforts to cope might have mimicked similar experiences that her mother had during adolescence. Her mother shared results from her own recent psychological evaluation, which described not only her ADHD and learning challenges but also her difficulty with depression. More interestingly, her mother's testing report noted her tendency to cope with painful feelings through intellectualizing and turning to humor and jokes. Like Joelle, her mother said that she, too, had been an "angsty kid," who had struggled in school and engaged in provocative behavior aimed at getting a reaction from her peers. Aside from genetic factors, it is not unreasonable to conjecture that Joelle, knowingly or unknowingly, may have identified with her mother in the context of her parents' separation. This loss was reportedly enormously painful for Joelle and may have exacerbated some of her earlier struggles with anxiety and impulsive control.

## ICD-10 and PDM-2 diagnoses

According to the. *International Statistical Classification of Diseases and Related Health Problems* (ICD-10; World Health Organization, 1992), Joelle met criteria for the following diagnoses:

F90.0 Attention Deficit Hyperactivity Disorder, combined presentation
F81.0 Specific Learning Disorder with impairment in academic fluency, manifested in impairment in reading rate & fluency
F81.2 Specific Learning Disorder with impairment in math fluency
F81.81 Specific Learning Disorder with impairment in written fluency
F82 Developmental Coordination Disorder, dysgraphia
F32.1 Major Depression, Single episode, Moderate with anxious distress

Rule-out included risk for the development of a Cluster B personality disorder. However, with the presence of significant affective distress and with her development in flux, it was premature to diagnose a personality disorder. Nonetheless, without sufficient ongoing treatment, of sufficient intensity, scope, and duration, Joelle was at risk for a worsening of her affective symptoms and behavioral instability.

Based on the *Psychodynamic Diagnostic Manual, Second Edition* (PDM-2; Lingiardi & McWilliams, 2017), I conceptualized Joelle's difficulties as follows:

**Mental functioning for adolescents (MA Axis)**: Moderate impairments in mental functioning
**Emerging personality patterns and syndromes in adolescence (PA Axis)**: Externalizing Spectrum

**Adolescent symptom patterns (SA Axis)**: Major Depressive Disorder, Attention Deficit/Hyperactivity Disorder, Executive Function Disorder, Reading Disorder, Mathematics Disorder, and Disorder of Written Expression.

## Implications and recommendations

### School issues: Setting, supports, and accommodations

Joelle had an IEP, which included special education pull-out services for reading and writing. She also attended OT. Parents were encouraged to consider smaller schools specializing in educating students with learning and academic performance challenges. Regarding her learning needs, the testing indicated that her primary difficulties included (a) processing, retrieval, and academic fluency, (b) handwriting and written output, (c) sustained attention, (d) organization and planning, and (e) disengagement and low motivation. A comprehensive IEP would need to address each of these areas.

### Fluency and processing speed

Joelle processed new information slowly. She retrieved information from long-term memory slowly. She read, wrote, and computed slowly. Her written output was meager and her handwriting barely legible. Her reading comprehension and math calculation skills were weak. The pull-out services she was receiving would need to continue targeting her problems in each area.

### Dysgraphia

Occupational therapy services should continue to address long-standing fine-motor regulation issues affecting handwriting speed and control.

### Sustained attention, organization, and planning

Joelle should receive teaching accommodations to help her maintain attention and limit distractions. She should have a resource class to help with organizing her notebooks, outlining chapters, and preparing study plans. She should be able to begin her homework with staff supervision and support.

### Disengagement and low motivation

Joelle should have regular appointments with the school counselor, who could liaison with parents and a therapist to help with Joelle's discouragement and disengagement from classroom learning. Classroom accommodations should include (but not be limited to) interventions to address inattention and distractibility; slow processing, retrieval, and academic fluency; and dysgraphia.

*Extended time*

A benchmark of 50–100% time extensions should be put in place for all classroom tests. She should be given a minimum of 50% extended time, with 100% if she demonstrates a need in specific classes. Splitting the difference and providing 75% extended time for high-stakes standardized testing would be reasonable and justifiable based on her demonstrably slow fluency on all academic tasks.

*Preferential seating*

Joelle should be routinely assigned front row seating in all her classes. She should be seated away from distracting peers and noisier parts of the room. Sitting close to the teacher should help her remain more engaged and on task.

*Use of notebook computer*

Joelle said she can type faster than she can write. She should be allowed to use a keyboard for all in-class writing tasks.

*Speech-to-text software*

When possible, Joelle should use assistive technologies for speech to text (STT). Resources include software such as *Dragon Naturally Speaking* and *Microsoft Speech to Text* (Ontario Teachers' Federation, 2020); retrieved from https://www.teachspeced.ca/speech-to-text-programs).

**Treatment interventions**

*Individual psychotherapy*

Individual psychotherapy had helped Joelle process and manage her emotions and was needed to help with psychosocial, family, and academic challenges she will continue to encounter throughout adolescence. I strongly encouraged continued individual sessions at the frequency recommended by her therapist. Parent guidance sessions were recommended. Whether these were to be conducted by her therapist or by a colleague, parents needed to remain actively involved in Joelle's treatment. Parent guidance sessions could help them understand Joelle's cognitive, learning, and psychosocial challenges, and simultaneously provide consultation around co-parenting and management decisions.

*Medication consultation*

I recommended that psychopharmacological consultation and intervention become a more active and integral part of the treatment plan. Starting with her inattention and impulsivity, Joelle had a range of symptoms that could be targeted for medication trials. The testing showed a great deal of affective pressure with symptoms of anxiety, depression, anhedonia, irritability, and sleep difficulties. Joelle had difficulties regulating or filtering distracting thoughts and impulses, including dark and morbid fantasies that can capture her attention. The adolescent psychiatrist should be someone who can work collaboratively with Joelle's psychotherapist and parents to form a cohesive outpatient treatment team.

## Feedback

Although I do not practice formal Therapeutic Assessment (Finn, 2007), I strive for all of my assessments to be therapeutic experiences for patients and their families. I initially asked parents what they hoped to learn about Joelle from the evaluation. They jointly expressed an interest in whether Joelle's processing and academic skills had improved since her first evaluation when she was in second grade. They also hoped to gain an understanding of her reckless behavior that had drawn such negative attention and threatened to lead to her expulsion. Separately, I had queried Joelle about what she hoped she would learn about herself. Typically, I phrase this question in the following way for children and adolescents:

> We both know that you weren't the one who contacted me to do all this testing. Your parents and therapist had questions that they hoped I could help answer in the work that we will be doing. But, you are going to spend several days with me doing all these tests. I wonder what you would like to learn about yourself. What questions do you have that I could help you figure out?

My question was designed both to establish rapport and forge an alliance, and, at the same time, assess the patient's psychological-mindedness and potential for self-reflection during the diagnostic work, and potentially in treatment, as well.

Joelle quickly responded to my question by saying, "Nothing. I'm here because I have to be." However, she was not content to let this question fall flat. After a pause, she added, "Well, I guess I'd like more answers about why I put myself in this hole to begin with." Here was a foothold, a small opening in which Joelle seemed troubled and perhaps a bit curious about her self-destructive behavior. I try to schedule two feedback sessions, one with the parents alone and the other with the patient and her therapist (if they have one). I had worked in this manner with Dr. P. before, and he was happy to arrange time to be present when I shared the findings and recommendations with Joelle. Her parents were receptive to the feedback. We reviewed findings, diagnoses, and recommendations for school planning and treatment. Her father was surprised to learn about her depression because he had been focused more on her poor grades and problem behavior. However, her mother was less surprised, sharing her suspicions that Joelle hid her sadness behind a tough girl persona.

She indicated that she had found some of Joelle's poetry, which had dark and morbid themes. Parents agreed that they needed to have a clinician with whom they could meet on a regular basis (at least monthly) to help them understand the underpinnings of Joelle's provocative behavior and to provide guidance regarding co-parenting issues. They were receptive to arranging a consultation with a child and adolescent psychiatrist to reassess the role of medications in her treatment. Finally, they agreed that a possible change to a smaller and more specialized school environment might be beneficial.

Prior to the feedback meeting, Dr. P. and I had discussed the evaluation and what I planned to share with Joelle during our joint feedback session. I began her session by reading a three-page summary I had written for her. I told her that I would read through it so that we could discuss the evaluation with her therapist present. Although it takes a bit more time, I have found it worthwhile to distill essential findings and recommendations and present them in a short letter format. Thus, Joelle's letter began, "Dear Joelle, I thought it might be more meaningful and personal if I summarized the findings and recommendations in a short letter that does not include distracting information and a lot of jargon."

Joelle listened intently as I read some parts of the letter verbatim and paraphrased other sections. We paused after each part and invited her reactions, questions, and comments. Somewhat surprisingly, she agreed wholeheartedly with my explanation about how she was in far greater emotional distress than anyone, even her therapist, had really known. At one point, she teared up when we began talking about how her behavioral problems were similar to some of the difficulties her mother reportedly had in high school. Joelle was not supposed to know about this; but, like most children who grow up with family secrets, Joelle knew far more about mother's learning and behavioral struggles than they had known.

The format of the session allowed Dr. P. to monitor Joelle's reactions to learning of the feedback, especially discussion about psychological and emotional issues that had led her to "put herself in such a deep hole." He reassured her that they would devote plenty of time to explore the issues raised in the evaluation and find less self-defeating ways for Joelle to deal with her sadness, anger, and frustration.

## Assessor reflections

Two years after Joelle's evaluation, her mother called to schedule an evaluation for Joelle's younger sister, Moira. Parents were concerned about Moira's grades and emotional regulation. At the end of our call, her mother indicated that Joelle was doing very well. They had changed schools, and she was working effectively with learning specialists. She had begun antidepressant medication a year ago and seemed to have a brighter, less irritable mood. The psychiatrist was considering the addition of a stimulant to help with residual inattentiveness. Most importantly, she had engaged in no further behavior that drew negative attention from school authorities. The lesson learned again from this kind of evaluation was to help parents and the school view behaviorally or learning disordered children and adolescents as more than the sum of their processing, learning, or behavioral symptoms. Although there are often clear educational and behavioral fires that will demand attention and appropriate interventions, it is always important to understand the internal experiences of the individual—not only the nature of cognitive, educational, and behavioral challenges that the youngster brings with her, but how her symptoms might serve her in paradoxical ways.

# References

American Psychiatric Association. (2013). *Diagnostic and statistical manual of mental disorders* (5th ed.). Arlington, VA: American Psychiatric Association.

BrainTrain. (2017). *IVA-2. Integrated visual and auditory continuous performance test.* North Chesterfield, VA: BrainTrain, Inc.

Delis, D. C., Kaplan, E., & Kramer, J. H. (2001). *D-K E F S. Delis-Kaplan executive function system.* San Antonia, TX: The Psychological Corporation.

Finn, S. E. (2007). *In our client's shoes: Theory and techniques of therapeutic assessment.* Mahwah, NJ: Erlbaum.

Goia, G. A., Isquith, P. K., Guy, S. C., & Kenworthy, L. (2015). *Brief-2. Behavioral rating inventory of executive function* (2nd ed.). Lutz, FL: Psychological Assessment Resources.

Lingiardi, V., & McWilliams, N. (2017). *PDM-2. Psychodiagnostic manual* (2nd ed.). New York: Guilford Press.

Meyer, G. J., Viglione, D. J., Mihura, J. L., Erard, R. E., & Erdberg, P. (2011). *Rorschach performance assessment system: Administration, coding, interpretation, and technical manual.* Toledo, OH: Rorschach Performance Assessment System.

Meyers, J. E., & Meyers, K. R. (1995). *Rey complex figure test and recognition trial.* Odessa, FL: Psychological Assessment Resources.

Morey, L. C. (1991). *The personality assessment inventory professional manual.* Odessa, FL: Psychological Assessment Resources.

Murray, H. A. (1943). *Thematic pperception test manual.* Cambridge, MA: Harvard University Press.

Ontario Teachers' Federation (2020). Speech to text programs. Retrieved from https://www.teachspeced.ca/speech-to-text-programs 9/3/2020.

Reynolds, C. R., & Kamphaus, R. W. (2015). *BASC-3. Behavioral assessment system for children* (3rd ed.). Duluth, MN: NCS Pearson.

Reynolds, C. R., & Voress, J. K. (2007). *TOMAL-2. Test of memory and learning* (2nd ed.). Austin, TX: PRO-ED.

Rothstein, A., Benjamin, L., Crosby, M., & Eisenstadt, K. (1995). *Learning disorders: An integration of neuropsychological and psychoanalytic considerations.* Madison, CT: International Universities Press.

Schrank, F. A., Mather, N., & McGrew, K. S. (2014a). *Woodcock-Johnson IV tests of achievement.* Rolling Meadows, IL: Riverside.

Schrank, F. A., Mather, N., & McGrew, K. S. (2014b). *Woodcock-Johnson IV tests of oral language.* Rolling Meadows, IL: Riverside.

Stetson, E. G., & Stetson, R. (2001). Educational assessment. In C. E. Walker & M. C. Roberts (Eds.), *Handbook of clinical child psychology* (3rd ed., pp. 125–150). New York: Wiley.

76    *James H. Kleiger*

Wechsler, D. (2009). Wechsler *individual achievement test, third edition (WIAT-III)*. San Antonia, TX: NCS Pearson.

Wechsler, D. (2014). Wechsler *intelligence scale for children, fifth edition (WISC-V)*. Bloomington, MN: Pearson.

World Health Organization (1992). *International statistical classification of diseases and related health problems* (10th Revision). Geneva: World Health Organization.

Wright, P. W. D., & Wright, P. D. (2015). *Special educational law* (2nd ed.). Hartsfield, VA: Harbor House Laws Press, Inc.

# 5 Psychoanalytic psychological testing in residential and hospital-based settings

*Jeremy Ridenour*

## Psychoanalytic psychological testing in residential and hospital-based settings

In this chapter, I describe the value and clinical utility of conducting psychological testing in a residential/hospital-based setting and the ways it can guide treatment conceptualization and intervention. I first review previous applications of psychological testing in residential and hospital-based settings and then present a case of an evaluation that I conducted at the Austen Riggs Center with a patient admitted because of psychotic symptoms. After summarizing the findings of the evaluation, I then detail how these contributed to treatment recommendations for a patient with complex psychiatric problems.

## Description of setting

The Austen Riggs Center (ARC) is an open psychiatric hospital and residential treatment center in Massachusetts. It is an open hospital because patients are not restricted by locks or privilege systems but instead are given the task of managing their safety and symptoms in a competent, collaborative manner. At ARC, we believe that relationships—not locked doors or coercive restraints—are what keep people truly safe and allow them to take charge of their lives. ARC's mission is to promote resilience and self-direction for individuals with complex psychiatric problems. Many of the patients at ARC are struggling with severe problems, including treatment-resistant depression, personality pathology, suicidal and self-injurious behavior, trauma, and psychosis. Treatment is guided by a psychodynamic orientation which prioritizes the developmental strivings of the individual; a belief that symptoms are meaningful and arise in particular social contexts; an appreciation for unconscious, irrational, and emotional processes that impact individuals and group systems; and a focus on the centrality of relationships. This framework guides not only individual treatment but the approach to medication, group and community work, family therapy, and psychological testing. At the core of ARC is the therapeutic community program and intensive four-times-weekly psychodynamic psychotherapy. Patients work with the same individual therapist throughout their stay, and individual therapy is a central focus of the treatment program. Therapists work on teams with members from various disciplines (e.g., psychiatry, psychology, social work, nursing, substance use counseling in an effort to provide integrated care that works to understand the patient across a variety of social contexts (Biel & Plakun, 2015). Every patient admitted to ARC commits to a six-week evaluation and treatment phase during which they complete a variety of assessments (e.g., psychiatric/medication evaluation, three-generation family history/social work, substance use assessment), including psychological testing. The psychological testing is used by the individual therapist and team members to coordinate treatment planning and to more deeply understand the ways in which the patient is engaging across the milieu. Often, patients will stay beyond the initial phase with the average stay being between 6 and 8 months. Sometimes, patients will step down to a lower level of care with programs that emphasize acquiring independent living skills, developing interpersonal relationships, and engaging in work or school.

Patients complete psychological testing in the third week of their stays at ARC. Every patient at ARC completes a standard battery of tests (Rapaport, Gill, & Schafer, 1945) that includes the Wechsler Adult Intelligence Scale— Fourth Edition (WAIS-IV; Wechsler, 2008), the Thematic Apperception Test (TAT; Murray, 1943), the Rorschach (Rorschach 1921/1951), and human figure drawings (HFD). The individual therapist writes the referral questions and submits them to me in my role as Director of Psychological Testing. Patients are eligible for re-testing after a year of treatment to assess changes in psychological functioning. Ridenour and Zimmerman (2019) described the significant contributions of ARC psychologists, including such luminary figures as David Rapaport, Roy Schafer, David Shapiro, and Richard Ford.

The ARC offers an accredited, four-year fellowship program for psychologists and psychiatrists who complete an involving formal adult psychoanalytic training and hospital-based psychotherapy. Psychological testing is an integral component of the fellowship training for psychologists. The majority of test reports are written by postdoctoral psychology fellows who work under supervision. The testing is usually conducted by a team of three postdoctoral fellows. Each fellow administers one test (WAIS-IV, TAT, Rorschach, HFD). The psychology fellow administering the Rorschach is responsible for writing the report. The team approach exposes the patient to different psychologists and allows us to understand the transference-countertransference dynamics that are evoked across a range of relational contexts (Schafer, 1954). After the data are collected and scored, I meet with the psychology fellows for a weekly two-hour seminar to analyze the data. We spend the first hour reviewing the WAIS-IV, HFD, and TAT. We devote the second hour to interpreting the Rorschach by analyzing formal scores, thematic content, as well as configuration and sequence. Subsequently, the fellow writing the report has an additional hour of individual supervision.[1]

The reports are usually only one-to-two pages and are written without reference to the patient's history (Shapiro, 2012). We do not interview the patient to collect psychiatric history, because this is addressed by other members of our multidisciplinary team during the treatment and evaluation phase. The testing reports are short, condensed psychodynamic formulations of the patient's strengths and vulnerabilities. Typical reports address constructs such as identity, self-esteem, developmental position, representations of significant others, defenses, thought processes, reality testing, emotional functioning, and suicide risk.

## Brief literature review of assessment applications in residential settings

Psychologists are often called upon in residential treatment to provide diagnostic clarifications and to assist psychiatrists with dilemmas. Patients in residential treatment often present with a variety of comorbid presentations that are difficult to categorize and require considerable time and effort to disentangle the influence of personality pathology, psychiatric symptoms, developmental trauma, and substance use. Within a residential setting, psychologists have an important responsibility to provide a thorough evaluation that accounts for the ego deficits and intrapsychic conflicts that have impaired the patient's functioning in outpatient treatment. However, conclusions from testing—which are sometimes at odds with those from psychiatric and other assessments— can also potentially contribute to conflicts among treatment team members about the nature of the patient's problems and diagnosis (Berg, 1984). Disagreements between team members, however, can be fruitful and can lead to a more synthetic and nuanced understanding. Testing conducted within a competent, integrated treatment team (de la Torre, Appelbaum, Chediak, & Smith, 1976) is an essential component of a complex, multimethod way of assessing patients. Psychologists in residential settings can collaborate with social workers, psychiatrists, and nurses to add perspective and insight that supplements other health professionals' assessments. Patients presenting for residential and long-term hospital-based treatment participate in individual psychotherapy, psychiatric, group, and milieu-based treatment. Schlesinger and Holzman (1970) outlined the therapeutic aspects of hospital milieus in long-term settings and suggest the ways an activity program within this setting can promote the development of the patient's ego capacity, educational interest, physical health, and interpersonal functioning. Psychological testing can facilitate treatment teams' recommendations for how the patient might engage in the milieu by outlining the patient's relative strengths, vulnerabilities, relational patterns, and areas of conflict. For instance, a patient who on the Rorschach shows impairments in reality testing in the context of affective dysregulation might be encouraged to engage in skills-oriented groups (rather than open-ended process groups) that promote emotional resilience to decrease psychosis proneness. Harty (1979) has written eloquently about the types of countertransference patterns that might emerge when working on psychiatric teams in a long-term setting. As treatment teams work to understand the patient's behavior across the various social contexts, the psychologist can utilize information from the testing to anticipate and understand transference–countertransference dynamics apt to play out in the treatment team.

The application of this literature to patients at ARC draws on the collaborative nature of the treatment setting. Patients are encouraged to engage in the therapeutic community program, which is comprised of a patient government system, a variety of groups (e.g., topic-oriented discussion groups, skills-oriented groups, and process groups), work, and artistic activities. Sometimes, patients will gravitate toward certain aspects of the therapeutic community program, while others avoid them altogether due to social anxiety. The treatment team often struggles to know how to engage with patients who present as withdrawn or uninvolved. For example, one patient continued to have significant tension with the nursing staff and often presented as guarded. During one shift, a nurse observed the patient loading her dirty clothes in the laundry and approached her to say hello. The patient became extremely hostile, verbally aggressive, and accusatory. The nurse was understandably shaken and perplexed by the interaction. We analyzed how the patient might be enacting a hostile maternal transference with the nurse. Additionally, in the team meeting, I recalled that the patient had offered a flagrantly thought-disordered response on Card IV: "A demon rhinoceros with decaying flesh. It is being shot by helicopter while standing on a boardwalk." I highlighted how aggression triggers her paranoia and stimulates the fear of fragmenting with this aggression. I wondered if the patient experienced the nurse as intruding, felt threatened by the nurse seeing her dirty clothes, was unable to generate alternative ways of understanding the nurse's intent, and responded aggressively, which erected a boundary against underlying shame/dirtiness. This is but one example of the way in which psychological testing supports treatment team collaboration in the service of understanding and supporting the patient.

## Case background

Although patients' backgrounds are generally not known by the testers when we write reports at the ARC, given my dual role in the admissions department and psychological testing, I was aware of the history and referral context of the patient who is the subject of the following case study. Mr. A was a 20-year-old cis-gendered man who was a successful student who had been admitted to a prestigious university with plans to become an architect. During the spring semester of his freshman year, he pledged at a fraternity and was subjected to considerable hazing that included physical abuse and sexual humiliation. In the wake of these events, he had a psychotic break characterized by paranoid delusions and auditory and visual hallucinations. He started to become worried about being sexually assaulted by men on campus and was eventually psychiatrically hospitalized before being referred to long-term residential treatment. He also reported having intrusive sexual thoughts about men and worried he might be gay. The auditory hallucinations involved voices mocking him about his sexuality and lack of masculinity.

Mr. A was referred to testing by his individual therapist to assess his vulnerabilities to psychosis. Additionally, the individual therapist asked for an assessment of his sexuality, representations of others and capacity for relatedness, and the nature of his difficulties with emotional regulation and the conditions under which he is better able to manage affect. Although most patients are tested by the postdoctoral fellows, sometimes staff psychologists evaluate patients independently based on the flow of admitted patients. As a result, I conducted all of the testing myself. I met with Mr. A for two 90-minute sessions. At the time of the evaluation, his medications included mood stabilizers and antidepressants.

## Rationale for battery

Mr. A's therapist requested that the testing assess four domains of Mr. A's functioning: (a) thought organization (i.e., ability to structure thought coherently and logically at an appropriate level of abstraction) and reality testing (i.e., the ability to perceive situations and people accurately), (b) representations of others and capacity for relatedness, (c) sexuality, and (d) emotional dysregulation and the contexts under which he is better able to manage feelings. We use a standard battery because it offers patients different tests with a range of structure (i.e., how clearly defined the expectations and guidelines are), ambiguity of stimuli, relational content, and emotional evocativeness (Bram & Peebles, 2014) that allows them to demonstrate their capacities and vulnerabilities. The WAIS-IV (Wechsler, 2008) allows for the analysis of intellectual functioning in a clearly defined task with unambiguous stimuli. The WAIS-IV provides a lens for understanding a person's thought organization in the context of a task that offers explicit guidelines. It can also be useful to elucidate personality dynamics that can break through in the content of the responses and during the interpersonal interaction on the WAIS-IV (Bram, 2017). For example, although some subtests directly provide relational content (e.g., verbal subtests), the majority of the tests do not and are also minimally emotionally and thematically evocative.

The TAT requires that the patient construct a narrative with beginning, middle, and end in which the mental states of characters are delineated. We offer the same ten TAT cards to all patients in this order: 1, 5, 14, Picasso,[2] 13MF, 12M, 2, 18GF, 10, and 9GF. The TAT is valuable to elicit prominent relational schemas and implicit mentalization skills that are required to navigate interpersonal interactions. Although the instructions provide some structure and guidance for responses, there is a moderate degree of ambiguity in the stimuli. Many of the characters are depicted in evocative situations that can elicit emotionally charged responses. Two psychologists rate the TAT stories using the Social Cognition and Object Relations Scale—Global Scoring Method (SCORS-G; Stein, Hilsenroth, Slavin-Mulford, & Pinsker, 2011).

We apply the SCORS-G to the TAT as a quantitative rating of the quality of social cognition, affective capacities, and interpersonal relatedness. Two SCORS-G subscales, in particular—Complexity of Representations of People and Understanding of Social Causality—evaluate the person's quality and differentiation of mental states of self and other and their ability to understand behavior in a logically coherent manner. We have found these SCORS-G subscales serve as a helpful indicator of the patient's psychological mindedness and capacity to engage in exploratory psychotherapy (Stein & Slavin-Mulford, 2017). We also compare individual profiles to local norms (mean scores among ARC patients on each of the SCORS-G subscales) to identify areas of relative weakness and strength. This supplements the in-depth qualitative analysis of the TAT. The TAT would assist me in addressing each of the referral questions, especially his representation of others, capacity for relatedness, and how he experiences his sexuality.

The Rorschach is the least structured task, which demands that patients generate responses to relatively ambiguous visual stimuli. The Rorschach is particularly valuable to assess thought organization and reality testing (Mihura, Meyer, Dumitrascu, & Bombel, 2013). Although the Rorschach might shed light on the more relational questions asked by the examiner (e.g., sexuality and representations of others and capacity for relatedness), the patient may or may not perceive human relationships on the Rorschach. Additionally, the chromatic cards on the Rorschach often provoke affective reactions. I expected that the Rorschach would be essential to determining conditions under which Mr. A would be more vulnerable to lapses in reality testing, thought organization, and emotional functioning. The chromatic determinants (FC, CF, C) and responses to the chromatic cards have been conceptualized and found to be associated with affective modulation capacities (Malone et al., 2013). I administered the Rorschach using the Comprehensive System (CS; Exner, 2003), and present data involving CS variables that have received the strongest meta-analytic support (Mihura et al., 2013). The data were interpreted in reference to the CS international norms (Meyer, Erdberg, & Shaffer, 2007).

Unlike most other assessment settings, we do not administer self-report measures. Additionally, our test reports do not reference the history of the patient, given that the assessment takes place in the larger context of a system-wide evaluation where the historical data are gathered and integrated. Instead, we prioritize understanding and elucidating the patient's unique intrapsychic world by examining how the patient thinks, feels, and perceives the world. We try to carefully delineate a phenomenological description of the patient's inner world. For instance, rather than categorizing someone as psychotic, we try to understand the conditions under which someone's thought and perceptual capacity break down and what enables them to recover (Bram & Peebles, 2014). Close attention to the test data (that goes beyond merely nomothetic analysis) allows us to appreciate the particular contexts for symptomatic exacerbation. Our aim is not to provide a psychiatric diagnosis but instead to capture ego functioning and personality dynamics.

# Summary of findings

I first provide a description of my testing interaction with Mr. A and then present the summary of findings according to the four parts of the referral question: (a) thought organization and reality testing, (b) representations of others and capacity for relatedness, (c) sexuality, and (d) emotional dysregulation and the contexts under which he is better able to manage feelings.

## Patient–Examiner interactions

Mr. A presented as bored, flat, and mildly frustrated. He appeared especially insecure, notably during WAIS-IV when he asked if he had "gotten dumber." He communicated this in a deadpan manner that minimized the potential shame underlying the question. He completed the performance-based tests quickly, especially the TAT. He appeared to put forth a good effort in the various tests. He did not ask many questions. I had met Mr. A three weeks prior when I admitted him to ARC as his admissions officer. Based on our past experience, we were easily able to establish rapport. During the admissions consultation, he had told me I was "smart" in comparison to previous doctors who were "idiots." Although he paid me a compliment, his detached demeanor did not communicate warmth. I had the experience that he was someone whose idealizing stance could easily become devaluing if he were to feel frustrated or ashamed.

## Thought organization and reality testing

Intellectually, Mr. A was highly intelligent. He obtained the following index scores on the WAIS-IV: Verbal Comprehension Index (VCI) was 120 (Superior, 91st percentile) and Perceptual Reasoning Index (PRI) was 119 (High Average, 90th percentile). He was particularly adept a tasks of verbal and nonverbal fluid reasoning, vocabulary, and visual problem-solving. His Working Memory Index (WMI) score was 108 (Average, 70th percentile) and slightly lower. His lowest score was 97 (Average, 42nd percentile) on the Processing Speed Index (PSI); the differences between his VCI and PSI and between his PRI and PSI were both statistically and clinically significant (base rates in the standardization sample for VCI-PRI and VCI-PSI differences were only 8% and 7.8%, respectively). Though still in the average range, Mr. A's processing speed was clearly an area of relative weakness and unusual in the context of his verbal and nonverbal strengths. It was unclear to what extent his lower processing speed was (a) secondary to his psychiatric illness and/or his medications versus (b) consistent with his premorbid cognitive functioning. Given the discrepancy between index scores, a Full Scale IQ was not a valid estimate of his overall intelligence. On the General Ability Index (a composite of the Verbal Comprehension and Perceptual Reasoning), he obtained a score of 123 (Superior, 94th percentile). This suggests that Mr. A can make use of his intellect under more structured and less emotionally evocative conditions. One implication of slower processing speed for therapy might be that his therapist maintains a somewhat slower verbal pacing in sessions to allow Mr. A time to process verbal exchanges. Despite his verbal capacities, he needs time to efficiently integrate information and can think abstractly when giving the time to consider his thoughts and the thoughts of others. There were no signs of thought disorganization of the WAIS-IV: His responses to the VCI subtests were coherent, focused, and at an appropriate level of abstraction.

On the TAT, Mr. A's stories were odd and seemed haphazard in their construction. For instance, in many of his stories, people suddenly died for reasons that often did not make sense. The plots of the narratives were often concrete or minimally elaborated (Understanding of Social Causality [Mean Score = 3.25]). On TAT Card 12M, he told the story of a boy who fell asleep while studying. The other boy responds by opening "his eyes or eyelids to wake him up so they can keep studying because he likes messing with him." In this story, the boy's action of trying to wake up the other one by opening his eyes or eyelids seemed bizarre, concrete, and sadistic. Many of his stories involved death, violence, and strange actions that seemed to illustrate some of his confused thinking in interpersonal situations.

On the Rorschach, Mr. A. was highly engaged (R=20; Lambda = 0.43, Blends = 8:20), and exhibited notable disturbances in terms of the organization of his thinking (WSum6 = 33, Lv2 = 5) and his reality testing (X-% = 0.30). He generated five severely confused and illogical responses: Three FAB2 and two INC2. For instance, on Card VII he perceived, "Two women with high pony tails looking at each other, maybe it's a caterpillar, a single, a double-headed caterpillar woman" (W+ Mp- 2 (H) INC2 PHR). Bordering on a contamination, this response highlights his tendency to confuse conceptual boundaries (in this case, between human and animal) when processing interpersonal information (the card-pull of Card VII) in ambiguous situations. Mr. A's other cognitive special scores were on chromatic cards, signaling his greater confusion when emotionally activated. Many of these responses involved primitive content such as blood, sexuality, and food (smashed tomatoes, gummy worms). He appears to be at the mercy of archaic urges that spill out of his mind with little ability to weave them together intelligibly. From a psychodynamic perspective, we might speculate that he has little ability to filter out of awareness primitive impulses, compromising his ability to properly organize information, leading to strained reasoning and primary process thinking (Ridenour, 2016).

Mr. A tends to experience his environment in a holistic manner, ambitiously accounting for many details when processing information (W:D:Dd=12:7:1). But as noted in the examples above, his style of taking in information in this way is associated with a misperception of the situation (X-% = 0.30, Xu% = 0.35), and he is prone to integrate the details in illogical ways (WSum6 = 33, Lv2 = 5). Interestingly, these slips in his reality testing and reasoning tended to be associated with a certain impulsive style involving his responding immediately to the blots without deliberation. But a notable strength was that Mr. A's second response to most cards often improved in terms of form quality compared to his first. Five of his negative form quality responses occurred on whole responses (X-% = 0.42 for W responses), indicating that when he tries to integrate more aspects of his environment, he is prone to misperceptions. Of note, four out of his six negative form quality responses included human content, suggesting that he is especially prone to interpersonal distortions and misreading people.

Despite the aforementioned vulnerabilities in reality testing, it is worth noting that his six responses on the achromatic Cards IV–VI were less pathological (X+% = 0.67, Xu% = 0.33, no special scores) and better displayed his strengths. It is possible to infer that these healthier responses were a function of the comparably less emotional valence of these achromatic cards.

In sum, Mr. A is intelligent and has notable cognitive strengths. However, on the TAT he demonstrated odd (sometimes bizarre) social reasoning and on the Rorschach, he was prone to repeated lapses in reality testing and thought organization. He seems particularly prone to disordered thinking when contending with his emotions and impulses. His perceptual distortions are more likely to occur in interpersonal contexts, suggesting his difficulty in reading others. These data could help contextualize Mr. A's psychotic break in a socially complex, traumatizing environment of his fraternity when facing negative feelings (e.g., humiliation and shame) and urges (e.g., sexuality) that were destabilizing.

### Representation of others and capacity for relatedness

To assess Mr. A's interpersonal capacities and relational schemas, I will present findings from the TAT and Rorschach. On the SCORS-G variables that were coded on the TAT, Mr. A's mean scores across the various eight dimensions were all within the average range for our patient population. Compared to a nonclinical college sample (Bram, 2014), Mr. A's scores on both Complexity of Representations of People (Mean Score = 3.20) and Understanding of Social Causality (Mean Score = 3.25) were approximately one standard deviation below average, suggesting that he tends to think about mental states and social interactions in a more concrete, simplistic manner. However, his lowest score relative to other patients was on the Emotional Investment in Relationships (EIR): Mr. A's Mean Score = 2.45; Average ARC Patient Mean Score = 2.87 (SD = 0.45). EIR is a measure of relational mutuality (or at the lower end, narcissism) with lower scores suggesting that the person prioritizes their needs over the needs of others and anticipates that others will do the same. This was evident in Mr. A's TAT stories involving men having affairs (Cards 5, Picasso), a boy sadistically pulling a prank (Card 12M), and a girl stealing another's diary (Card 9GF). Mr. A also told multiple stories about people dying suddenly often after moments of physical or emotional intimacy (Cards 13MF, 18GF). These stories reveal Mr. A's implicit relational expectations of harm or being used. It is reasonable to infer that the story about the stolen diary reveals his belief that he cannot trust others with his private thoughts due to his worries that others might turn against him and violate his confidence. Moreover, his stories illuminate his struggles with sustaining relational contact and his expectation that intimacy will either be short-lived or damaging.

Mr. A's Rorschach protocol included two Reflection responses, pointing to his proneness to self-referential thinking, grandiosity, and a strong need for interpersonal mirroring/validation to bolster his shaky self-esteem. What was the FQ of these two responses? That would add more information on whether reality testing declines when he becomes too focused on himself. This might contextualize the compliment he paid me as "smart" during the admissions consultation: Perhaps he wished that I would also affirm his intelligence, despite his manifest worry on the WAIS-IV that he had gotten "dumber." Mr. A's human representations were notably distorted (GHR:PHR = 1:6; four of his 6 PHRs involved poor form quality; M-=3), suggesting he is prone to misperception and poor judgment in interpersonal interactions. At the same time, he appears interested in others (H = 6) despite his potential for misperception (M- = 3) and misunderstanding (e.g., his aforementioned Card VII response involving human content alongside INC2). A consistent finding across the Rorschach (more evident than on the TAT) was his interpersonal needfulness and painful longing. Although his TAT stories illuminated his mistrust and fearfulness, Mr. A's Rorschach revealed someone grappling with considerable interpersonal needs. Many of his responses featured food imagery (e.g., tomatoes, gummy worms) and childlike responses (man with a rattle, babies on a blanket). These would each be scored on the Rorschach Oral Dependency scale (ROD; Bornstein & Masling, 2005).[3] In addition, Mr. A offered three responses coded for Texture, which is elevated and suggests significant distress related to unmet relational needs. We might hypothesize that Mr. A experiences his basic dependency needs as unmet met as a result of his social confusion and feelings of mistrust. Finally, I wanted to comment on his response to Card III. He saw two women spinning together on a merry-go-round. "They're in love and their hearts are going out of their chest. They kind of have beaks. These are their hearts, literally a heart shape" (D+ Mau 2 H, An, Cg 4.0 FAB1, INC1, PHR). Mr. A struggles to manage the affectively arousing color of Card III, which results in disordered thinking (hearts out of chest, women with beaks). This illustrates his difficulties in thinking logically and perceiving situations conventionally under conditions of greater interpersonal and emotional intensity.

From these data, we can conclude that Mr. A does not feel that he can let his guard down and expects that relationships will be rife with betrayal. He focuses on his own needs and likewise believes others will do the same (EIR = 2.45). Though he is interested in people and implicitly/unconsciously longs for connection and caretaking (T=3; RODs), he anticipates he can lose others in the blink of an eye, which might contribute to his difficulty trusting others. When in closer contact, he becomes so overwhelmed that he feels like he is coming apart at the seams, and he is prone to interpersonal distortions and misjudgments (GHR:PHR=1:6; M- = 3). Given the perils of intimacy, he avoids relying upon others and instead tries to soar over his problems like a "beautiful moth flying above a mountain, but the wings are bleeding" (Card VIII—Do2, FMa.FCu A, Bl MOR). Despite his herculean efforts to be self-sufficient, his disordered thinking prevents him from being able to successfully manage. Underneath this counter-dependent stance, Mr. A is filled with painful needs that he cannot communicate to others because of his fears of falling apart and being betrayed. That he is prone to misperceiving others further contributes to his alienation.

### Sexuality

Findings regarding sexuality are more limited because he did not produce explicit sexual content on the Rorschach. It is possible that he produced more sexual content on the TAT (in contract to the Rorschach) because he was more emotionally activated by the evocative interpersonal situations depicted on the cards. On the TAT it was notable that five of his ten stories included sexual plots (Cards 2, 5, 10, 13MF, and Picasso). Although some of these cards do pull for explicit sexual narratives (e.g., Picasso, Card 13MF), the other cards pull for themes of separation from family and personal ambition (Card 2), fear and curiosity (Card 5), and intimacy (Card 10). It is meaningful that Mr. A's sexual concerns were evoked even in response to interpersonal contexts that typically do not evoke them. In two stories, women caught men having affairs. The men were depicted as reckless, selfish, and "dumb." On Card 13MF, a man slept with a woman, but she died unexpectedly in the night, causing him to become paranoid that the police would try to "pin it on him." On Card 10, he told the story of two male lovers whose relationship conflict was resolved through sexual activity occurring in the "shadowy part of the card." Finally, Mr. A's Card 2 narrative was of a young woman who is attracted to the farmhand, more typically an incidental or ignored character in stories to this card.

These stories suggest that sexuality is a prominent concern, even if it is often lurking in the outskirts of his mind "in the shadows." He seems drawn to sexuality, though it is associated with fears of punishment (Card 13MF). He anticipates that men will often use sexuality in reckless ways that can lead to ruinous consequences (Cards 5, Picasso). He also turns to sexuality as a way of managing interpersonal conflict or feelings of aloneness. On Card 2, a young woman turns away from her thwarted dependency needs to develop a private sexualized connection with a man. Mr. A might resort to using sexuality in moments of interpersonal conflict or distress, given his discomfort expressing his relational needs. Finally, Card 10 is generally viewed as a man and woman embracing (Eron, 1950). However, Mr. A perceived two men who were engaged in a sexual act. This perceptual distortion of the stimulus might reveal his sexual anxieties about men that were activated by the sexual humiliation in his fraternity and the subsequent homoerotic concerns he experienced after his psychotic episode.

*Emotional regulation*

There were three notable trends in how Mr. A communicated and represented emotions on the TAT. First, Mr. A's stories suggest that he is uncomfortable with expressing any feelings of vulnerability or sadness. On Card 1, a boy who does not want to play the violin pretends to have practiced. When prompted to comment on his feelings, Mr. A stated that the boy is "bored, frustrated and maybe concerned that he is not good at the violin." This emotional sequence captures the ways that Mr. A presented in his interactions during the testing appointments. He appeared listless and slightly annoyed, but he uses this disengaged posture to cover over underlying feelings of shame and insecurity. Second, many characters acted out in aggressive ways before speaking about their anger to others. This raises questions about Mr. A's proclivity to taking impulsive action before acknowledging his distress to others. Third, Mr. A's stories provide evidence of the defenses he uses such as minimization (suppressing the negative impact), devaluation (referring to characters as dumb), and acting out (e.g., repeated references to people taking impulsive actions to manage difficult situations; Cards 9GF and 14).

On the Rorschach, Mr. A's three Morbid responses were all paired with color as a determinant. This suggests that Mr. A is struggling with a sense of vulnerability and dysphoria that gets activated when he feels emotionally aroused. A sequence of responses to Card II illustrates his problems with affect regulation. In the first response, he saw two bear faces (D2) with "floating creepy faces and their necks are cut off with some creepy aura" (Wo mp 2 A INC2, MOR). This was followed by "Two bears that are bloody. It's pretty self-explanatory. This would be blood flying out top of its head and blood dripping out of the hands. The marks on it are blood (E: Blood?) The fact that it's red" (D+ ma.CFu 2 A, Bl INC1, MOR). In the first response, he saw two bears, but he focused on the top red (D2) that are "floating creepy faces." This provides a window into the possible dissociation between affect (represented in the severed red head) and the bear's body. Mr. A is initially unable to integrate his emotions into his experience, and instead they hover in the background like some menacing threat. In the subsequent response, there is similar content, but now the red is exploding out of the bodies. The blood is "flying" out of the head, dripping from the hands, and also covering the body. There are four points to note about this response:

1. Mr. A says that this is "self-explanatory" which illustrates his difficulty taking a step back and reflecting upon his perceptions and the ways others might see it differently. Although this might be self-evident for Mr. A, it is an unusual, morbid, and thought-disordered response.
2. Affective arousal again cannot be integrated into the form and instead is leaking out everywhere, suggesting how it results in impulsive behaviors and leaves Mr. A feeling damaged and broken.

3. Mr. A describes that blood is dripping out of the bears' hands, which is a mild thought-disordered response (the INC1 for bear's hands). We could hypothesize that he feels like he has blood on his hands and might harbor feelings of guilt or badness.
4. Finally, it is worth noting that three of Mr. A's first four responses included bears. This type of thematic perseveration is uncommon and highlights a certain ruminative cognitive style.

Integrating TAT and Rorschach findings, the former revealed the ways that Mr. A's presentation was tough, covers over dysphoria with anger, and how he is more prone to communicate his aggression in action rather than verbally; and the latter provided evidence of the extent that emotions flood him. When emotionally aroused, he is apt to feel overwhelmed, broken, and unable to manage (MOR = 3). Moreover, he struggles to think in an organized manner, perceive situations accurately, and contain his impulses. To avoid this affective chaos, he attempts to steel himself with an aggressive front and primitive defenses such as devaluation and denial to avert emotions that might destabilize him. He seems best able to manage emotional stimulation when he can maintain a sense of control and avoid feeling too exposed and vulnerable.

## ICD-10 and PDM-2 diagnoses

Our test reports generally do not include such a descriptive diagnosis but instead try to describe the characteristic personality style and the level of personality organization (in line with the P and M Axes from the PDM-2, Lingiardi & McWilliams, 2017). In addition, the S axis was added for this particular case. The PDM-2 diagnoses were:

P Axis:    Narcissistic personality
M Axis:    Major/severe defects in basic mental functions
S Axis:    Unspecified psychotic disorder

The descriptive *International Classifications of Diseases and Related Health Problems, 10th Revision* (ICD-10, World Health Organization, 1992) diagnoses were:

Unspecified psychotic disorder
Rule out Posttraumatic stress disorder (PTSD)

## Implications and recommendations

The testing findings offered important considerations to Mr. A's treatment team and therapist. First, Mr. A is guarded for good reasons. He is highly anxious and fearful of being hurt or betrayed by others. His proneness to being emotionally flooded and overstimulated is associated with vulnerability to disorganized thinking, impaired reality testing, and poor impulse control. Thus, I highlighted that his therapist and other team members should be sensitive to the boundaries of therapeutic relationship by assuming a neutral, professional stance, as noting that an overly warm inviting posture might arouse sexuality, which could exacerbate paranoia. Given his emotional guardedness and vulnerabilities to dysregulation, therapy should proceed at a slow pace to facilitate trust, as Mr. A gradually allows himself to share his feelings. I recommended that the therapist might anticipate that Mr. A will often return to a more defended, angry stance in moments when he feels exposed. At the same time, I alerted his treaters that despite Mr. A's seemingly detached demeanor, underneath he is hungry for connection and yearns to be understood. Second, Mr. A's interpersonal approach is characterized by narcissistic and paranoid traits that others will likely experience as off-putting and cold. We might anticipate that the therapist might expect to be idealized (like I was in testing as an "intelligent doctor"), devalued when he feels exposed, and feel a pull to offer mirroring/affirmation. His dominant interpersonal style enables him to maintain a sense of control and interpersonal safety. However, he is prone to misread situations and is hypervigilant to threat. I underscored that his therapist ought to be sensitive to his interpersonal misperception and strive to be transparent and frank with him (McWilliams, 2011). The therapist could also strive to provide clear descriptions of her thought process to enable Mr. A to better manage the needs and concerns that could get activated in the transference. Too much ambiguity will likely exacerbate his paranoia. Third, Mr. A is extremely smart and engaged. He might be able to connect more around his intellectual or creative interests. In this context, his thinking is clearest. Furthermore, his needs for intimacy can be met in a less direct, threatening manner.

## Feedback

After I wrote the report, the therapist reviewed the findings with the patient. I heard from the therapist that the report was helpful in illuminating Mr. A's emotional world and vulnerability to losing distinction between his mental states and the mental states of others when in close contact. I learned from the therapist that while the patient could appreciate how he buried his needs and "soft emotions" underneath his anger, he mocked the term "soft emotions," a term I had used in the report to capture feelings of vulnerability and sadness. At ARC, therapists generally weave the findings of the report into the general feedback from the treatment and evaluation phase which often includes contextualizing the patient's psychiatric symptoms in their developmental history. At this point, the therapist provides a psychodynamic formulation of the patient's core conflicts, and the report can be integrated into those findings.

The treatment team appreciated learning about the pervasiveness of psychotic thought processes that came through on testing, given that they were trying to determine whether his problems were a reflection of PTSD or an underlying psychotic process. The nursing staff also integrated the findings and found them useful because they had previously felt frustrated given their inability to connect with Mr. A, who presented as passive, frustrated, or annoyed. During meetings with the nursing staff, he would often complain about others without revealing much about his needs. Now they could understand that Mr. A led with his aggression in order to self-protect against feeling too vulnerable or ashamed.

Of note, I also served as Mr. A's individual therapist for a couple of sessions while his therapist was away on vacation. He had requested to work with me because of our previous contact in admissions and psychological testing. We touched upon many themes central to the test report, including his difficulties sharing his sadness with others and his lack of faith in others.

In the community program, Mr. A had a reputation of being a cold person who made cruel comments that cut people down to size. He rarely expressed his wishes, though he readily shared his annoyance with others. He was given feedback by his peers that by only expressing his anger, people were not learning more about who he was. This feedback seemed consistent with the test report, which included a description of his guarded, mistrustful posture. For instance, Mr. A's difficulties acknowledging his more vulnerable feelings due to his worries about being betrayed contributed to his more defensive posture that he assumed in various groups in the community program.

## Assessor reflections

The assessment experience was quick and, in many ways, unremarkable. Mr. A's affective flatness covered over any feelings or concerns that might have been present during the testing. He was most open in revealing his insecurity on the WAIS-IV and seemed nervous that he might come across as unintelligent or unknowledgeable. During the Rorschach, his problems became more readily apparent. I recall feeling concerned for Mr. A, given the level of cognitive disorganization and psychic pain that he was communicating through his morbid, thought-disordered responses. Interpreting the data was challenging, at times, especially due to some of his odd thinking, perceptual distortions, and morbid responses. I was especially aware of applying my analytic thinking on the Rorschach to try and understand his poor form quality responses and what it might reveal about his unconscious concerns. As noted above, many basic developmental themes emerged around oral dependency, a sense of vulnerability and damage, and the perils of intimacy. I am always interested in interpreting what the Rorschach responses might reveal about preconscious or implicit concerns that might not be readily apparent based on someone's self-report. Mr. A was no exception. As I administered the testing, he appeared listless, uninterested in the task, and mildly frustrated. However, his responses on the Rorschach highlighted the profound need/fear dilemma he is facing that is common for many individuals experiencing psychotic processes (Burnham, Gladstone, & Gibson, 1969). On the one hand, his hostility and fearfulness provide him much-needed distance though they contribute to his alienation and loneliness (Fromm-Reichmann, 1959). On the other hand, his needs are terrifying as he worries about interpersonal intrusion or neglect. The data gave me a more empathic understating of a person who was more psychologically "online" than he readily communicated verbally and behaviorally.

Unlike other reports written at ARC, this case was distinct in two ways. First, I was aware of Mr. A's history and the context that led to his admission to ARC. Although all reports are written with some knowledge of the patient in mind (given that recently admitted patients are discussed in clinical staff meetings), I was in the unusual position of having served as Mr. A's admissions clinician. Our prior connection from the admissions consultation might have enabled Mr. A to reveal more of his primitive thought process and disorganization during the testing sessions. This would be consistent with Exner, Armbruster, and Mittman's (1978) finding that patients tested by their own therapists produced longer, richer protocols in which they revealed significantly more sexual content. On the other hand, given that he seemed to idealize me, it is unclear if he felt pressured to censor his Rorschach responses to minimize more shameful sexual content. Second, I conducted all the testing by myself. It would have been interesting to have Mr. A tested by men and women to see how he might have approached the tasks differently with different psychologists.

While writing the report, I tried to highlight the dilemma of someone who is both desperately worried about their mind breaking down, crippled by shame, and cynical that others could help. Psychological testing can provide a guiding formulation to appreciate how the patient's symptoms often represent efforts to adapt to vexing developmental challenges. How can Mr. A maintain his dignity and sense of pride while also having the courage to face the losses and anguish of his current psychiatric crisis? Psychological testing, especially from a psychodynamic approach that values both the adaptive and the destructive forces inherent to experience, can provide a context for people's deepest existential dilemmas.

## Notes

1 See Biederman, Ridenour, and Biel (2019) for more information about training and supervision in the fellowship.
2 This card was originally included as Card 8 in the B Series of the TAT (see Rapaport et al., 1945).

## References

Berg, M. R. (1984). Teaching psychological testing to psychiatric residents. *Professional Psychology: Research and Practice, 15*(3), 343–352.
Biedermann, C., Ridenour, J., & Biel, S. (2019). Psychodynamic psychological testing in the mental health inpatient setting: A way of listening, learning, and holding patients and psychotherapists. In M. Turel, M. Siglag, & A. Grinshpoon (Eds.), *Clinical psychology in the mental health inpatient setting: International perspectives.* New York: Routledge.

Biel, S., & Plakun, E. M. (2015). Psychodynamic systems of residential treatment: Another view from Riggs. *Psychodynamic Psychiatry, 43*(1), 91–116.

Bornstein, R. F., & Masling, J. M. (2005). The Rorschach oral dependency scale. In R. F. Bornstein & J. M. Masling (Eds.), *Scoring the Rorschach: Seven validated systems* (pp. 135–157). Mahwah, NJ: Lawrence Erlbaum Associates Publishers.

Bram, A. D. (2014). Object relations, interpersonal functioning, and health in a nonclinical sample: Construct validation and norms for the TAT SCORS-G. *Psychoanalytic Psychology, 31*(3), 314–342.

Bram, A. D. (2017). Reviving and refining psychodynamic interpretation of the Wechsler intelligence tests: The verbal comprehension subtests. *Journal of Personality Assessment, 99*(3), 324–333.

Bram, A. D., & Peebles, M. J. (2014). *Psychological testing that matters: Creating a road map for effective treatment.* Washington, DC: American Psychological Association Books.

Burnham, D. L., Gladstone, A. I., & Gibson, R. W. (1969). *Schizophrenia and the need–fear dilemma.* New York: International Universities Press.

de la Torre, J., Appelbaum, A., Chediak, D. J., & Smith, W. H. (1976). Reflections on the diagnostic process by a clinical team. *Bulletin of the Menninger Clinic, 40*(5), 479–496.

Eron, L. D. (1950). A normative study of the thematic apperception test. *Psychological Monographs: General and Applied, 64*(9), i-48.

Exner, J. (2003). *The Rorschach: A comprehensive system: Basic foundations* (vol. I, 4th ed.). New York: Wiley.

Exner, J. E., Jr., Armbruster, G., & Mittman, B. (1978). The Rorschach response process. *Journal of Personality Assessment, 42*(1), 27–38.

Fromm-Reichmann, F. (1959). Loneliness. *Psychiatry, 22*(1), 1–15.

Harty, M. K. (1979). Countertransference patterns in the psychiatric treatment team. *Bulletin of the Menninger Clinic, 43*(2), 105–122.

Lingiardi, V., & McWilliams, N. (Eds.) (2017). *PDM-2. Psychodynamic diagnostic manual.* New York: Guilford Publications.

Malone, J. C., Stein, M. B., Slavin-Mulford, J., Bello, I., Sinclair, S. J., & Blais, M. A. (2013). Seeing red: Affect modulation and chromatic color responses on the Rorschach. *Bulletin the Menninger Clinic, 77*(1), 70–93.

McWilliams, N. (2011). *Psychoanalytic diagnosis: Understanding personality structure in the clinical process.* New York: Guilford Press.

Meyer, G. J., Erdberg, P., & Shaffer, T. W. (2007). Toward international normative reference for the comprehensive system. *Journal of Personality Assessment, 89*(Suppl. 1), S201–S216.

Mihura, J. L., Meyer, G. J., Dumitrascu, N., & Bombel, G. (2013). The validity of individual Rorschach variables: Systematic reviews and meta-analyses of the comprehensive system. *Psychological Bulletin, 139*(3), 548–605.

Murray, H. A. (1943). *Thematic apperception test: Manual.* Cambridge, MA: Harvard University Press.

Rapaport, D., Gill, M., & Schafer, R. (1945). *Diagnostic psychological testing monograph series* (vol. 1). Chicago, IL: Menninger Clinic.

Ridenour, J. M. (2016). Psychodynamic model and treatment of schizotypal personality disorder. *Psychoanalytic Psychology, 33*(1), 129–146.

Ridenour, J. M., & Zimmerman, B. (2019). The evolution of psychological testing at the Austen Riggs center: A theoretical analysis. *Journal of Personality Assessment, 101*(1), 106–115.

Rorschach, H. (1921/1951). *Psychodiagnostics: A diagnostic test based on perception* (5th ed. rev.). Oxford: Grune & Stratton. (Original published 1921).

Schafer, R. (1954). *Psychoanalytic interpretation in Rorschach testing.* New York: Grune & Stratton.

Schlesinger, H. J., & Holzman, P. S. (1970). The therapeutic aspects of the hospital milieu. *Bulletin of the Menninger Clinic, 34*(1), 1–11.

Shapiro, D. (2012). Theoretical value of psychological testing. *Journal of Personality Assessment, 94*(6), 558–562.

Stein, M., Hilsenroth, M., Slavin-Mulford, J., & Pinsker, J. (2011). *Social cognition and object relations scale: Global rating method (SCORS-G).* Unpublished manuscript, Massachusetts General Hospital and Harvard Medical School, Boston, MA.

Stein, M., & Slavin-Mulford, J. (2017). *The social cognition and object relations scale-global rating method (SCORS-G): A comprehensive guide for clinicians and researchers.* New York: Routledge.

Wechsler, D. (2008). Wechsler *adult intelligence scale-fourth edition* (WAIS-IV). San Antonio, TX: The Psychological Corporation.

# 6   A psychoanalytic approach to custody evaluations

*Diana S. Rosenstein*

## Description of setting

Custody evaluations are psychological evaluations ordered by the court when there are issues about parenting capacities that cannot be resolved by the litigants in consultation with their attorneys or by a negotiation or conciliation process by the various agencies of the court. Evaluations are ordered in a small number of cases, with most of the cases within this group referred because of high conflict between parents, opaque information about the parties, or when there are serious allegations that hold significant consequences for custodial parenting (Johnston & Campbell, 1988). This group of parents has been noted to be outliers in terms of the intensity of their post-divorce enmity toward one another and personality disturbance, even in the context of divorce, which is notorious for reactivating traumas and emotional conflicts from earlier in the parents' lives and causing otherwise well-functioning parents to behave in uncharacteristically emotional and aggressive ways (Johnston & Campbell, 1988).

The following case was part of a full custody evaluation conducted in my independent practice. The evaluation was court-ordered. Parents signed contracts with me that specified the evaluation procedures and fees. I use the same procedures in all my custody evaluations in order to be comprehensive and complete in obtaining the information needed, and to demonstrate my evaluative neutrality. For this evaluation, I interviewed each parent separately, several times, as to their view of the custody dispute, their view of their own emotional health and parenting capacity, their view of the emotional health and parenting capacity of the other parent, their view of the development and emotional health of the child, and their view of the relationships among all of the family members. Information regarding physical abuse of any family member, particularly a child, mental health, or substance abuse problems was of concern. Parents also provided their own individual history and that of the child's development, as well as practical information regarding living arrangements, managing complex family schedules, transportation, arrangements for alternative childcare, if needed, and relationships with extended family. I interviewed the children who were old enough to participate in a conversation about their experiences with each parent. This interview included the children's views on life in each parental residence, their relationships with each parent, and their own emotional state and development.

In addition to the aforementioned interviews, families participated in observations of the children with parents at their respective homes and in the evaluator's office. For very young children (i.e., under five years) and children with limited verbal capacities, I extend the observation sessions and do not interview them because they cannot meaningfully participate in an interview. I reviewed other sources of information such as the children's grades, police reports, texts and emails between the parents, and previous evaluations. By phone, I interviewed other parties (known as "collaterals") who provide information on various family members, such as teachers, therapists, neighbors, extended family, and friends. I gathered information on the parents' coparenting abilities via their reports of their coparenting relationship and reviewing the emails and text communications they have with one another. Each parent also completed the Rorschach (Exner, 2003) and the Minnesota Multiphasic Personality Inventory—Second Edition (MMPI-2; Butcher, Graham, Ben-Porath, Tellegen, & Dahlstrom, 2001). The children who were old enough completed the Rorschach. At a separate re-evaluation six months later, I interviewed both parents extensively, observed the father with the children, and spoke to a therapist working with the father and one of his family members who provided childcare.

## Brief literature review

A psychoanalytic perspective has had a long history in all aspects of child welfare litigation and child custody disputes are no exception. Anna Freud worked closely with a group at the Yale Child Study Center in the early 1970s to apply a psychoanalytic understanding of child development to legal issues in child welfare, such as custody in divorce, foster care, and adoption (e.g., Goldstein, Solnit, Goldstein, & Freud, 1996). The work of Freud and collaborators led to the adoption of the best interests of the child as the standard in all types of child welfare proceedings, though the psychoanalytic underpinnings of this concept are not widely recognized. Because of their seminal work, it has become commonplace in custody and most child welfare work to put a consideration of the child's developmental and emotional needs, and the parents' ability to meet those needs, at the heart of any assessment of children, even though most practitioners do not consider themselves to be psychoanalytically trained.

What then, can a psychoanalyst contribute to child custody evaluations in current professional practice? Psychoanalysts come to custody work with the basic psychoanalytic principles of a developmental approach and the role of the unconscious in determining behavior. Specifically, they use the ideas that unconscious thoughts and feelings influence conscious thoughts, feelings, and behavior; that the past influences the present and is likely to be re-enacted or repeated in the present; that the human mind works via defenses that can lead either to adaptation or to maladaptation; that fantasy plays a role in the development and can bias the appreciation of reality; that there is internal conflict among agencies of mind; and that the workings of the mind are multi-determined. In clinical practice, psychoanalysts focus on the interplay of transference and countertransference in the psychoanalytic process, using free association and the analysis of defenses to uncover underlying fantasies that determine the individual's narrative about themselves and their place in the world. The psychoanalytic approach also offers a perspective on the structure of the individual's mind; that is, the quality of their ego functions and defenses. This orientation, which is less obvious to untrained observers, can be at odds with the needs of the legal system to provide information to the court that is based on objective, rigorously obtained information and evidence from which determinations about issues that are life changing can be made. In this chapter, I aim to demonstrate how a psychoanalytically informed custody evaluator can go about meeting the standards of evidence for the legal system, while using all of the basic concepts inherent in a psychoanalytic understanding.

A well-structured custody evaluation will not just make a recommendation for physical custody time of the children but will focus on the evaluation of specific questions related to parenting capacity of each parent, as well as the psychological state and well-being of the children and parents. In order to understand a parent's capacity for parenting, an evaluation is required of that parent's psychological functioning, life history, and adaptation to the other tasks of adulthood, such as work and sustaining relationships. According to Demby (2009, p. 477), "From a psychoanalytic perspective, the capacity for parenting is viewed as an outgrowth of a parent's object relationships defensive structure, ego functioning, superego functions, and unresolved developmental conflicts" (p. 477). Demby (p. 480) also notes the importance of attending to the "degree and pathology of narcissism, capacity for reflective self-awareness, and ego strengths and weaknesses." As is true in all areas of health care in recent years, there has been an emphasis on using empirically derived measures from which to draw conclusions about the important determinations in custody disputes (Gould & Martindale, 2009). Although these efforts help to correct what can be misuses of personal biases and subjective recommendations on the part of some evaluators, in practice there are severe limits on the degree of empirical certainty that can be derived from a custody evaluation. In fact, there are no well-validated measures of parenting behavior and capacities in the literature at this time, though there have been many attempts at a variety of self-report and observational measures (e.g., Ackerman, 2010).

Custody evaluations focus on the future of the child's relationship with each parent and on the child's development (Erard, Singer, & Viglione, 2017). From my point of view, there are multiple, interrelated factors that must be assessed in the course of a custody evaluation: (a) for parents, the psychological functioning of each parent; the emotional capacity for parenting; and the capacity to work cooperatively with each other for the welfare of the child; and (b) for the child, the state of their emotional, physical, social, and academic development; the quality of their relationship with each parent, potential step-parents, and siblings; and the quality of the relationship between the parents themselves. All relevant information gathered in the evaluation contributes to this assessment, formulated as parenting plans and recommendations for legal custody (decision-making regarding medical, educational, religious, and other important aspects of the child's life) and physical custody (where the child will live and by what schedule), as well as therapeutic interventions for the parents or children to facilitate the success of the parenting plan.

It is the skill of the custody evaluator, based on the integration of an almost overwhelming trove of information about the family, which determines the quality of the custody evaluation. A thoughtful, useful, unbiased, and complete custody evaluation depends upon the evaluator's deep knowledge—based on a thorough reading of the pertinent literature and clinical experience—of such central disciplines as child development, parenting, family dynamics, parent-children relationships, marital dynamics, individual psychodynamics, multiculturalism, psychological assessment, and psychopathology. In addition to these considerations, the custody evaluator with a psychoanalytic orientation relies also on an integrated and sophisticated understanding of appropriate laws and legal customs as well as an understanding of the complex interplay of psychological functioning and those standards. Psychoanalysts are well suited to working with highly charged transference/countertransference dynamics based on their experience of analyzing and synthesizing free associations for both thematic content and defenses against hidden thoughts and feelings. Similarly, in custody evaluations, the evaluator can listen to the participants' narratives in a similar dual manner; both for direct information, but also for what is not said for self-protective purposes, for the underlying themes, and how those themes connect to or are repetitions of the history of the participant's life. For example, how are the unresolved issues and conflicts carried over from childhood played out again in the marital relationships and in the relationships between the parents and their children? Do those conflicts limit that parent's capacity to put the child's needs ahead of their own repetition of conflict? The better the evaluator's understanding of the dynamics of each parent, as well as their strengths and limitations in parenting, the better the evaluator is in making recommendations to the court that will have a chance of ameliorating conflict in the custody situation. For example, the custody evaluator speculates about whether the assessment provided sufficient evidence to determine a parent's ability to utilize, as intended, various recommendations, including motivation for psychotherapy, parent education, and other provisions of mental health care associated with custody disposition. Additional questions include (a) Does the parent evidence the requisite psychological openness to be able to rethink their own actions and make changes? (b) To what degree has the parent experienced a temporary regression in their defensive processes as a result of the psychological insult of the divorce, which might then be predictive of their ability to resume more adequate functioning once the divorce conflict is settled? Or is the parent so narcissistically impaired that it is important for them to continue the conflict, or inflict it on their children, in order to bolster their fragile self-esteem?

## Case background

The case was referred for a custody evaluation by mutual agreement among both parents and their attorneys. After the marital separation, Mrs. F retained primary physical custody of the children and Mr. F had severely limited time with the children for about a year, based on Mrs. F's concerns about his capacity for aggression against the children. He petitioned the court for more time with the children after a failed attempt to negotiate a new custody plan. Because Mr. F's emotional state was of most serious concern in this evaluation, the focus of this report will be on the evaluation of him and his parenting.

## Rationale for battery

According to the American Psychological Association (APA) Guidelines for Child Custody Evaluations in Family Law Proceedings (2010) and the Association of Family and Conciliation Courts (AFCC) Model Standards of Practice for Child Custody Evaluation (2006), the best practice for custody evaluations involves obtaining information from multiple independent sources, either to corroborate or to provide additional information for the evaluation. Therefore, information gathered from direct interviews, self-report inventories, documents, and from standardized testing are all necessary to provide multiple independent sources of information leading to incremental validity of the conclusions drawn in the evaluation.

In a custody evaluation, as in any well-crafted assessment, one uses multiple sources of data—psychological testing, interviews of parents, children, and other parties to the conflict, as well as observation and self-report—to answer broader questions that are often directly asked by the parties ordering the evaluation (Erard et al., 2017). A custody evaluator is most often asked to use the evaluation to assess the quality of parenting behavior; here, the impact of parent emotional and psychological functioning on parenting should also be described. Following Erard's (2005) comments about the utility of the Rorschach test in custody evaluations, I used the Rorschach in the following ways: (a) What does the Rorschach say about the quality of the parents coping style and object relations, their ability to regulate affect, or to problem solve? (b) Can each of these aspects of parental psychology help the child negotiate not only the difficulties inherent in parental separation but the child's ongoing developmental conflicts? Erard (2005) refers to these as "highly relevant intermediate questions" (p. 123) that can be answered using standard Rorschach data such as the parents' affect regulation capacity, impulse control, frustration tolerance, self-reflective capacity, empathy, and all of the other characteristic defenses, dynamics, and capacity for object relations. Similar specific sets of questions can be answered about the child's psychological health, including specific questions about the effects of the divorce and specific custody plans on the child's development—such as can the child cope with multiple transitions between parental homes or what will be the emotional effect on the child of separations from the non-custodial parent.

Most custody evaluations use some type of psychological testing for both parents and children. For this evaluation, I administered the Rorschach and the MMPI-2 to both parents. Because of their ages, the older three children completed only the Rorschach, and none of the children completed the MMPI-2 (Butcher et al., 2001). The Rorschach was scored and interpreted using the Comprehensive System (CS; Exner, 2003), consistent with variables supported by Mihura, Meyer, Dumitrascu, and Bombel (2013) and interpreted according to the 2007 international norms (Meyer, Erdberg, & Shaffer, 2007). The MMPI-2 was scored using forensic norms for litigants in custody evaluations (Butcher et al., 2001). I selected these two tests because they are among the most commonly used psychological tests in custody evaluations, both tests are psychometrically sound, and both have computer scoring and interpretation available. The literature for both tests takes into account test-taking biases in custody litigants in scoring and interpretation. For example, on various versions of the MMPI, custody litigants typically underreport psychopathology and psychological distress, presenting themselves with self-serving and self-aggrandizing biases (Kauffman, Stolberg, & Madero, 2015; Strong, Greene, Hoppe, Johnston, & Olesen, 1999). Custody litigants demonstrate elevated levels of repression and denial, lack insight, lack awareness of their effect on others, and present with emotional restraint and restriction (Caldwell, 2005) as well as elevations on scale Hy (Hysteria), Pd (Psychopathic Deviant), and Pa (Paranoia) (Ellis, 2012; Semel, 2015). Singer, Hoppe, Lee, Olesen, and Walters (2008) showed that child custody litigants' Rorschach protocols reflected their clinical description in the literature:

> They showed marked deficits in managing interpersonal conflict; problematic ability to modulate, control and tolerate their own affective experience; and difficulties in engaging collaboratively in problem solving. Their emotional constriction may be a function of the difficulties that they have in processing complex affective states and leads to a defensive and constricted posture. Additionally, deficits in coping are primarily the result of their inability to engage with others emotionally and the difficulties these litigants have in processing complex feelings associated with the divorce." [This group tends to show] defensiveness, self-focus, a lack of capacity for empathy and a distortion of others' motives.
>
> (p. 460)

Both the MMPI-2 and Rorschach are methods of assessing personality and psychopathology that bypass the response biases inherent in instruments with more face validity. Particularly in the context of these evaluations, where the pressure to win custody of the children often becomes an incentive for parents to either unconsciously bias or consciously manipulate their presentation of self to be psychologically healthier than is actually the case, tests that cannot be manipulated and that accurately measure test-taking bias and validity are of particular importance. Because the interview of the parties provides a great deal of information about how they view themselves psychologically and symptomatically, self-report inventory instruments of symptoms are redundant and therefore unnecessary. Even so-called "objective" tests, such as the MMPI-2, have strong aspects of such self-report bias (Meyer & Kurtz, 2006). Erard et al. (2017) view all self-report measures as coming from a single source of information, providing for shared variance, counter to the ethical obligation of evaluators to use multiple independent sources of information toward an assessment conclusion. Erard described the Rorschach as a "systematic observation of performance in stressful circumstances, personality in action, in addition to what people say about themselves" (p. 213) and is particularly useful when the individual assessed cannot or will not provide objective information about themselves. They view the Rorschach as a test of an individual's ability to perform psychologically in a "novel, ambiguous, yet provocative stimuli and requires impromptu decision-making under stressful conditions" (p. 214). The test elicits anxiety and observes the individual's psychological processes in managing that anxiety. The Rorschach can also show thematic preoccupations, and in the sequence of responses, display the individual's emotional reactions and how they defend against them.

## Summary of findings

### Interviews

The family consisted of the parents and their four children, ranging in age from adolescent to young elementary school. Mr. F was in late middle-age and worked in a technical field. Mrs. F worked part time in an office. The parents had been experiencing ongoing tensions in their relationship from its outset, with at least one failed attempt at marital therapy. There was a sense that they had settled on a relationship with one another when their options for finding a more suitable partner had run out, and they both wanted to start a family. The marriage ended after an argument over the children as well as Mrs. F's refusal to be sexually intimate. During the argument, Mr. F threw objects at her, missing her, and hit the wall with his hand, culminating in grabbing Mrs. F, but not injuring her. Mr. F stated that he tried to deescalate their argument by physically forcing Mrs. F to leave their home. Mr. F recalled that he would typically be the one to walk away from an argument with Mrs. F in order to calm things down, but now he wanted to stand up for himself. In retrospect, Mr. F recalled that he was frightened by the fact that he had laid his hands on his wife. Mr. F acknowledged that sometimes he yelled at various family members, which he viewed as normal behavior, and also caused minor property damage in the home, such as throwing small objects or punching walls, the importance of which he minimized. He was careful to state that he did not hurt anyone, though acknowledged that he "put his hands" on Mrs. F during the final argument and once pushed his adolescent son. Mr. F implied that his behavior could be much worse if he were not holding himself to a mature standard of behavior. He justified his anger and aggression as a response to the way in which Mrs. F or the children related to him.

Mr. F viewed Mrs. F as derogatory of his strenuous efforts to support the family, overly demanding of him as both a provider and partner in parenting, overly involved with her family of origin, demeaning of his decisions regarding parenting and, worst of all, lacking sexual interest in him. He felt dismissed and controlled by Mrs. F, particularly with respect to the process of determining custody of the children. He felt that Mrs. F coddled the children by having low expectations of them academically, socially, and professionally, so that they were not learning to be as independent and risk-taking as he felt they should be. He justified his anger and yelling at the children as necessary to overcome Mrs. F's lax discipline of the children and to teach the children to respect him.

In Mrs. F's view, Mr. F had a long history of being verbally and emotionally abusive toward her, calling her names, throwing objects at her and at the wall, kicking objects and the dog. They argued frequently in front of the children. She believed that the younger children were afraid of him because he yelled at them for minor infractions. Mrs. F recalled that Mr. F's physical aggression toward her was far worse than he had described, causing her to fear for her life. She feared that he would now turn his anger and aggression from her onto the children.

The children's responses to Mr. F varied depending upon their age and developmental stage. Both adolescent boys were verbally aggressive with friends and with one another, repeating the verbal aggression they observed in their father. The older of the adolescent boys often provoked his father into arguments to get Mr. F's attention and was very angry and distrustful because he felt emotionally abandoned and harshly punished by Mr. F over the years. The younger adolescent boy largely ignored Mr. F. The pre-adolescent daughter believed that Mr. F favored her brothers and ignored her. She tried to interact with Mr. F as little as possible and was very attached to Mrs. F. The youngest child expressed love for Mr. F but was observed to be fearful of him at times. On observation, Mr. F was playfully engaged with this child, but would suddenly grab the child, albeit playfully, in a manner that seemed to make the child momentarily fearful. At the re-evaluation observations, Mr. F's ability to playfully engage all his children was in evidence, as was his ability to tactfully discipline them without anger or coercion.

Many family members on both sides were interviewed, as well as several neighbors and professionals involved with the family. As an expression of the poverty of his social life, Mr. F provided the names of no friends to contact. As is typical, these interviews supported the parent with whom the individual was aligned, biasing their interpretation of their observation of the parents and children to sustain their loyalty to the respective parent. Therefore, Mr. F's family downplayed his problems with the expression of anger and blamed his outbursts on Mrs. F or the children for provoking him. Mrs. F's family exaggerated the dangerousness of Mr. F's anger and worried about a future escalation in his anger without Mrs. F there to modulate him. Several neighbors had observed Mr. F yell at the children, though one of the children's coaches observed Mr. F to be appropriate when helping to coach children on the team.

During the evaluation, Mr. F presented as extremely polite, respectful, serious, intelligent, distraught over the relative absence of his children, and determined to prove that was not a violent threat to his children. His impatience over the need for the evaluation and the slow process of the legal system came through directly and indirectly as his subtly demeaning of me by questioning whether an evaluation was necessary or whether I could provide any useful information. At other times, Mr. F impressed me as haughty and arrogant, as he extolled the characteristics that he and his extended family could offer the children, such as their independent thinking, self-sufficiency, and familial cohesiveness. Mr. F also displayed a great deal of underlying vulnerability and inadequacy, which he experienced as painful, evoking sympathy in me. At other times, he stirred in me an inchoate sense that he was strange, emotionally isolated, and potentially menacing. It was this contrast between the Mr. F's vulnerability and genuine interest in being the best possible father (and having already taken steps to improve his parenting through classes and therapy) and his explosiveness and strangeness that made a sophisticated understanding of his personality and ego capacities all the more necessary, if the best interests of the children were to be protected.

Mr. F came from hard-working, blue-collar parents, whose struggle for financial stability took precedence over attending to the emotional needs of the children. Mr. F's father was harsh with his own sons with the ostensible aim of instilling a strong work ethic and the resilience needed for a world that he saw as hard and unyielding. Like Mr. F, his father could also be verbally, but not physically, abusive, and also be playful and fun. Mr. F had some awareness of re-enacting some of his own father's more troublesome behaviors, but with less intensity, so therefore considered himself to be a better parent than his father. Mr. F's love for his own father was evident in the care that Mr. F took in describing the values that his father instilled in him of hard work, taking care of one's family, and teaching sons to be men. Mr. F thought of women in marriage as equal partners but had been willing to allow his wife to stay home to take care of the children while he proudly took the responsibility of supporting the family. He did not condone any violence toward women, a part of his father's moral code.

When asked about the trigger for his aggression toward his wife, Mr. F pointed to his wife's indifference to him one morning, stimulating his conscious thought that she neither cared about him nor desired him sexually. His wife's statements in their subsequent argument sparked old feelings of rejection by his own father, who routinely told him that he was "a nothing" and "insignificant." Mr. F was surprised by his violent reaction to his wife. Adding to his shame was a feeling that he had violated not only his own standards of conduct but the strict standards of his father that a man should never physically hurt a woman. This violation led Mr. F to think that his own father would have rejected him if he were still alive. Because Mr. F was surprised and upset that he had put his hands on his wife, without outside prompting, he initiated therapy for anger management immediately after the marital separation and believed that he had learned a great deal about his anger and aggression from that therapy.

### Mr. F's psychological testing

I used psychological testing to address several key questions bearing on his parenting:

1.  How pervasive were Mr. F's aggressive impulses and emotional reactivity? Did he have sufficient ego strengths and flexible defenses to manage his affect in a mature way?
2.  To what extent was Mr. F able to think logically and perceive situations within the range of consensual reality? Under what conditions and to what extent did the quality of his thinking deteriorate? Assuming some regression as a result of the custody process, did he show a capacity to recover better adaptive functioning?
3.  How did Mr. F's self-perception and personality affect his ability to reflect on himself and his parenting behavior? To what extent did he show interest in and an ability to empathize with his children? To what extent did he display openness to rethink his actions with his children and make changes? Or was it necessary for him to bolster his self-esteem with denial?

*Questions about Mr. F's management of aggression and other emotions*

On the MMPI-2, Mr. F produced a defensive profile in which he consciously attempted to inhibit the expression of aggression, as evidenced by a mild, relative elevation on the Inhibition of Aggression subscale (Hy5 T = 63) and low scores on the Anger Subscales, Explosive Behavior (ANG1 T = 52); and Irritability (ANG2 T = 41). On the Rorschach, however, Mr. F showed himself not only to be highly reactive to more intense and complicated emotional stimulation (Afr = 0.91) but that this reactivity (i.e., on the more affectively evocative and complex fully chromatic Cards VIII–X) was associated with an increased likelihood of: His emotion overwhelming his ability to think (CF = 1), difficulty taking into account the big picture (W = 0), a sense of helplessness and loss of control (m = 2), one of which was in a blend with the CF), and the stirring of volatile/aggressive ideas (Card VIII "lion or tiger" and "cross-section of a volcano" coded for Fi; Card X "exploding fireworks" coded for Ex), and mildly illogical reasoning (INC1 = 1).[1] It was encouraging, though, that none of these data points associated with vulnerability to aggressive impulses and emotional dysregulation and were associated with human content or human movement responses, converging with Mr. F's report of efforts to keep intense feelings from spilling over interpersonally. Also hopeful were findings that he was a man motivated to mitigate his aggressive impulses interpersonally, that is, he was highly interested in people, capable of delaying impulses, and not lacking in his capacity for empathy (Human content = 7; M = 6).

Mr. F's Rorschach suggested that his efforts to manage emotions spanned a range including somatizing (An = 3, all on chromatic cards), intellectualized distancing (Art = 2, both on the fully chromatic Card X), and efforts to minimize vulnerability and aggrandize himself (i.e., narcissistic defenses; Fr + Rf = 2, PER = 2, all reflections and PER on chromatic cards). There was some evidence that his intellectualizing could only sustain him for so long before he eventually became overwhelmed and dysregulated: His two Art responses with good form quality on Card X were followed by the "fireworks exploding" response coded ma.CFu Ex (indicating overwhelming affect, helplessness, a mild lapse in reality testing, and breakthrough of primitive impulses). These Rorschach findings strongly paralleled reports by Mr. F and several collaterals, as well as my experience of Mr. F, as a man who seemed angry and had an inchoate sense of menace about him. Though the Rorschach data showed Mr. F to have some vulnerability to emotional dysregulation in the experience of anger, both the Rorschach data and his history showed that he generally had the ability to confine his expression of anger to verbal channels, punctuated by infrequent instances of aggression toward objects (e.g., throwing small objects and punching walls) though only once toward a person (his wife).

*Questions about Mr. F's logical thinking, accurate reality testing, and resilience*

On the MMPI-2, Mr. F showed no indication of lapses in logical thinking or reality testing (Pa T = 37; Persecutory Ideas [Pa1] T = 40; Schizophrenia [Sc] T = 45; Lack of Ego Mastery [Sc3] T = 42; Bizarre Sensory Experiences [Sc6] T = 41; Psychotic Symptomatology [BIZ1] T = 44; Schizotypal Characteristics [BIZ2] T = 41). Mr. F's approach to the Rorschach pointed to a problem-solving style marked by difficulty taking in the bigger picture (W = 4 among 21 responses; W = 0 on fully chromatic cards) and not pulling ideas together to form more complex and nuanced understanding (DQ+ = 2; none on fully chromatic cards). Consistent with his presentation on the interview and his MMPI-2 profile, Mr. F's Rorschach revealed no indication of his having a thought disorder, that is, illogical, incoherent, or tangential thinking (WSum6 = 2). This finding is tempered somewhat by a technically nonscorable response that Mr. F offered during the Inquiry to his popular butterfly response to Card V:

I do see something else I didn't see before. Off to the side, it looks like two alligators on the side of the [butterfly] wings. Actually, the butterfly overlaid on the alligator and only see the head overlaid on the alligator and only see the head portions. I say that you don't see any more the alligator and the shading. If it was correctly done, the alligators would be shaded. They were opposite shades.

I had a difficult time following this response. Were I to attempt to score it, I would puzzle about a CONTAM (contamination) versus INCOM2 (severe incongruous combination) and consider a DR2 (deviant response) for the confusion of his communication. This response underscored that under the surface of seeming conventionality (the easy popularity of the Card V butterfly with no cognitive special score), Mr. F showed some potential for lapsing into thinking that could become illogical and confused. It was notable too that his cognitive regression was associated with the intrusion of aggressive content (the alligator that he did not see in the Response phase). To Mr. F's credit, though, this was his only such lapse, showing a capacity for resilience.

Though Mr. F showed no signs of grossly distorted reality testing (XA% = 0.90; X − % = 0.10)—and he exhibited the ability to perceive situations in the most conventional ways (P = 5)—his Rorschach also revealed a vulnerability to take in experiences with an unusual or idiosyncratic spin that (though again, not distorted) was somewhat off from the way others do (Xu% = 0.48). The latter converged with MMPI-2 data showing a tendency toward nonconformance (Social Imperturbability [Pd3] T = 63). It is reasonable to speculate that at least at times his unique perspective made it difficult for others to understand or empathize with him. Conversely, it is conceivable that he might be inclined to dismiss the perceptions of others when they do not resonate with his own, further contributing to or exacerbating interpersonal misunderstanding. One example, occurring after his separation from his wife, involved Mr. F's decision when picking up his kids for a visit to park his car across the foot of her driveway. Mrs. F experienced this as intimidating (i.e., blocking her ability to leave if she felt he threatened her), while he focused on the ease with which the children could enter his car. Not surprisingly, conflict ensued from this misunderstanding.

*Questions about Mr. F's self-perception, capacity for self-reflection, and ability to adapt parenting*

Mr. F responded to the MMPI-2 in a defensive manner, portraying an overly positive self-image of good psychological adjustment, excessive virtue, and self-responsibility (Lie [L] T = 65; Correction [K] T = 66; Superlative Self-Presentation [S] T = 65). That is to say, he expressed his conscious view of himself as psychologically healthy, as is very common in custody evaluations. He viewed himself as an independent person, who was somewhat nonconforming, open to new experiences, and willing to take risks in life (Pd T = 59). As noted earlier, on the Rorschach Mr. F was motivated to mitigate his aggressive impulses interpersonally; that is, he was highly interested in people, capable of delaying impulses, and not lacking in his capacity for empathy (Human content

= 7; M = 6). Also noted earlier was the fact that his Rorschach pointed to tendencies toward self-absorption ("somebody dancing" mirrored on the opposite side on Card III), embeddedness in his own point of view, and aggrandizement (Fr + rF = 2; PER = 2).

There were also some indications on the Rorschach of Mr. F's difficulties with interpersonal closeness. Notably, his representations of people were often marked by physical proximity but lacked engagement. This was the case on both Cards VII and IX where his responses were "two faces … looking away from each other." Mr. F elaborated his percept on Card IX as "more like a caricature, like Laurel and Hardy," (scored for unusual form quality), which can be understood as thrice distanced: Once, by the faces looking away from each other; second by making them caricatures; and third, by referencing historically distal figures. On the Rorschach overall, therefore, Mr. F showed a generally benign view of relationships, with no direct expression of aggression, though with a limited ability to permit himself the closeness he desired in relationships.

In order to test Mr. F's self-reflective ability, during the interview, I pointed out to Mr. F that he had frightened his youngest child by picking him up without warning. My feedback could be viewed in a psychoanalytic context as a kind of confrontation (Auchincloss & Samberg, 2012, p. 43), which was likely to arouse anxiety and resistance. His defensive response was that I only considered him to be physically intrusive because I was predisposed to believe that he was a physical threat, based on Mrs. F's statements. This statement was a potential counterindication to therapy. In contrast, however, Mr. F demonstrated some interest in self-reflection when he initiated therapy for anger management on his own accord shortly after separation, because he felt that he had lost control of his anger by putting hands on his wife. Mr. F seemed to be interested in learning to relate better to his children, though with some impediments. Based on these data points, Mr. F's self-reflective ability appeared variable, with greater self-reflective ability under conditions when he did not feel criticized or his self-esteem to be threatened.

### ICD-10 and PDM-2 diagnoses

According to the *International Classification of Mental and Behavioral Disorders, Tenth edition* (ICD-10; World Health Organization, 1992), Mr. F met criteria for:

**F43.25**, Adjustment Disorder with mixed disturbance of emotions and conduct r/o F60.81 Narcissistic Personality Disorder

Based on the *Psychodynamic Diagnostic Manual*, Second Edition (PDM-2; Lingiari & McWilliams, 2017), I conceptualized Mr. F as follows:

**Level of personality organization**: Borderline
**Personality syndromes (P Axis)**: Narcissistic, arrogant/entitled type

**Mental functioning (M Axis)**: Moderate constrictions and alterations in mental functioning

**Symptom patterns (S Axis)**: Adjustment disorder with mixed disturbance of emotions and conduct

## Implications and recommendations

I recommended that Mr. F's physical custody time with the children be gradually increased over a six-month period, and with the assistance of a coparenting counselor (a type of joint therapist who deals specifically with issues of coparenting the children), to assess the success of his increased time to monitor him and reassure Mrs. F. The coparenting counseling could also address the difficulties that each parent had in communicating with one another regarding the children; that is, Mrs. F tended to react negatively to any of Mr. F's custody requests because she believed him to be a threat to her and to the children, as well as tending to inhibit the children's independence. Mr. F. approached Mrs. F as if she was demeaning him and his parenting by having to coordinate the children's care with him. An increase in Mr. F's custody time was contingent on Mr. F's following two primary therapeutic recommendations: (a) more consistent attendance at anger management class and application of techniques to identify relationship triggers to feelings of anger and to shore up weak controls over the expression of anger when affectively stimulated, and (b) begin psychotherapy with a psychodynamically oriented therapist who would help him step back from himself in order to see the bigger picture of his experience and to make connections regarding his perceptions, his behavior, and the perceptions of others that he did not connect. The therapist could help him explore the limits in his nuanced understanding of interactions with others and their reactions to him; to explore his defenses against recognition of the aggression implied or enacted in his behavior; to understand the childhood origins of his anger which were being re-enacted, and to help him work through the narcissistic injury he felt at having his parenting criticized and restricted. This recommendation grew out of the assessment of Mr. F as periodically interested in and intellectually curious about himself and his children when he felt in control over the process and did not feel as if he was being scrutinized and criticized. His testing showed an ability to inhibit his anger at and aggression with others, and his interview showed better inhibition when he was not feeling affectively threatened or controlled in relationships. Based on these observations, I thought he might be able to come to understand and gain better control over his anger and aggressions in therapy. In addition, in the time between the evaluation and re-evaluation six months later, Mr. F had demonstrated an ability to control his anger with the children. Therefore, I believed that a therapist who approached him with an attitude of respect and empathy might be able to make enough of an alliance with Mr. F that he could hear feedback on the quality of his relationships with the children and with Mrs. F and allow him to use avenues of relating other than resorting to anger, force, or aggression. Mr. F's sense of narcissistic vulnerability needed this level of empathy in which he felt that his point of view about parenting was being valued and respected. Mr. F had many parenting strengths from which to build stronger relationships with his children and demonstrated a commitment to improving those relationships.

## Feedback

At the end of the evaluation, I sent a lengthy report (about 50 pages) to the respective attorneys and the judge, detailing the information gathered from all sources, including the test data, resulting in conclusions and recommendations for a custody plan and treatment. The parents read the report with their lawyers. I do not have formal post-evaluation feedback with anyone in order to maintain my neutrality for potential testimony in court or potential re-evaluation. Testimony would be requested by one of the parents, allowing me to then discuss the findings of the report with that parent and representing attorney in preparation for court. My testimony will typically explain the findings of the report in greater detail to all present in court. There are times, however, where I provide feedback to the parents during the course of the evaluation in order to test their capacity to reflect on themselves. Recall Mr. F's response to my feedback about frightening his youngest child during play.

Despite his attitude of externalizing blame, Mr. F had engaged in anger management prior to the evaluation and did follow all of the treatment recommendations of the evaluation. At the follow-up re-evaluation six months later, Mr. F stated that he did not recall the conclusions from the original report. However, he had clearly benefited from the treatment, because he was demonstrably less angry and less frightening to the children. Mr. F's lack of memory for the conclusions of the report may have indicated that he had internalized the conclusions of the report and internalized the effects of his psychotherapy, but defensively excluded the ideas from consciousness in order to disavow his feelings of vulnerability at being scrutinized during the evaluation, bolstering his self-esteem. Because he was able to spend more time with the children, Mr. F was also less overtly angry with Mrs. F and with all aspects of the legal system, including the evaluator. His lessened anger may have also resulted from therapeutic efforts, but he defensively believed that his own efforts alone had improved his parenting. Mr. F's vulnerability to threatened self-esteem required additional therapeutic work.

Psychoanalytically oriented custody evaluators must write their reports with the limitations of the court in mind so that the evidence presented in the report and the inferences drawn from that evidence meet the higher standard of proof that is necessary for material introduced into a legal setting. Therefore, interpretations made from the evidence presented do not go far beyond the data themselves. However, a psychoanalytically informed report can diplomatically point the parents toward their psychological contributions to the custody conflict. The report can point psychologically minded attorneys toward a negotiated settlement of the case. Keeping the psychological best interests of the children in mind and bolstered by the custody evaluation report supporting those interests, the attorneys can help the parents to begin to grapple with their own psychodynamic issues that have led them to put their unresolved marital issues and coparenting differences ahead of the needs of their children. Negotiated settlements are obviously preferable in that they keep the parties out of court, reducing time, expense, and acrimony, but also are more likely to be successful because the parties are more likely to feel that their concerns have been heard and addressed.

In this case, the psychologically minded attorneys used the report to convince their respective clients to come to a negotiated and satisfactory agreement based on the recommendations in the report. The agreement included the more limited follow-up evaluation six months later. That re-evaluation verified Mr. F's improved parenting, enabling him to negotiate even more physical custody time with the children.

## Assessor reflections

This evaluation was particularly rewarding because, despite his very concerning emotional difficulties, Mr. F chose to make use of the therapeutic recommendations in order to improve his parenting. I was somewhat surprised by his ability to make progress, given his difficulties with self-awareness and occasional devaluing attitude toward me, because I was not sure that his strong motivation to improve his relationship with his children could overcome these difficulties. The ability to re-evaluate him and observe his good outcome was also gratifying because re-evaluations usually happen in custody cases where there is an intractable conflict between the parents. In this case, Mrs. F requested a re-evaluation because she did not trust that Mr. F had indeed improved his parenting, and Mr. F wanted his improvement documented. What was most challenging about this evaluation was trying to determine the potential for future aggression by Mr. F, since the prediction of violence is always difficult and the stakes for the children were so high. Sorting through my counter-transference feelings of empathy toward this man's vulnerability, while at the same time feeling that he was somewhat strange and unnerving, was also quite challenging. Mr. F's determination to improve his parenting and to normalize his relationships with his children was persuasive to me. He followed my treatment recommendations to deepen his engagement in therapy, where he could hopefully be able to learn more about his capacity to frighten others unintentionally and use anger to control others when he felt passive and inadequate. Ultimately, the empathy I felt toward his struggle to connect with his children, and his ability at times to honestly convey to me his lack of understanding of his own loss of control and the fear he evoked in others, allowed me to believe that he might be able to make use of psychotherapy.

As is typical of all custody cases, I have more dynamic speculations than would be appropriate from an evidentiary perspective to put in the report. In this case, I discussed in the report the parenting behavior that Mr. F learned by positive and negative example from (i.e., identifications with) his own father. Though these dynamics might never be discussed directly at any time in court or in the evaluation, they are part of the background of a psychoanalytic viewpoint that informs all of the evaluator's thinking during the case (Gunsberg, 2009). As analysts, we consider every piece of information or communication from the patient at the manifest level, hypothesize about the latent, unconscious, fantasy-driven meaning of the communication, and look for evidence to support or refute our hypotheses.

## Note

1  By contrast on Cards I–VII, Mr. F's protocol had no CFs (FC = 1), W = 4, no Ms, and no responses with such volatile content (the only aggressive content was the less immediate and more muted "ominous dragon" on Card IV), and no cognitive scores.

## References

Ackerman, M. J. (2010). *Essentials of forensic assessment* (2nd ed.). Hoboken, NJ: Wiley.

American Psychological Association. (2010). Guidelines for child custody evaluations in family law proceedings. *American Psychologist, 65*(9), 863–867.

Association of Family and Conciliation Courts. (2006). *Model standards of practice for child custody evaluation*. Madison, WI: Association of Family and Conciliation Courts.

Auchincloss, E. L., & Samberg, W. (2012). *Psychoanalytic terms & concepts*. New Haven, CT: Yale University Press.

Butcher, J. N., Graham, J. R., Ben-Porath, Y. D., Tellegen, A., & Dahlstrom, W. G. (2001). *Minnesota multiphasic Inventory-2 manual for administration, scoring, and interpretation* (revised ed.). Minneapolis, MN: University of Minnesota Press.

Caldwell, A. (2005). How can the MMPI-2 help child custody examiners? *Journal of Child Custody, 2*(1/2), 83–117.

Demby, S. (2009). Interparent hatred and its impact on parenting: Assessment in forensic custody evaluations. *Psychoanalytic Inquiry, 29*(6), 477–490.

Ellis, E. M. (2012). Are MMPI–2 scale 4 elevations common among child custody litigants? *Journal of Child Custody, 9*(3), 179–194.

Erard, R. E. (2005). What the Rorschach can contribute to child custody and parenting time evaluations. *Journal of Child Custody, 2*(1/2), 119–142.

Erard, R. E., Singer, J. S., & Viglione, D. J. (2017). The Rorschach in multimethod custody evaluations. In R. E. Erard & F. B. Evans (Eds.), *The Rorschach in multimethod forensic assessment: Conceptual foundations and practical applications* (pp. 210–241). New York: Routledge.

Exner, J. E. (2003). The Rorschach: A comprehensive system: *Basic foundations and principals of interpretation* (vol. I, 4th ed.). New York: Wiley.

Goldstein, A., Solnit, A., Goldstein, A., & Freud, A. (1996). *The best interests of the child: The least detrimental alternative*. New York: Free Press.

Gould, J. W., & Martindale, D. A. (2009). *The art and science of child custody evaluations*. New York: The Guilford Press.

Gunsberg, L. (2009). Living and working in two worlds: The psychoanalyst in the office, and the psychoanalyst as forensic expert in the courtroom. *Psychoanalytic Inquiry, 29*(6), 442–464.

Johnston, J. R., & Campbell, L. E. G. (1988). *Impasses of divorce*. New York: Wiley.

Kauffman, C. M., Stolberg, R., & Madero, J. (2015). An examination of the MMPI-2-RF (Restructured Form) with the MMPI-2 and MCMI-III of child custody litigants. *Journal of Child Custody, 12*, 129–151.

Lingiardi, V., & McWilliams, N. (Eds.) (2017). *PDM-2. Psychodynamic diagnostic manual*. New York: Guilford Publications.

Meyer, G. J., Erdberg, P., & Shaffer, T. (2007). Toward international normative reference data for the comprehensive system. *Journal of Personality Assessment, 89*(Suppl. 1), 201–216. *Journal of Child Custody, 12*(2), 129–151.

Meyer, G. J., & Kurtz, J. E. (2006). Advancing personality assessment terminology: Time to retire "objective" and "projective" as personality test descriptors. *Journal of Personality Assessment, 87*(3), 223–225.

Mihura, J. L., Meyer, G. J., Dumitrascu, N., & Bombel, G. (2013). The validity of individual Rorschach variables: Systematic reviews and meta-analyses of the comprehensive system. *Psychological Bulletin, 139*(3), 548–605.

Semel, R. (2015). MMPI-2 clinical scale 6 (Paranoia) and restructured clinical scale 6 (Ideas of persecution) in child custody litigants. *Journal of Psychology and Clinical Psychiatry, 2*(4), 1–4.

Singer, J., Hoppe, C. F., Lee, S. M., Olesen, N. W., & Walters, M. G. (2008). Child custody litigants: Rorschach data from a large sample. In C. B. Gacono & F. B. Evans (Eds.) & N. Kaser-Boyd & L. A. Gacono (Collaborators), *The LEA series in personality and clinical psychology. The handbook of forensic Rorschach assessment* (pp. 445–464). New York: Routledge/Taylor & Francis Group.

Strong, D. R., Greene, R. L., Hoppe, C., Johnston, T., & Olesen, N. (1999). Taxometric analysis of impression management and self-deception on the MMPI-2 in child-custody litigants. *Journal of Personality Assessment, 73*(1), 1–18.

World Health Organization. (1992). *The ICD-10 classification of mental and behavioral disorders: Clinical descriptions and diagnostic guidelines*. Geneva: World Health Organization.

# 7 Psychoanalytic assessment in a forensic setting

## A case of an incomplete murder-suicide

*Ali Khadivi*

Forensic psychology involves the application of the science of psychology into the law (American Psychological Association, 2013). Forensic psychologists are often called to conduct evaluations of individuals in a civil or criminal legal proceeding. Psychologists who practice forensic psychology utilize a multi-method assessment that includes clinical interviews, psychological testing, and review of medical records, legal documents, and collateral information (Heilbrun, Marczyk, DeMatteo, & Mack-Allen, 2007).

When court appointed or retained by counsel, forensic psychologists work within a psycho-legal and adversarial context where all aspects of the assessment (i.e., procedures, scoring, inferences, and language of the report) are scrutinized at a very high level. The psychologist's expertise is challenged by opposing counsel, and outcomes can come with dire consequences for the plaintiff or defendant. Court-related evaluations that involve criminal cases operate under legal jurisdiction, and psychologist-evaluators must be familiar with state laws and responsive to the specifics regarding forensic psychology practice as addressed in the standards of the Ethical Principals of Psychologists and Code of Conduct (American Psychological Association, 2002) and Specialty Guidelines for Forensic Psychologists (American Psychological Association, 2013).

The setting can also vary: Evaluations might be conducted at a private practice office, law firm, psychiatric facility, or in a correctional setting. There may or may not be third parties observing the evaluation for the purpose of recording the clinical interview or to ensure the defendant's or psychologist's safety. Procedures for managing communications with attorneys and the court involve a working knowledge of legal matters and an understanding of what is and is not permissible for evidentiary purposes, including tests and measures whose psychometric properties are acceptable in court.

## Description of setting

I conducted this psychological evaluation inside a correctional facility in a major city. At the request of the correctional authorities, I conducted the examination in a small office inside the jail that had a desk, two chairs and a large window, which allowed the officers to observe the evaluation from a distance. The defendant was not in handcuffs and no other person was present in the room.

The audience of the report was the presiding judge on the case, the district attorney's office, and the defendant's counsel. The case involved my work with Joanna (pseudonym) a 32-year-old woman, separated from her husband, who was incarcerated because she had planned a murder/suicide. She murdered her 4-year-old daughter and then attempted a planned suicide. Her suicide attempt involved overdosing on multiple different pills. She survived her suicide, was arrested, and charged with murder in the second degree.

Joanna entered a plea of guilty. A private defense counsel retained me to conduct a sentencing evaluation. The aim of this type of forensic evaluation is to identify mitigating factors that potentially impact the length of the sentence. Mitigating factors are predispositions, events, and proclivities that may negatively impact one's psychological functioning, including affect regulation, impulse control, self-esteem regulation, interpersonal and moral development (Cunningham, 2010). From a psychodynamic perspective, these are important areas to assess as ego functions (Lingiardi & McWilliams, 2017).

## Brief literature review of psychodynamic assessment in forensic settings

The use of psychodynamic thinking has long been advocated and applied to criminal forensic psychological practice. Meloy (1992), for example, in his classic study of psychoanalytic theory and forensic testing, and in using extensive case analyses that included psychological test data, illustrated a psychoanalytically informed understanding of the pathological attachment patterns underlying violent crimes. Psychodynamically informed psychological evaluations are particularly helpful in sentencing evaluations because it can potentially enrich the understanding of the defendant's developmental history, nature of attachments, sense of self, psychological vulnerabilities, and defensive processes. Finally, in cases involving a violent crime, psychoanalytic thinking can provide an explanation as to the motive for the crime, target of violence, and the nature and the manner in which the crime was committed (Meloy, 1988; Welldon, 2011). However, a major challenge for the psychoanalytically oriented forensic psychologist is integrating psychoanalytic concepts into a forensic report and during testimony in language that is acceptable, comprehensible, and defensible in court.

## Case background

Joanna was born into an intact family. She reported no developmental or behavioral problems as a child. Her father worked as a manager in a large factory. Her mother was a homemaker. She has one younger sister. Joanna described her home environment as "a living hell." She witnessed her father repeatedly verbally and physically abusing her mother. Although she reported no history of physical or sexual abuse, her father subjected her to constant emotional abuse, including comments about how bad she looked. She felt "humiliated" and "undesirable." She found comfort in her mother. She described her relationship with her mother as "very close," like a "best friend." Both parents died, however, within two years of each other. Her mother died of cancer when Joanna was 18-years-old and about to graduate from high school. She noted that her mother's death was another loss in a series of losses for her when things were looking to improve. She stated, "The rug was pulled from under me again." Her father reportedly developed alcohol problems after the death of his wife. He died two years later in a motorboat accident. She stated that there was no reason to think the accident was a suicide. She described her relationship with her father as distant until just before his death, though she had been hoping that their relationship would improve.

Displaying resilience in response to these two losses, Joanna excelled academically and completed four years of college. She obtained an undergraduate degree in Communications. Following her college graduation, she obtained a job at a public relations firm and maintained steady employment without work-related difficulties.

Joanna had no previous criminal history or any legal problems. Joanna reported no major medical illnesses. Her only surgical operation was a breast augmentation one year prior to her marriage. Joanna smoked marijuana "on and off," about once a week for approximately two years in her mid-20s. She denied using any other drugs. From ages 19 to 24, she drank nightly with her friends while "clubbing," but denied drinking on the job or missing work due to partying the night before a workday. She reported no other drug use. Joanna had a limited psychiatric history prior to the crime.

Interpersonally, Joanna had always been very social, had many friends, both close friends and acquaintances. She had maintained some of these friendships for over 20 years. She had a series of intimate relationships dating back to age 15. She indicated that her boyfriend cheated, and when she confronted him, he physically assaulted and threatened her. As an adult, she had a history of having multiple relationships, mostly sequentially, although there were relationships during which she would "cheat" because she did not trust her boyfriend and would, subsequently, "cheat first." Several of these relationships included both verbal and physical altercations in which she was beaten. She was described by her co-workers as being extremely hard-working and giving, but also someone who expected much in return and could be hurt or angry if she did not feel her generosity was reciprocated.

Joanna met George (pseudonym), the father of her now-deceased daughter and the man with whom she was in a custody battle, at a party. Although there was no initial attraction, several months later they began dating, and she "fell in love." George was an "aspiring artist" who came from a prominent and wealthy family. His family supported him as he pursued his career in photography. George was divorced and had a son whom he saw every weekend. Joanna indicated that the first six months of her marriage were "great." However, Joanna stated that shortly thereafter she found that she was having to "babysit" George's son on weekends, while he traveled for "artistic retreats." She indicated that they argued frequently about his behaviors such as his going through her picture albums or her phone because he was jealous of her past intimate relationships. She "felt taken advantage of." She considered leaving after eight months if the relationship did not improve, but she became pregnant with her daughter. She described being "shocked" upon discovering the pregnancy but stated that her pregnancy was a "beautiful thing." Having had abortions in the past for which she felt that perhaps she had been punished, Joanna was now "delighted" with her pregnancy and anticipating motherhood. Joanna stated, however, that her relationship with George was deteriorating, noting that George was even more "inconsiderate" of her needs, particularly toward the end of her pregnancy. Joanna stated that she was "forced to go out" when she was supposed to be on bed rest for bleeding. Even under these circumstances, Joanna anticipated that George would be around when she was induced, but he "left after their daughter was born." She noted that she "was by [herself] ... and felt abandoned" while he was busy painting or going to art galleries with his friends. It was, in her words, "not fair." Joanna continued feeling "abandoned," with associated anxiety and crying, and what she termed as "no helping" from George over the care of their newborn daughter. During the course of their marriage, they would alternate between her apartment and George's house several times per week. She complained that George was always "insulting ... verbally abusive ... and trying to egg [her] on" when she would pick up or drop off her daughter. She told her doctor that she "couldn't be with this guy" and that she was not sleeping or eating well. Her doctor diagnosed postpartum depression but also referred Joanna and George for marital counseling. George reportedly refused to attend couple's therapy. Joanna had six months of therapy in conjunction with Zoloft and made some progress. Xanax was prescribed at a later point.

Approximately one year after the birth of her daughter, she left George. A few weeks earlier, she described having a fight about cell phone use that led to a call to the police in which George accused her of attacking him with a phone. She began to believe that George was "trying to get [her] in trouble." She moved with her daughter to an apartment nearby. Joanna noted that the reason he would want to get her in trouble was to take her daughter. She reported that when her daughter turned 4, he told her, "If you ever leave, I will do everything to not let you take her" and told her he had seen a lawyer. Two years later after she left George, the custody and visitation proceedings began. Joanna noted that she was concerned that her daughter came home with bruises and cuts and was worried about who was watching her, knowing that George was not home very much. She reported that in later years, her daughter would say that she "did not want to go with Dad." She stated that "week after week" her daughter would say that she wanted to "stay with Momma." As the years passed, Joanna became increasingly concerned that she would lose her daughter to George. She believed that George and his family were powerful and well connected, and that she would receive unfair treatment in court with regards to custody. In fact, soon after, Joanna was informed by her attorney that the court was leaning toward ruling in George's favor. She believed that a ruling in his favor was a sign that she was going to lose custody. Over the course of the ensuing weeks, she reported that she was convinced that George was going to get custody, that he was doing it "to hurt [her]," and that her daughter was not safe when he was with George. Months before, she obtained additional Xanax in preparation for the murder/suicide. She had not made the final decision to go forward, but the purchase gave her some sense that she was taking action.

After the first court appearance, Joanna became anxious that the court may rule against her. She stated, "I decided that I wasn't going to let George take my daughter from me." She was "so angry" at George as well as feeling "sad" and "so scared" of "losing [her] daughter." She stated that she did not want her daughter to be with George and for her to live without her. She became increasingly depressed and felt hopeless about the case. She stated, "Something is happening to my daughter. I need to take her with me. Nobody is going to separate us."

On a Thursday, two days prior to the instant offense (i.e., the case being tried by the court), Joanna received a call at her office from her attorney, who reported that the judge was not allowing her to take her daughter on an overseas vacation as she had wished. She took this information to mean that her quest for custody was hopeless. That same day, she "cleaned [her] office, took her pictures down and left a suicide note stating, 'By the time you read this, my daughter and I will be in heaven together.'" The next day, she told friends to pick up things from her apartment and acted like "nothing was happening." She went to a local pharmacy to buy additional pills (Benadryl and Tylenol). She went to the post office and mailed a letter to George about what she was about to do, stating that she intended the letter to be hurtful. On Friday, she called her sister and asked her to come on Sunday morning so they could have brunch together. Her stated reason for this was to have someone find the bodies on Monday morning before they would begin to decompose. On Saturday afternoon, she played with her daughter for a couple of hours. Sometime later in the evening, Joanna began to give her cough medicine mixed with crushed Xanax and Benadryl and Tylenol to sedate her. She then took "all the pills" in her Xanax bottle and several other medications. Her next memory is of waking up in the hospital. Her sister decided to surprise her with the news of her engagement, and she came Saturday evening. She called 911 when she found Joanna and her daughter unresponsive.

Joanna was taken directly to a local hospital, where she was treated and evaluated. The toxicology report noted both benzodiazepines (e.g., Xanax) and cough medicine in her blood and urine. She was noted to have an "altered mental status," with "drowsiness" and "trouble concentrating." She was placed on observation for a suicide attempt and given charcoal to drink in order to empty her stomach of some of the medications she had taken. Upon waking up, she asked what had happened to her daughter and was told that she had died. In the psychiatry consult note, she was documented as having told the doctors that she "wanted to be 'together' with her 4-year-old daughter, and at peace with her mother and father in heaven." She reported that her husband was "verbally and emotionally abusive" and was "derisive, degrading and debased her for many years." She reported feeling "hopeless ... trapped and desperate." On mental status examination she was "lethargic, but oriented," and "crying, and distraught." Her mood was "depressed, and hopeless." She expressed suicidal ideation. She was diagnosed with Major Depression and placed on suicide watch. She was discharged into the custody of the police and taken to a county jail. Upon admission to the jail, she was noted to be tearful and having thoughts of hurting herself. She was diagnosed with adjustment disorder with mixed depressed mood and anxiety r/o unspecified personality disorder" (American Psychiatric Association, 2013). She was initially placed on suicide watch for one week. She was prescribed Ativan on an as-needed basis. The records indicate that she had concerns about losing the custody battle and not wanting to live without her daughter. One week later, she was placed back on suicide watch, after a correctional officer found a rope that she had made with a piece of cloth from her clothes and the bed sheets.

I evaluated Joanna two months after the instant offense for approximately 7.5 hours across three days. She was living in a single jail cell and was no longer on suicide watch. She stated that being in jail was like being "on another planet," a place with which she had "no familiarity," but that the hardest part of being in jail was missing her daughter. She reported no physical assault in the jail. Her primary symptom was difficulty sleeping. She was seeing a therapist once a week and was taking Abilify and Remeron.

## Rationale for battery

The battery included a clinical interview, including history and mental status examination. Given the forensic context of this evaluation I administered two different tests to assess the possibility of feigning (gross exaggeration or fabricating) symptoms of psychopathology. The Structured Interview of Reported Symptoms, Second Edition (SIRS-2; Rogers, Seward, & Gillard, 2010) is a fully structured interview used to measure feigning of symptoms of mental illness. Ackerman (2010) holds that the SIRS-2 is considered to be the best single instruction for the detection of malingering. It is standard practice in the assessment of feigning to also include a multi-scale self-report inventory. In this case, I administered the Personality Assessment Inventory (PAI: Morey 1991, 2007), which also provides information about symptom exaggeration. The other goal of the evaluation was to evaluate personality functioning and dynamics likelihood of psychological trauma as potential mitigating factors. As such, in addition to the PAI, I also included the Rorschach Comprehensive System (CS; Exner, 2003) to measure more implicit personality functioning.

Although the use of the Rorschach in forensic context is not without its challenges and controversies (see Khadivi & Evans, 2012), when the Rorschach is used in a clinically appropriate manner and as part of a multi-method forensic assessment, it does not encounter significant challenges in the courtroom (Gacono & Evans, 2008; Erard & Evans, 2017).

## Summary of findings

### *Approach to assessment*

On clinical interview, Joanna was cooperative, open, and forthcoming. She was also fully engaged with the psychological testing portion of the evaluation. The pattern of Joanna's PAI scores indicated that she attended to test items consistently (Inconsistency [INC] T = 55, Infrequency [INF] T = 47) without evidence of either symptom over-reporting (Negative Impression Management [NIM] T = 77, Malingering Index [MAL] T = 57, and PAI Rogers Discriminate Function [RDF] T = 39) or under-reporting (Positive Impression Management [PIM] T = 43). In short, she produced a valid PAI profile. Similarly, on the Rorschach, Joanna also was fully engaged with the test and produced a valid protocol (R = 27, Lambda = 0.59, Zf = 14).

On the SIRS-2, which yields five classifications (Genuine Responding, Feigning, Indeterminate-Evaluate, Indeterminate-General, and Disengagement), Joanna's performance showed that she was fully engaged with the measure. In addition, she did not have any elevations on any of the primary scales of the SIRS-2. Overall, her pattern of scores was consistent with genuine responding.

### *Thinking and reality testing*

With respect to Joanna's reasoning abilities, her Rorschach responses indicated that she was capable of thinking logically as indicated by very few cognitive special scores suggestive of a more serious ideational disturbance (WSum6 = 2, Level 2 = 0). She also demonstrated intact reality testing, which indicates that she is capable of seeing others and events in a conventional and accurate manner (P = 6, XA% = 0.81, X-% = 0.15, Xu% = 0.11) and reported no psychotic symptoms on the interview or on the PAI (Schizophrenia [SCZ] T = 54, Schizophrenia-Psychotic Experiences [SCZ-P] T = 56), or paranoia (Paranoia Persecution [PAR-P] T = 57).

### *Affect regulation*

Joanna's Rorschach revealed her preference for using thought, rather than emotion, when responding to problem-solving situations. She is more inclined to think through problems rather than react with strong emotionality, although there are times when emotions are experienced more intensely. (EB = 8:2, EBPer = 4.0, FC:CF+C = 2:1, C = 0, FQo on all responses with color as a determinant). She also showed a tendency to intellectually distance from (2AB+Art+Ay = 4) and restrict (C':Sum C = 5:2) emotions, which limits her ability to fully experience and understand her feelings. Limitations in affect expression and awareness results in uncertainty about affect recognition, leading to distress and moodiness without depth, range, and insight into various emotional states. As a result, she is prone to experience conflicting emotional states (two color-shading blended responses, FC.C'F and FY.FC) that can lead to stress or mood fluctuations. In addition, there were clear indications of an underlying oppositional stance and resentment (S = 4, S- =3, AG = 3 with FQ- = 1) that potentially impair her judgment.

Joanna showed a proclivity toward significant depressive experiences in the areas of dysphoric mood (C' = 5, three of which were C'Fo, two were FC'o and FC'-, and one was FC'u), suggesting periodic disturbances associated with upsurges in dysphoric affect that affected the accuracy of perception; painful, but not disorganizing ruminative or introspective thought FVo = 1; FDo = 1; MOR = 2 with FQo and no cognitive special scores). The MOR responses speak to negativity but not to a degree that disorganizes her thinking. Consistent with her self-report, her Rorschach reflected considerable emotional distress, which was causing her to become more vulnerable to unpleasant and negative emotions.

Consistent with negative affect, Joanna's PAI profile scores showed multiple, significant elevations on scales that measure depression (Depression [DEP] T = 73), anxiety (Anxiety Related Disorder [ARD] T = 75), and stress (Stress [STR] T = 86). This pattern of elevated scores is most consistent with an individual who is reporting severe past psychological trauma (ARD T = 75) and experiencing environmental stress (STR T = 86). As such, she is in a highly distressed state of mind, feels pessimistic (DEP T = 73), and experiences recurrent suicidal thoughts (Suicidal Ideation [SUI] T = 77). The PAI also indicated the likelihood that Joanna is a very rigid individual who is compulsive and has a strong need to control any situation she encounters (Obsessive-Compulsive [ARD-O] T = 78). In addition, she had difficulty dealing with change in her routine and unexpected events may bring her significant anxiety and stress. In response to anxiety, she had a strong proclivity to engage in obsessive rumination or compulsive behaviors.

### Object relations

Interpersonally, Joanna reported that she has been involved in volatile, unstable, and negative relationships (Borderline Features Negative Relationships [BOR-N] T = 71) that have left her hurt, depressed, and resulted in an uncertain sense of self. In relationships, she perceived herself as someone with a strong need for affiliation (Warmth [WRN] T = 65). She experienced interpersonal conflict as anxiety-provoking and may need to control the relationship as a way of managing anxiety. Individuals with similar PAI profiles are overly sensitive, inflexible (ARD-O T = 78), and somewhat controlling (Dominance [DOM] T = 63). Joanna also showed mistrust in relationships and a tendency to be hypervigilant (Paranoid Hypervigilance [PAR-H] T = 71). Although the Rorschach hypervigilance index (HVI) was not positive, she met most of the criteria for that index (Zf>13, S>3, H+(H)+Hd+(Hd)>6 , and Cg>3); she did not, however, meet the requirement of T = 0. Overall, however, this finding was consistent with PAI results suggestive of a tendency toward hypervigilance and mistrust (PAR-H T = 71).

### *Self-perception*

Joanna viewed herself as very ineffective (PAI DEP-C T = 70), filled with self-blame (Rorschach V = 1), and diminished self-esteem (PAI Mania Grandiosity [MAN-G] T = 38). However, there are also implicit signs of a tendency to be overly self-absorbed, with strong narcissistic personality features (Fr+rF = 4), which renders her vulnerable to misperceiving, and feeling hurt (two of the Fr+rF were associated with FQ-, and one was associated with a MOR). She is attentive to others but more likely responds to selective parts of other people, rather than primarily integrating various details of a person into a multidimen-sional individual (H:(H)+Hd+(Hd) = 6:6, all FQo). That is, she experiences herself as fragmented and may have difficulty integrating positive and negative views of herself into a coherent self-representation. She easily becomes self-absorbed ("this a woman looking at a mirror and admiring her butt," "she is looking at a mirror wiping her black color makeup from her face"). As such, she is prone to experience narcissistic injuries in which her feelings of self-worth may drop suddenly in response to rejection, loss, or perceived slights. She may react with depression (C' = 5, V = 1) or oppositionality (S = 4, S- = 3) that can diminish her perception of reality and impair her judgment.

## ICD-10 and PDM-2 diagnoses

According to the *International Classification of Mental and Behavioral Disorders, Tenth edition* (ICD-10; World Health Organization, 1992), at the time of the instant offense Joanna met criteria for:

F43.23 Adjustment disorder with Depressed and Anxious mood.

This diagnosis reflects the perception that her emotional state was a direct reac-tion to her circumstances at the time (i.e., the loss of her daughter). Joanna was clearly emotionally disturbed with a strong proclivity toward depressive expe-riences, but symptoms were not persistent or pervasive enough to meet the full ICD-10 criteria for either Major Depressive Disorder or an anxiety disorder

From the vantage point of the *Psychodynamic Diagnostic Manual, Second Edition* (PDM-2; Lingiari & McWilliams, 2017), the following diagnoses were applicable to Joanna:

**Level of Personality Organization**: Borderline
**Personality Syndromes (P Axis)**: Narcissistic and paranoid

**Mental Functioning (M Axis)**: M06; 19–25 Significant defects in basic mental functions

**Symptom Patterns (S Axis)**: Adjustment disorder with depressed mood and anxiety; suicidal and homicidal ideation

Joanna's life history is an important component in understanding her reaction to the custody battle in which she was mired and over which she was very upset. Her response to the call from her attorney was a trigger event that led to the eventual criminal act. Joanna had a longstanding history of both actual and perceived victimization by her own account and as corroborated by her sister. She had been emotionally abused by her father, witnessed domestic violence in the home, and was physically assaulted by her first boyfriend, who later threatened her life, requiring her to contact police. Her later relationship history is also significant for physical and emotional abuse. Consistent with others who have experienced victimization, Joanna was hypervigilant about being victimized again both by people with whom she had intimate relationships with, as well as by life itself. She noted, for example, that she was often concerned that boyfriends might cheat on her, so she explained her own infidelity as a protective maneuver, i.e., she would do it preemptively as well. In a very different vein, she discussed the deaths of her mother and father, both as significant losses, but also as examples of how "the rug was pulled out from under [her] again." She was predisposed to seeing herself as not getting a fair break, which clearly has echoed in her experience of the custody battle over her daughter with George.

Psychological testing confirmed a rigid and compulsive person prone to depression and anxiety, with a predisposition toward volatile interpersonal relationships, in which she often feels disappointed and hurt. She appears to be a self-oriented individual who sees the world and others in terms of how her needs are being met (or not).

For Joanna, the loss of custody of her daughter was intolerable. For her, this loss represented more than just the loss of daily physical access to her daughter. Given her personality and interpersonal vulnerabilities described above and having suffered the death of her mother (for whom she was still visibly grieving), and (from her perspective) was "best friends" with, her daughter was her primary intimate relationship and emotional support. The joy of caring for her daughter and being with her was what she lived for. In addition, her hypervigilance about being victimized extended to concerns about her daughter, and she was very suspicious that her daughter was not safe at George's home. Finally, the loss of custody of her daughter was yet another experience of emotional abuse by George, who she perceived as pursuing custody merely to hurt her. She was anxious about her daughter's well-being, depressed about being alone, and furious at her abuser George. Her past relationship with her father and other men further enraged her.

The call from her attorney on Thursday was the final straw. Although he merely told her that there was not yet a formal resolution to her request to travel outside of the United States, what Joanna heard was that there would never be a resolution, that George had won again, and that the ultimate loss of custody was inevitable. Already predisposed to experience a narcissistic injury, she reacted with self-directed anger and narcissistic rage directed at George, and completed plans to kill her daughter as well as herself. In doing so she would exact revenge on George for his abuse, protect her daughter from further danger at her father's home, and avoid the loss of her daughter. Her actions over the weekend and on the day of the instant offense reflected her continuing ability to plan in an organized fashion. However, at that time, these plans were her only solution to an intolerable emotional state. On the day of the instant offense Joanna was in an intolerably angry, depressed, and most importantly, hopeless state of mind when she decided her only way out was to take her own life and that of her daughter.

## Implications and recommendations

The defense counsel reviewed a copy of the completed report before it was sent to the court and to the district attorney's office (DA). It is not common to make recommendations in mitigating forensic psychological examinations. However, ideally, Joanna would have benefited from a psychodynamically informed therapy with a self-psychology theoretical orientation advocated by Feldmann, Johnson, and Bell (1990). They argue that in violent crimes there is a "cofactor" which is a person or persons who elicits the violence by influencing an individual who has primitive personality and narcissistic pathology. As such, given the psychological test findings, I believed she would benefit from a therapy that would focus on the trauma of murdering her daughter in the context of a narcissistic injury and unstable interpersonal relationship. The findings from psychological testing indicate that Joanna is likely to be motivated by her current distress to enter therapy. However, her narcissistic self-absorption coupled with her hypervigilance and interpersonal instability may make establishing a therapeutic alliance challenging. Furthermore, she has limited self-reflection and has a tendency to distance herself from her emotional experience. Based on these findings she is more likely to respond to empathic statement and mirroring and is less likely to respond favorably to a more exploratory, confrontational, object relational approach to the treatment of narcissist pathology that is advocated by Kernberg (1984).

## Feedback

I provided ongoing feedback throughout the evaluation to Joanna's attorney. However, given the forensic nature of the evaluation and at the request of her attorney, I did not provide Joanna herself with the feedback. I had informed Joanna that prior to the evaluation she might not receive feedback. I received a follow-up call from Joanna's attorney that she was sentenced to 20 years-to-life and would serve at least 18 years in prison. The judge considered Joanna's mitigating factors and rejected the district attorney's request to sentence her to life without a parole.

## Assessor reflections

I found the psychoanalytic perspective on suicide as outlined by Karl Menninger (1938) crucial in understanding this case. Menninger (1938) proposed that suicide is an interplay of three wishes; a wish to die (depressed), a wish to be killed (guilt), and a wish to kill (revenge). Joanna's murder/suicide clearly reflected a complex interplay of those wishes and enhanced my understanding of the dynamic of self- and other-directed violence.

Assessing a person charged with the murder of a child is never easy. One must be aware of countertransference reactions to such cases and make an active effort to stay objective and consider all available evidence. Sugarman's (1981) conceptualization that countertransference is a source of data in psychological assessment is especially helpful. It allowed me to process my reactions while maintaining an empathic stance toward the defendant, the deceased daughter, and the grieving father. In examining my countertransference, I found Racker's (1957) model of conceptualizing countertransference reactions most helpful. Racker explains that therapists can have two distinct types of identifications with their patients. They can have a concordant identification in which they identify with the patient's self-representation, which can potentially lead to over-identification with the patient. In contrast, the clinician can have a complementary identification in which they can identify with unwanted aspects of the patient that are projected onto others. In the latter case, the clinician identifies with other people in the patient's life, which can potentially result in the loss of empathy toward the patient. I found myself initially to have a concordant identification, which allowed me to be empathic and helped to see her perspective. As I continued with the evaluation, I also felt anger toward Joanna and I recognized that I was in a complementary countertransference, where I was identifying with how others, including her husband, might have experienced her and her actions. I continued to vacillate between the two distinct counter-\transference reactions. It was in this process that I was able to simultaneously see Joanna, on one hand, as a self-absorbed, angry, narcissistic person who took the life of her little daughter, while on the other hand, I experienced her as a traumatized, hurt, depressed person who experienced the potential loss of the custody of her daughter as unbearable.

## References

Ackerman, M. J. (2010). *Essentials of forensic assessment* (2nd ed.). Hoboken, NJ: Wiley.

American Psychological Association. (2002). Ethical principles of psychologists and code of conduct. *American Psychologist, 57*(12), 1060–1073. doi:10.1037/0003-066X.57.12.1060.

American Psychiatric Association. (2013a). *Diagnostic and statistical manual of mental disorders* (5th ed.). Arlington, VA: American Psychiatric Association.

American Psychological Association. (2013). Specialty guidelines for forensics psychologists. *American Psychologist, 68*(1), 7–19. doi:10.1037/a0029889.

Cunningham, M. D. (2010). *Evaluation for capital sentencing.* New York: Oxford University Press.

Erard, R. E., & Evans, F. B. (2017). *The Rorschach in multi-method forensic assessment.* New York: Routledge.

Exner, J. E. (2003). *The Rorschach: A comprehensive system: Basic foundations and principles of interpretation* (vol. 1, 4th ed.). New York: Wiley.

Feldmann, T. B., Johnson, P. W., & Bell, R. A. (1990). Cofactors in the commission of violent crimes: A self-psychology examination. *American Journal of Psychotherapy, XLIV*(2), 172–179.

Gacono, C. B., & Evans, F. B. (Eds.) (2008). *The handbook of forensic Rorschach assessment.* New York: Routledge/Taylor & Francis Group.

Heilbrun, K., Marczyk, G., DeMatteo, D., & Mack-Allen, J. (2007). A principles-based approach to forensic mental health assessment: Utility and update. In A. M. Goldstein (Ed.), *Forensic psychology: Emerging topics and expanding roles* (pp. 45–72). Hoboken, NJ: John Wiley and Sons.

Kernberg, O. F. (1984). *Severe personality disorders: Psychotherapeutic strategies.* New Haven, CT: Yale University Press.

Khadivi, A., & Evans, F. B. (2012). The brave new world of forensic Rorschach assessment: Comments on the Rorschach special section. *Psychological Injury and Law, 5*(2), 145–149. doi:10.1007/s12207-012-9134-7.

Lingiardi, V., & McWilliams, N. (Eds.) (2017). *Psychodynamic diagnostic manual* (2nd ed.). New York: Guilford Press.

Meloy, R. M. (1988). Violent and homicidal behaviors in primitive mental states. *Journal of American Academy of Psychoanalysis, 16*(3), 304–382.

Meloy, R. M. (1992). *Violent attachments.* Northvale, NJ: Jason Aronson.

Menninger, K. (1938). *A man against himself.* New York: Harcourt, Brace & World.

Morey, L. C. (1991). *Personality assessment inventory professional manual.* Odessa, FL: Psychological Assessment Resources.

Morey, L. C. (2007). *Personality assessment inventory professional manual* (2nd ed.). Lutz, FL: Psychological Assessment Resources.

Racker, H. (1957). The meaning and uses of counter-transference. *Psychoanalytic Quarterly, 26*(3), 303–357.

Rogers, R., Sewell, K. W., & Gillard, N. D. (2010). Structured *interview of reported symptoms second edition* (SIRS-2): Professional manual. Lutz, FL: Psychological Assessment Resources, Inc.

Sugarman, A. (1981). The diagnostic use of counter-transference reactions in psychological testing. *Bulletin of Menninger Clinic, 45*(6), 473–490.

Welldon, E. V. (2011). *Playing with dynamite: A personal approach to the psychoanalytic understanding of perversions, violence and criminality,* The forensic psychotherapy Monograph series. New York: Routledge.

World Health Organization. (1992). *The ICD-10 classification of mental and behavioral disorders: Clinical descriptions and diagnostic guidelines.* Geneva: World Health Organization.

# 8 Simple questions with complex answers

## Digging deeper into primary care assessments

*David J. York and Alan L. Schwartz*

Over recent decades, a number of converging trends have led to the ascendancy of pharmacologic and cognitive-behavioral treatments and the corresponding marginalization of psychodynamic approaches in medical practice settings. At a broad level, the values of psychodynamic practice (including an intensive focus on understanding an individual's contemporary subjective and interpersonal experience with reference to his/her developmental experiences) have been seen as incompatible with the values of modern hospital-based care, including a focus on physical symptoms, measurable change, and acute outcomes. While some of the criticisms of psychoanalysis and its practitioners have been warranted (e.g., see Bornstein, 2001), on a number of fronts, increasingly sophisticated, often empirically based inquiries into its general conceptual validity and clinical effectiveness have revealed psychodynamic approaches to assessment and treatment to be powerfully effective, particularly for complex or difficult clinical problems and when effects are assessed over time, with psychodynamic treatments demonstrating stronger effects that increase over time, while the benefits of non-psychodynamic treatments tend to decrease over time (Shedler, 2010). More recently, Kivlighan et al. (2015) did not confirm Shedler's findings of psychodynamic superiority but found that psychodynamic treatments are at least as effective and enduring in their benefits as non-psychodynamic treatments. Accordingly, the relative advantages of psychodynamic approaches to treatment are being considered by contemporary hospital-based practitioners (Yuppa & Meyer, 2017).

Recent overviews of psychological assessment in medical settings (e.g., Altmaier & Tallman, 2013) indicate that historically hospital-based psychological assessments have focused largely on symptoms, taxonomic diagnosis, or specific variables believed relevant for a particular patient population. We have had the good fortune of successfully advocating with a healthcare organization for the value of a psychoanalytically informed, collaborative assessment approach. In this chapter, we apply this approach to a case involving the differential diagnosis of Attention Deficit Hyperactivity Disorder (ADHD), a referral question posed by our primary care colleagues with increasing frequency as behavioral health becomes increasingly integrated with traditional medical services. As demonstrated below, the psychodynamic approach with a unique focus on understanding internal motivations, prohibitions against such motivations, and associated defensive mental operations facilitates the expansion of the scope of inquiry beyond categorizing individuals according to symptoms into the unique, often-complex subjective world of the individual. Indeed, a growing body of literature indicates that the psychodynamic perspective enhances clinical empathy and informs more nuanced, individualized treatment strategies across domains of psychological inquiry, including the conceptualization and treatment of ADHD (e.g., Conway, Lyon, Silber & Donath, 2019), trauma (e.g., Schottenbauer, Glass, Arnkoff and Gray, 2008), and somatic expression of psychic distress (e.g., Busch & Sandberg 2014), each of which is relevant to this case.

## Description of setting

The assessment described in this chapter took place within the context of a primary care practice embedded in a large, nonprofit hospital system. Within the practice, there are three dedicated mental health professionals who function in the role of Behavioral Health Consultants (BHC), one of whom is a psychologist who specializes in psychological assessment. The clinical role of the BHC is consistent with the Primary Care Behavioral Health (PCBH) model, the purpose of which is to support Integrated Behavioral Health (IBH); that is, the active, complementary collaboration between behavioral health and primary care providers within the same setting (Robinson & Reiter, 2017). In such an integrated practice, the BHC is the mental health expert on the primary care team and provides immediate collaboration, consultation, and access for patients through their medical providers. BHCs are typically introduced to patients by their primary care physicians during office visits, referred to as a "warm hand-off"; this direct connection provides an opportunity for the BHC to assess the patient's needs, provide consultation regarding treatment planning to the primary care team, as well as provide psychoeducation and interventions for the patient during their initial contact (Robinson & Reiter, 2017). Consistent with the PCBH philosophy, psychological assessment in the primary care setting remains limited to the use of symptom-oriented screening tools such as the nine-item Patient Health Questionnaire (PHQ-9; Kroenke, Spitzer & Williams, 2001) or the seven-item Generalized Anxiety Disorder scale (GAD-7; Spitzer, Kroenke, Williams, & Lowe, 2006). Requests for assessment to establish or provide a differential psychiatric diagnosis, understand personality factors, or examine cognitive functioning to guide treatment are referred to a wait list. This system allows the psychologist to function within the streamlined role of the BHC while in the primary care practice but also to provide comprehensive full-battery assessments through the psychological assessment service.

## Brief literature review

There are many challenges for the assessment psychologist in IBH, including the rapid pacing of primary care life, which resists the standard depth and breadth of the assessment process, the focus on overt symptomatology, the high value placed on expeditious screening, and the limited opportunities for feedback (Schwartz & York, 2017). Assessment in this setting is most often brief screening to identify symptoms (Dobmeyer, 2018), and individuals can be prone to view themselves in a superficial, symptom-based manner and seek immediate solutions to problems rather than considering more complex psychological factors. Thus, when assessment is undertaken within medical settings, the practitioner and process can be subject to being idealized, misconceived, marginalized, or devalued by clients and other healthcare professionals.

One clinical phenomenon easily susceptible to these challenges is ADHD; American Psychiatric Association, DSM-5 Task Force, 2013). It is often a diagnosis toward which patients—and healthcare professionals—can gravitate in the service of avoiding awareness of psychological factors in favor of a purely neurobiological conceptualization (Schwartz, 2011) that minimizes psychodynamic factors (e.g., Gilmore, 2000). We present the case of an assessment involving a question of ADHD to illustrate the manner in which a number of these themes can play out in a psychological assessment conducted within a medical setting.

## Case background

Mr. S was a 26-year-old, healthy single male of South Asian descent who was in the care of Dr. W, his primary care physician (PCP). Mr. S's mother contacted Dr. W's office and asked that the PCP, not a nurse, call Mr. S. He was in medical school and had recently been experiencing difficulty concentrating, depressed mood, and "mood swings." In their meeting with Dr. W, Mr. S reported that for the prior two months he had been experiencing difficulties with attention and concentration, shifts in mood ranging from lethargy to mild agitation, and difficulties with sleep onset that he attributed to racing thoughts. He reported drinking alcohol moderately on weekends but no pattern of alcohol or other substance abuse. His symptoms improved with exercise. He did not report a history of hyperactivity, problems with anger or conduct, or suicidal ideation. Dr. W assigned a diagnosis of Adjustment Disorder with Mixed Anxiety and Depressed Mood and prescribed bupropion (a norepinephrine or dopamine reuptake inhibitor for mood regulation) and quetiapine (an atypical antipsychotic medication used in an off-label manner to assist with sleep). Dr. W suggested restricting caffeine and alcohol and encouraged Mr. S to attend a scheduled initial psychotherapy appointment. Over the next two months, Mr. S described better focus though more mood variability, as well as hypersomnolence. In response, Dr. W increased Mr. S's bupropion and cut back on his nightly quetiapine. A few months later, Mr. S's mood was improved; however, he now reported episodes of tachycardia along with hypersomnolence, the latter of which he tried to address with large quantities of caffeine, but then he remained awake until late at night. In response to Mr. S's request for additional medication to treat his heart palpitations, Dr. W wondered if such symptoms might be related to anxiety as well as his increased caffeine intake and ordered blood work and a Holter monitor before making any further medication changes. Mr. S's lab work was normal; he did not complete Holter monitoring. Four months after the initial diagnosis, Mr. S had discontinued both medications after experiencing them as having too much of a negative effect on his academic performance. Dr. W recommended a trial of sertraline and scheduled a follow-up visit in a month. Mr. S did not follow up regarding the plan to consult a psychotherapist.

Several weeks later, Mr. S took a leave of absence from medical school and moved back home. Now, Dr. W referred the patient to Dr. A's psychological assessment service, specifically to Ms. Q, a graduate psychology trainee.[1] Dr. W noted that although Mr. S had reported a recent history of depressive-like symptoms (e.g., decreased focus, mild agitation, variable mood, reduced motivation, poor sleep), he had not observed any of these symptoms during office visits. Thus, the assessors understood Dr. W's referral question to be "Can this young man's stress and functional impairment be attributed to depression and/or are other factors contributing to his presentation?"

On the first day of the assessment (and on each subsequent day), Mr. S arrived late. Although he demonstrated an engaged attitude during the clinical interview, at times it was hard for Ms. Q to follow Mr. S's report of his experiences. During test administration, Mr. S laughed nervously when he was unsure about how to answer certain test items. He seemed fatigued as the testing went on, and actually fell asleep while completing one of the performance-based cognitive tests. During the feedback session, Mr. S explained that he experiences this type of fatigue with any task of sustained attention.

Developmentally, Mr. S recalled himself as having been sheltered as a child and focused exclusively on school work. Mr. S acknowledged very good grades in school, though reported needing "stars and stickers" to help motivate him early on. But he was unable to recall any symptoms of inattentiveness, impulsivity, or hyperactivity at home or in school during his grade school years. Mr. S reported that he earned mostly As in high school. Mr. S studied chemistry in college and he started working for a biotechnology company. He earned a few Bs in college subjects in which he had less interest. In college, he described experiences of difficulty with switching tasks, forgetting to hand in assignments, and losing things and began to see himself as having ADHD.

Mr. S had his first dating relationship in college. After the breakup, he became depressed and had suicidal thoughts with a plan. He called a suicide hotline and conveyed that he would never commit suicide because he sees it as selfish and that he loves life. In the run-up to college graduation, Mr. S was trying to decide between attending medical school versus pursuing a job. Mr. S wanted to take a year off after college, but his parents did not support this plan. His transition to medical school was difficult. He struggled with depression and distractibility in the wake of his relationship breakup. Mr. S saw a psychotherapist at medical school but disengaged after not finding his initial session helpful. He expressed the wish that psychotherapy would involve his being asked difficult questions.

In the clinical interview, Mr. S exhibited what seemed like grandiose thoughts such as when he recalled that his motivation for going to medical school was to "change medicine." Mr. S reported that during his first year of medical school, despite usually being an "exceptional student," his efforts to study were impeded by low motivation, difficulties with focus, and procrastination. Mr. S's accounts of his difficulties in medical school were variable: At times, he described making merely average grades after bearing down hard in his studies; whereas, at other times, he described how he had fallen far behind his peers. The evaluators wondered if Mr. S was conflating average grades with falling far behind, suggesting concerns associated with his sense of adequacy. Feeling so far behind his peers, eventually, Mr. S took a medical leave.

Mr. S described a highly conflictual family of origin. During his senior year in high school, his mother discovered that his father had an extramarital affair. She became severely depressed though she also had manic-like phases, including episodically screaming and threatening suicide. His father would yell back and break things. Mr. S described his father as acting out "like a child." There was also some unspoken pressure from his close-knit ethnic/cultural/ religious community for his parents to stay together and for his mother to forgive his father, lest the community would abandon her. His father was unemployed for a year and then obtained a job requiring him to move several hours away. His parents eventually reconciled. Mr. S described the emotional milieu of the family household as "toxic," when on leave from medical school, his return home to live there had made him the focus of his mother's care.

## Rationale for battery

In accordance with optimal assessment practice (Meyer et al., 2001) and building upon foundational psychoanalytic assessment procedures such as the clinical interview and careful observation of the patient-assessor relationship (Schafer, 1954), the assessors constructed an individualized, multi-method battery of tests. Although some consistency exists in choice of types of tests (almost all batteries include methods ranging from structured assessment of cognitive abilities through low-structure performance tests of personality), specific tests are chosen according to the referral question(s) generated by the referring party, the client and the assessment psychologist. even minimal cues to guide or direct an individual's behavior (Bram, 2017).

In discussing the purpose of the current assessment and dovetailing with the collaborative assessment model (Finn, Fischer, & Handler, 2012), Mr. S was asked to identify his own questions to be answered by the assessment process. He questioned whether he may be suffering from ADHD. After the initial clinical interview, three primary assessment hypotheses about how to understand Mr. S's symptoms and difficulties functioning were identified: (a) Dr. W's question about possible depression; (b) Mr. S's question about undiagnosed ADHD; and (c) the assessors' question about the extent to which cognitive and/or personality factors account for Mr. S's current struggles. The evaluators aimed to clarify the underlying developmental disruption(s) (Bram & Peebles, 2014; Peebles, 2012) accounting for the emergence of acute symptomatology at the point in Mr. S's development when he was closest to achieving functional autonomy and sought-after regard from his parents (Erikson, 1994). Peebles (2012) outlined four non-mutually exclusive paradigms of underlying developmental disruption that facilitate conceptualization of psychological factors that are manifested in symptoms and DSM diagnoses: (a) structural weaknesses, (b) trauma, (c) conflicts and splits, and/or (d) maladaptive character patterns. Different patients may share a set of symptoms and the same DSM diagnosis, but each may be understood as having a different underlying developmental disruption. Identifying the nature of the disruption sharpens the conceptualization of what needs to be addressed in treatment and how that might be achieved (Bram & Peebles, 2014). So even as the assessors sought to determine whether Mr. S met DSM criteria for a depressive disorder, they were as interested in using testing to clarify the underlying psychological factors driving his symptoms. Note that Mr. S's question about whether he has ADHD involves ruling out the possibility of a very specific structural weakness (i.e., a brain-based impairment in executive functioning; Barkley, Murphy, & Fisher, 2008).

In order to address Mr. S's concerns about the possibility of ADHD, the assessors selected (a) a self-report instrument, the Conners' Adult ADHD Rating Scales—Long Version (CAARS—L; Conners, Erhardt, and Sparrow, 1999), (b) a collateral-report measure, the CAARS—L Observer Rating Form, completed by Mr. S's younger brother and a close friend, and (c) a performance-based test designed to assess mental focus and behavioral control, The Integrated Visual and Auditory Continuous Performance Test— Second Edition (IVA-2; Sandford & Sandford, 2019). In order to account for intellectual or learning factors that can give rise to performance difficulties in medical students (Quirk, 1996), two other performance-based measures, the Wechsler Abbreviated Scale of Intelligence—Second Edition (WASI-II; Weschler, 2011) and a set of core reading subtests (Word Attack, Letter-Word Identification, Sentence Reading Fluency, and Passage Comprehension) from the Woodcock Johnson Tests of Achievement Fourth Edition; (WJ IV ACH; Schrank, Mather, & McGrew, 2014) were administered. The verbal subtests of the WASI-II doubled as structured performance-based measures of personality functioning (Rapaport, Gill, & Schafer, 1946; Bram, 2017). Because of practical considerations of time constraints and incremental validity, the assessors chose to administer the WASI-II in lieu of the full WAIS-IV (Wechsler, 2008).

To address the questions about depression and underlying developmental disruption, the assessors include two self-report inventories, the Personality Assessment Inventory (PAI; Morey, 1991) and the NEO-Personality Inventory—Third Edition (NEO-PI-3; Costa and McCrae, 2010). Particularly within the medical setting and with referrals regarding the question of ADHD, we find it helpful to administer the PAI as one way to consider each patient's broad pattern of reported psychiatric symptomatology. The PAI provides information regarding an individual's experience of symptomatology and the presence of stressors, behavior patterns, traits, and dispositions relevant in considering treatment priorities and options. In addition, the PAI was specifically chosen because (a) its items and scales map onto DSM categories in a way that would help illuminate the presence or absence of a depressive disorder and (b) it is helpful in determining the role of maladaptive character patterns. To complement the psychopathology orientation of the PAI, the NEO-PI-3 was included to examine Mr. S's standing along a set of universal personality dimensions and to determine if potentially problematic personality facets might be acknowledged in response to the NEO-PI-3's manifestly more benign, potentially less defense-activating items (compared to the PAI). In addition to these self-reports, the assessors selected the Rorschach Performance Assessment System (R-PAS; Meyer, Viglione, Mihura, Erard, Erdberg, 2011) and Thematic Apperception Test (TAT; Murray, 1943). The TAT set comprised Cards 1, 2, 3BM, 4, 6BM, 7BM, 8BM, 10, 13MF, and 14, a set routinely used by Dr. A. with male patients. These performance-based methods were included to assess various implicit aspects of personality functioning such as reasoning, reality testing, affect regulation, sense of self, and orientation to relationships.

## Summary of findings

In this section, we organize the test findings according to their relevance to each of the three referral questions that the battery of tests was designed to address. For each question the assessors reviewed all multi-method findings relevant to each question and, again, consistent with a psychoanalytic assessment approach, utilized formal scores, content themes, analysis of temporal sequences, convergent and divergent data configurations, and analysis of patient-assessor interactions (e.g., Bram, 2015).

### *Possible undiagnosed ADHD?*

The amalgam of Mr. S's test behaviors and responses revealed the extent to which Mr. S had invested in a narrative of himself as having ADHD (i.e., a structural weakness), despite considerable evidence in support of alternative explanations for his difficulties. Although Mr. S's self-report on the CAARS was consistent with ADHD (DSM-IV Inattentive Symptoms subscale T = 75, DSM-IV Total ADHD Symptoms scale T = 65), collateral reports by his brother and his friend were entirely within normal limits (respectively, brother's scores were T = 58 and T = 55, friend's were T = 45 and T = 46). In addition, although Mr. S's performance fell below the first percentile on omnibus indices of attentional focus and impulse/response regulation on the IVA-2, a 15-minute-long, multi-modal computerized test of sustained attention and impulse control, Ms. Q observed that Mr. S repeatedly evidenced gross somnolence, closing his eyes and apparently drifting to sleep during administration of the IVA-2. These observations led to a parsimonious and not uncommon causal hypothesis—hypersomnolence likely due to disrupted sleep—about what accounted not only for Mr. S's report of acute attentional problems but for the disparity between self- and observer-report of ADHD symptoms. That is, Mr. S's self-report may have reflected his awareness of his state of degraded mental alertness, particularly if its effects were more prominent when faced with challenging mental tasks. In contrast, his friend and his sibling would not have had access to Mr. S's internal states and may not have observed him in contexts that most elicited performance difficulties. The assessors concluded that Mr. S did not meet ADHD criteria but would benefit from a medical assessment for a sleep disorder.

In addition to evidence of a possible sleep disorder, clues regarding other factors contributing to Mr. S's medical school difficulties were evident in his pattern of performance, qualitative as well as quantitative, on measures of global intellectual capacity and academic skills. Mr. S's performance on the WJ IVACH revealed no areas of gross weakness across tasks assessing reading (all subscale scores $\geq$ 108) and his performance on the WASI-II (Full Scale IQ-4 [FSIQ-4] SS = 115, Performance IQ [PIQ] SS = 119, Verbal IQ [VIQ] SS = 108) placed him in the average-to-high average range with regard to intellectual capacity. Although his performance on visuospatial tasks (PIQ) was commensurate with the average IQ of medical students (generally estimated to be around SS = 120; Matarazzo & Goldstein, 1972; Hauser, 2002), his performance on verbal tasks was less robust, indicating that though he possessed the gross cognitive abilities necessary to succeed in medical school, he was likely to require greater time and effort—in short, high levels of conscientiousness—to succeed in medical school. The contrast between Mr. S's elevated ambitions "to change medicine" and his more modest intellectual capacities set him up for inevitable frustration, disappointment, pressure, and a sense of falling short and wounds to his self-esteem.

### Depressive disorder?

As with most ADHD referrals, the assessors utilized the PHQ-9 and GAD-7 screening data to consider the potential contribution of depressive or anxiety disorders to Mr. S's complaints regarding concentration and motivation: The evaluators were impressed first by the prominence of mood symptoms relative to ADHD-specific symptoms. On the PHQ-9 (total score = 15, moderately severe), Mr. S reported experiencing concentration difficulties for several days during the prior two weeks, while he reported experiencing five other major depressive symptoms more than half of the days (but only one—disrupted sleep—nearly every day) during the prior two weeks. In contrast to his score on the PHQ-9, Mr. S attained a score of 6 on the GAD-7, placing him in the mild range of anxiety, with this score largely attributable to reporting annoyance or irritability nearly every day for the prior two weeks. Similarly on the PAI, Mr. S's score on the Thought Disorder Subscale of the Schizophrenia Scale (SCZ-T, T = 61), and the Activity Level Subscale of the Mania Scale (MAN-A, T = 60), the two PAI subscales most associated with a bona fide diagnosis of ADHD (Musso et al., 2011; Watson & Liljequist, 2015), were merely commensurate with his moderately elevated overall level of distress (Mean Clinical Elevation [MCE], T=60) suggesting that his experience of difficulties with concentration and motivation were related to his general experience of distress rather than to a primary attentional impairment.

In contrast, though none of his core clinical scale scores indicated a specific clinical syndrome in any of the domains assessed by the PAI, Mr. S's scores on four of the 11 clinical scales, including Depression (DEP, T = 68), Mania (MAN, T = 66), Borderline Features (BOR, T = 66), and Alcohol Problems (ALC, T = 68) were mildly to moderately elevated, indicating diffuse symptomatology. These impressions were further validated when application of the PAI structural summary approach (Morey & Hopwood, 2007) failed to identify a clear match between Mr. S's pattern of scores and those associated with major depression, dysthymia, and bipolar disorder. The evaluators interpreted these findings as providing further disconfirming evidence regarding ADHD as well, indicating that Mr. S's functional difficulties and distress were associated with a broad, complex set of symptoms and concerns rather than simply reflecting the presence of a single discrete clinical syndrome. Additionally, more so than during the interview, Mr. S acknowledged that recent alcohol use (Alcohol Problems; ALC, T = 68) may have adversely affected his functioning. Further, when directly compared to the DSM-V criteria for major depressive episodes, Mr. S reported sufficient number of symptoms (depressed mood, disrupted sleep, disrupted appetite, fatigue and diminished energy, diminished self-esteem), but he did not report experiencing these symptoms for most of the day nearly every day. Rather, the relatively short duration and moderate frequency and intensity of his reported symptoms were more consistent with the DSM-V diagnosis of Adjustment Disorder with Depressed Mood. However, in light of the above findings, the assessors concluded that Mr. S's functional difficulties and experiential distress could not be fully understood as simply an "Adjustment Disorder" but, as will be elaborated in the next section, appeared to reflect a more complex set of developmental, intrapsychic, and interpersonal factors.

### Developmentally based dynamic personality factors?

The evaluators considered Mr. S's report of his history as well as his interpersonal behavior during the clinical interview to be striking in a number of ways. Based upon their experiences with Mr. S, they developed a series of questions to be answered by the assessment, all of which represented various aspects of the larger question of "What psychological factors might account for the emergence of acute symptomatology and functional impairment during the first year of medical school in someone with a history of generally intact social and academic functioning?" These included questions such as:

1.  To what extent did Mr. S experience the long-standing conflicts between his parents as overwhelming and even traumatic? If so, how do such factors affect his current functioning, particularly with regard to self-image, relationships, reasoning, and ability to perceive people and situations accurately?
2.  Are Mr. S's current difficulties related to internal conflict or split—between competing wishes or desires, some of which he suppresses, denies, or even stringently disavows (see Bram & Peebles, 2014)—stirred by current developmental demands? More specifically, was his functioning disrupted by his experience of mixed, unintegrated, conflicting feelings evoked the closer he came to achieving autonomy, success, and recognition from his parents?
3.  Rather than primary deficits in attentional control, does Mr. S exhibit other enduring structural weaknesses or deficits in core psychological capacities (e.g., relatedness, reality testing, etc.) that might contribute to his current difficulties?
4.  Might Mr. S's current difficulties represent the manifestation of maladaptive patterns of perceiving, thinking, and relating (i.e., character patterns) that negatively impacted his functioning in medical school? If so, perhaps such patterns had been unchallenged or perhaps even contextually adaptive in previous settings?

Answering these psychodynamic questions was deemed crucial to the generation of meaningful treatment implications. Along similar lines, the assessors also wondered about how to understand the appeal to Mr. S of the notion that his difficulties were attributable to ADHD.

### The influence of trauma?

Although Mr. S did not self-report a subjective sense of trauma (e.g., PAI Anxiety Related Disorder; ARD-T, T = 48), his responses to the relatively unstructured, performance-based Rorschach indicated the presence of significant implicit distress and dysphoria (YTVC' SS = 122), and his TAT responses pointed to the possibility that such distress may be linked to ongoing preoccupation with his parents' long-standing marital conflicts. The most compelling of these occurred in response to Card 3BM of the TAT (depicting a person, often seen as female, slumped on the floor), where Mr. S described, "A lady who loves her family, but dad doesn't really 'get her.' Her husband, I guess husband, slapped her." The assessors were struck by the fluidity and seeming lack of awareness with which Mr. S's perceptual set shifted from "dad" to "husband," in the course of his narrative of domestic violence; this possibly self-referential lapse in the coherence of his narrative raised the possibility, albeit tentative, that Mr. S might be communicating his experiences of his own father's physical violence toward his mother. Moreover, the assessors noted the slip in Mr. S's cognition—which did not occur in his other narratives—was associated with the traumatic content evoked by Card 3BM.

Mr. S exhibited a similar response pattern on the Rorschach, as his most cognitively impaired response was also in configuration with content involving authority and aggression. Specifically, two of Mr. S's four cognitive codes occurred on his first response to Card IV:

> An alligator with a smoky, billowy cloak ([FAB1], like an alligator evil overlord [INC2] (CP) Yes, I couldn't not see the eyes at the top. Looks like some type of reptile. I said overlord—it's part of the outfit it's wearing. Royal, exuberant, flares out like Renaissance times have parts of their coat flare out. [Dd99 A,Ay,Cg,Fi Sy—ma.Y INC2, FAB1 AGC]

This response illustrates how for Mr. S internal representations of authority figures ("overlord") are associated with feelings of danger (AGC), anxiety (Y), and helplessness (m) as well as with deteriorations in reality testing (FQ−) and logical reasoning (FAB1, INC2). In addition, these concerns were also entwined with a certain grandiosity ("lord," "royal," "exuberant") and possible identification with the aggressor (AGC).

Although there is not sufficient convergence of data to indicate that Mr. S is suffering full-blown post-traumatic symptoms, his TAT 3BM story and Rorschach Card IV response suggest he is vulnerable to at least moments when concerns about the danger of authority figures can intrude and disrupt his functioning. It is possible to speculate that the experience of being in medical school—with his need to interact with physicians/professors in authority and the prospect of his becoming such an authority figure himself—played some role in the regression in his cognitive and adaptive functioning.

### The presence of internal conflicts or splits?

Mr. S's pattern of scores within the PAI and across the PAI and performance-based measures pointed to his tendency to split off or disavow psychological aspects of his distress. Specifically, his self-report on the PAI indicated his experience of physiological activation (Anxiety—Physiological [ANX-P], T = 72), yet he was less inclined to report experiencing his anxiety psychologically (ANX T = 60, and ARD-T = 48; converging with his relatively low score on the GAD-7). Mr. S's Rorschach also pointed to his tendency to experience his distress more somatically (An SS = 133). But his Rorschach also pointed to more anxiety and other psychological distress than he self-reported (YTVC' SS = 122), and his TAT stories were replete with anxious concerns about guilt and ineffectiveness as well as his efforts to distance from such feelings. For example, in response to Card 1 (depicting a boy contemplating a violin), which typically evokes concerns around mastery and achievement, Mr. S described a protagonist who is

> messed up. He's disappointed in himself. He felt bad but didn't know how to deal with emotion. He tried to read a book he enjoys, but it's not working. He hurt a friend by accident. He's trying to do homework but is distracted because he's upset and doesn't know how to make it right.

Similarly, on Card 13MF (depicting a man, downturned head buried in his arm, standing over a woman lying on a bed) Mr. S responded:

> One of our older doctors … and he just lost his patient. He feels like he failed her. He knows he has to be strong, have a strong face. He has to assure her husband that he's done everything he could but he feels that he could have done more and if he did more, she wouldn't be dead. He feels guilty even though he rationally knows there wasn't anything. Story ends with him going to tell the husband with the image of confidence and sadness—the image that husband needs him to be— but keeps his true feelings within him.

In these two responses, Mr. S identified protagonists who perceive themselves as responsible for losses and harm, attempt to contain and mask inner turmoil without help from others but find themselves plagued by disruptive feelings of guilt and regret that need to be hidden from others. Consistent with this hypothesis, Mr. S's R-PAS profile illuminated his proneness to self-criticism (V SS = 126). The assessors considered the possible interface among Mr. S's apparent experience of chronic interpersonal hostility during his upbringing, his view of himself as responsible for having harmed others and his preoccupation with feelings of guilt, a common set of thoughts, feelings, and beliefs experienced by individuals who have witnessed chronic domestic conflict or violence (Stuewig & McCloskey, 2005; McCoy, Cummings, & Davies, 2009).

Furthermore, Mr. S offered the following response to the last TAT card administered, Card 14 (depicting the silhouette of a person juxtaposed against a bright space often construed as a window):

> Younger brother of Peter Pan. Wendy and older brother are all off to college. He's flying the coop. It's just him in the house. He still dreams, and they're all grown up now. Dreaming he could go back to Neverland, dreaming he could go back but knowing it may not be what he wants. He knows it might not be right. It's a memory that makes him happy.

The evaluators viewed some convergence between this TAT response and Mr. S's Rorschach Card IV response of the "alligator overlord," which was not too far afield from the Captain Hook-crocodile dynamic from the *Peter Pan* story.[2] Barrie's (1957) iconic story of children escaping from impending demands of adulthood and, though not likely known to the author himself, has been understood as Barrie's efforts to metabolize his own series of childhood traumas (Birkin, 2003). Along similar lines, the evaluators considered this TAT story to be a "telling response" (Lerner, 2005, p.272) and conjectured that it reflected Mr. S's use of imaginative, regressive, disavowing fantasy to mitigate against the emotional impact of the domestic distress he experienced during childhood as well as anxieties about moving into adulthood. As Mr. S was unable to recognize the various developmental and psychological components of his distress (indicated in his TAT and Rorschach responses) that contributed to his autonomic over-arousal and cognitive concerns (i.e., symptoms leading to his focus on ADHD), the evaluators concluded that Mr. S had split off these aspects of his experience from his conscious awareness.

*Structural weaknesses in core psychological capacities?*

Mr. S's educational history and his performance on structured tests of intelligence and academic skills provided ample evidence that his neurocognitive capacities were solidly developed (WASI-II FSIQ-4 SS = 115, all WJ IV-ACH reading subscale scores ≥ 108). Furthermore, his R-PAS profile revealed him to possess average levels of differentiated and integrated thinking (Complexity SS = 104). However, several areas of structural weakness were evident in Mr. S's personality test responses, and these weaknesses appeared to reflect the impact of chronic exposure to his aversive, interpersonal environment on foundational psychological abilities. When conceptualized as trauma-related, such structural weaknesses might be considered to occur at the "firmware" level (i.e., algorithms that are stored in memory and control a device or organism at an embedded level in an enduring manner but that can be "updated" if desired) versus at the "hardware" level (i.e., the physical device or organism itself).

First and foremost, Mr. S's capacity for relatedness appeared to be underdeveloped. His TAT stories were notable for the absence of representations of benevolent, trusting relationships. There were other indications in his Rorschach that he has not internalized representations of people that he can call upon in times of distress and that he does not have well-developed empathy (M SS = 83). Further, his experience of relationships is fraught with misunderstanding, confusion, conflict, and vulnerability (PHR/GHR SS = 132).

Second, Mr. S's responses indicated weaknesses in his capacity to regulate his emotions. In comparison to his ample cognitive capacities (FSIQ SS = 115), Mr. S's R-PAS profile showed a modest set of ego capacities and coping skills (MC = SS = 90). Moreover, there was evidence of Mr. S's vulnerability to having emotions flood and disrupt his cognition and problem-solving (C SS = 124). As noted earlier, Mr. S was also inclined to experience and express his emotional distress somatically rather than psychologically (An SS = 133; PAI SOM-C T = 66).

Third, Mr. S's R-PAS profile revealed a weakness in his capacity to maintain accurate reality testing under conditions of being more on his own to make sense of situations that are less familiar and offer fewer external guidelines and expectations and less opportunity for feedback (FQ−% SS = 143). Moreover, under such conditions, he even exhibited difficulty picking up on what is fairly obvious to others (Populars [P] = 0 SS = 56). Configurational analysis (Bram & Peebles, 2014) illuminated that his vulnerability to perceive situations in more distorted ways was exacerbated to the extent he was stirred by anxious or dysphoric emotions: For responses in which he made use of one or more YTVC' determinants, his FQ−% was 0.67; in the absence of those determinants, his FQ−% was 0.19.

### *The contribution of maladaptive character patterns?*

From early on in the clinical interview onward, aspects of Ms. S's interpersonal style raised the question of possible maladaptive character patterns. His demeanor vacillated between anxiousness and overconfidence and devaluation. For example, Mr. S expressed his belief that the field of medicine was "dumb" and that he could change it to make the patient and doctor experience better. During the feedback session (detailed further below), Mr. S actively refuted the findings presented by Ms. Q in a way that she experienced as devaluing her efforts to understand him, raising her internal anxiety around concerns regarding whether or not she had managed to fully capture his experience. The NEO-PI-3 offered further support for the hypothesis of a characterological element to Mr. S's difficulties functioning. Specifically, comparison of Mr. S's NEO-PI-3 facet score profile to conceptually and empirically based prototype NEO-PI-3 facet profiles for each of the categorical DSM-V personality disorders using an empirical coefficient of fit (McCrae et al., 2001; Costa and McCrae, 2010) revealed very high (>0.90) correspondence between Mr. S's NEO-PI-3 personality facets and those characteristic of individuals diagnosed with Narcissistic Personality Disorder (NPD). As defined within the five-factor model, people with NPD manifest very low levels of Modesty, Altruism, Tender-mindedness, and Straight-forwardness, all facets of Agreeableness, reflecting an antagonistic disposition. Simultaneously, they exhibit high levels of Openness to Fantasy (wishes for unlimited power, beauty, etc.) and Neurotic Self-Consciousness (hypersensitivity to constructive feedback) as well as Neurotic Hostility (Widiger, Trull, Clarkin, Sanderson, & Costa, 2002). Mr. S's pattern of scores matched the NPD prototype for six of these seven facets. Convergent with these NEO PI-3 findings, Mr. S's PAI profile underscored further narcissistic characteristics: Demanding and easily frustrated (PAI Mania-Irritability [MAN-I] T = 69); sensitive to slights and prone to hold grudges (PAI Paranoia-Resentment [PAR-R] T = 69); and underlying self-criticism and brittle self-esteem and tenuous sense of identity (PAI Mania-Grandiosity [MAN-G] T = 58, PAI- Depression-Cognitive [DEP-C] = 64], PAI Borderline Features-Identity Problems [BOR-I] T = 68). Interestingly, the finding of Mr.

S's interpersonal egocentrism was somewhat culturally uncharacteristic of people of his South Asian ethnicity. (Konstabel, Realo, & Kallasmaa, 2002).

## ICD-10 and PDM-2 diagnoses

In the International Classification of Diseases and Related Health Problems (ICD-10; WHO, 1992), Mr. S's symptoms meet criteria for

F43.21 Adjustment Disorder with Depressed Mood
F10.10 Alcohol Abuse Disorder
        r/o sleep disorder.

Within the framework provided by the *Psychodynamic Diagnostic Manual—Second Edition* (PDM-2; Lingiardi & McWilliams, 2017), the following diagnoses are applicable to Mr. S:

**Level of personality organization**: Borderline level
**Personality syndromes (P Axis)**: Narcissistic personality
**Mental functioning (M Axis)**: Moderately impaired
**Symptom patterns (S Axis)**: Adjustment disorder and Substance-Related
        disorder

## Recommendations

First and foremost, the findings of Mr. S's underdeveloped capacity for relatedness needed to be taken into account in formulating a treatment plan. It was not a given that Mr. S would be able to readily engage in a safe, trusting, collaborative alliance with a therapist. In retrospect, it was not surprising that he had past difficulty connecting with a therapist and even in following up on the recommendation for therapy. It would be important for a therapist to recognize from the outset that building a therapeutic alliance would take time. Related to this, from the outset the therapist would do well to take into account Mr. S's narcissistic vulnerabilities—that is, his sensitivity to feeling misunderstood, criticized, and slighted—and work to repair inevitable ruptures in the alliance (Safran & Kraus, 2014). Given Mr. S's representations of relationships with authority figures as fraught with danger, fear, and hostility, the potential for power struggles between him and his therapist would not be surprising. To strengthen collaboration in the alliance, it could be helpful to predict this possibility to him (based on the test findings) and discuss with him whether the two of them might agree to work together to try to understand and resolve such dynamics if and when they unfold.

Recognizing the extent that Mr. S needed to split off and disavow developmental and psychological aspects of his distress would be important for the therapist so as not to prematurely confront and interpret. Instead, the task would be to gradually and tactfully encourage his curiosity. The hope would be that over time, Mr. S would be assisted to access his anxieties and guilt about becoming a successful adult (including escapist, regressive fantasies) and understanding the developmental roots of these experiences in his tumultuous and sometimes violent family environment. It would be important for the therapist to take seriously and address Mr. S's concerns about symptoms. Along these lines, there could be room to integrate psychoeducational and skill-building interventions from cognitive-behavioral therapy (CBT) or dialectical behavior therapy (DBT). For example, this might include teaching him about the connections among thoughts, feelings, behaviors, and physiology or offering him self-regulation skills (e.g., relaxation or mindfulness). But the therapist should not lose sight that relational elements of therapy would be central to help him stay engaged in the short term and, over time, develop more adaptive and satisfying ways of interacting with others. Recognizing that implementing this kind of therapeutic plan would not be easy, the evaluators recommended that, if possible, Mr. S would benefit from a referral to a therapist experienced in working with complex, difficult-to-treat patients.

In addition to the recommendation for psychotherapy, anticipating that Mr. S would be disappointed in not receiving his wished-for ADHD diagnosis, the evaluators provided him with a list of broad, globally beneficial behavioral strategies from the ADHD literature (e.g., parsing daily schedule into discrete time increments allowing intensive focus interspersed by breaks; systematic self-reward for attaining personal behavioral goals; potential use of an executive function coach to provide guidance if self-directed efforts are unsuccessful). Mr. S was encouraged to discuss these strategies further with the therapist recommended to him.

Although the evaluators did not find support for full-blown major depressive disorder, Mr. S's struggles with dysphoric symptoms were compelling enough that they encouraged him to reconsider antidepressant medications, particularly those with known attention-optimizing characteristics. Finally, for Mr. S's sleep problems, the evaluators recommended a follow-up meeting with Dr. W to discuss a referral to a board-certified sleep specialist for further assessment, including the possibility of an overnight sleep study. If a sleep disorder (e.g., sleep apnea, restless leg syndrome) were to be diagnosed, appropriate medical treatment could mitigate and even resolve the neurocognitive symptoms contributing to Mr. S's hypothesis about ADHD.

## Feedback

In many ways, Mr. S's behavior during and after the feedback session with Ms. Q supported hypotheses developed over the course of testing. As he had done previously, Mr. S arrived 15 minutes late. Mr. S's presentation was remarkable in one specific way: Intermittently and repeatedly he typed into his mobile phone as he listened to Ms. Q. In the spirit of the broadly collaborative assessment framework we teach, Ms. Q reviewed the referral questions and described the results. However, after Mr. S's use of his phone continued and she noticed feeling put off and distanced from him, Ms. Q wondered whether such behavior reflected Mr. S's feelings of anxiety or shame. Ms. Q expressed curiosity regarding this behavior, and Mr. S reported matter-of-factly that he had been taking notes about the findings. Mr. S resumed taking notes and asked brief clarifying questions; however, for the most part he did not engage reciprocally in discussion. After Ms. Q had spent over an hour providing the integrated, synthesized results, she then asked Mr. S to share his thoughts and feelings. Curtly, Mr. S stated that he disagreed with Ms. Q's conclusion that a diagnosis of ADHD was not supported. He then asked her to review the specific findings with him. Although taken aback given that she had just gone over the findings with him, Ms. Q retained hope that Mr. S might still be engaged in dialog so that he would be able to metabolize the findings and recommendations. So Ms. Q spent an additional 45 minutes showing Mr. S his test scores, interpreting them, and reiterating her recommendations. At the conclusion of the session, Mr. S appeared to reluctantly accept the findings, agreed to follow up with Dr. W, and stated his willingness to consider psychotherapy. Ms. Q provided him with referrals to a psychiatrist and psychotherapist thought to be a good match. Ms. Q also encouraged Mr. S to call the assessors should he wish to further discuss the findings, conclusions, and recommendations. When the report was completed, Ms. Q sent it to him with a questionnaire requesting feedback regarding Mr. S's experience of the assessment. Mr. S neither called nor completed the questionnaire.

Rather than seeking an appointment with one of the experienced psychotherapists recommended by the assessors, after the session Mr. S promptly contacted Dr. W's BHC with his impressions of the feedback, whereupon he was referred to the outpatient behavioral health practice at the hospital. Within two weeks, Mr. S was scheduled for an intake with Dr. K, a female psychiatry resident who happened to be—like Mr. S—the child of South Asian immigrants. On intake, Dr. K found Mr. S to be pleasant but noticed that, like many men from South Asian cultures, his use of body language, facial expression, and paralinguistic cues conveyed a usually subtle, but sometimes overt sense of superiority (e.g., Zare, 2007). Unfortunately, because the assessment report had not yet been scanned into the electronic medical record and the referral was not known to the evaluators, Dr. K did not initially have access to the findings from this evaluation.

Mr. S appeared to feel more comfortable with Dr. K. He openly acknowledged that cultural and familial attitudes had stigmatized participation in mental health treatment. He disclosed that he had used a friend's capsules of the stimulant Adderall, which he believed provided him with relief from depressed mood, improved his concentration, and (seemingly inexplicably) helped him sleep better. Perhaps in response to Dr. K's shared cultural background and the more directive and structured format of medication-focused psychiatric consultations, Mr. S acknowledged a history of ingesting cannabis via vaporizer and recent episodes of excessive alcohol abuse. Further, after describing his parents' severely dysfunctional relationship, Mr. S reported that he was "inspired" by his younger brother's recent move from the family home to his own apartment. Dr. K started a trial of antidepressant medication and, rather than formally evaluating him or referring him out for a sleep consultation, recommended that Mr. S use melatonin to help regularize his sleep-wake cycle and arranged to meet with Mr. S at monthly intervals.

In addition, Mr. S started supportive psychotherapy with Ms. T, a licensed clinical social worker in the clinic assigned to provide time-limited psychosocial interventions to patients in outpatient psychiatric treatment. After completing her own intake evaluation and reviewing the report of the psychological assessment, Ms. T began by trying to help Mr. S develop more effective organizational and time-management strategies. In their second session, Mr. S acknowledged his experience of anxiety in social situations, and Ms. T encouraged him to reflect upon his relationship with his parents, particularly his mother, whom Mr. S acknowledged had experienced several episodes of severe suicidality. Mr. S elaborated that he had become deeply invested in securing and maintaining his mother's safety. In apparent response to Ms. T's explorations into intrapsychic and interpersonal material, Mr. S canceled his next session and did not schedule a follow up. Although the evaluators had taken into account that it would not be easy to keep Mr. S in treatment, it appeared that this therapist may not have heeded some of the most essential recommendations from the report. Notably, she may have moved too quickly into emotion-laden material that Mr. S had been warding off and not attending to the alliance with the requisite degree of pacing and sensitivity.

Mr. S's relationship with Dr. K followed a similar trajectory. Over the following three months, Mr. S attended appointments inconsistently, complained of ongoing symptoms, and repeatedly requested stimulants. After reviewing the psychological assessment report, Dr. K declined to prescribe stimulants. Tensions came to a head when, in his fifth visit with Dr. K, after reporting that he had been feeling better, Mr. S again requested stimulant medication. Although Mr. S initially accepted Dr. K's offer to prescribe Wellbutrin, an atypical antidepressant with known attention-improving qualities, two weeks later he called Dr. K and left a lengthy and impassioned phone message in which he dismissed the psychological assessment finding on the grounds that he had been severely depressed at the time and that diagnosing ADHD as an adult is difficult. Dr. K advised Mr. S that she would discuss his concerns with her supervisor and follow up at their next visit. In the next session Dr. K and her supervisor, Dr. V, interviewed Mr. S and advised him that he did not meet criteria for ADHD and they were not willing to prescribe stimulants. Instead, Dr. K offered to start CBT with Mr. S and to increase the dose of Wellbutrin. Mr. S agreed to the increase the dosage of Wellbutrin, but, as might have been anticipated by test findings, did not accept Dr. K's overture regarding CBT.

When Mr. S met with Dr. K two months later, he reported feeling significantly better than he had at the start of her treatment of him and stated that he therefore no longer wished her to prescribe him Adderall. Mr. S acknowledged that his continued participation in treatment conflicted with his mother's concerns about social stigma. Further, while comments such as "an hour of my time can be three hours of an average person's time" belied his ongoing use of narcissistic defenses against threats to self-esteem, Mr. S proudly announced that he had rented an apartment and moved out of his parents' house. In addition, Mr. S reported that as he prepared his return to medical school he was also exploring more science and technology-based medical career options (rather than clinical options) that a medical degree might afford him.

## Assessor reflections

The case of Mr. S illustrates the ways in which patients can often, with varying degrees of conscious awareness and intent, gravitate toward particular medical diagnoses. We found Mr. S's references to the *Peter Pan* story to be particularly intriguing. We understood these references to illuminate Mr. S's unconscious concerns about moving into adulthood. Recall this combination of findings: (a) Mr. S's wishful regressive reversal of roles on TAT Card 14 (Mr. S identified with a younger sibling who remains in a place of magical omnipotence, while the older sibling faces adulthood) and (b) the anxiety about being damaged in response to aggressive, competitive strivings condensed in the Captain Hook-costumed reptile of Rorschach Card IV. These findings pointed to internal distress about relinquishing fantasies of magical, never-ending youth and moving toward the challenges of adulthood. Thus, we conceptualized Mr. S's strong investment in the medicalized ADHD diagnosis as serving his unconscious self-protective efforts to disavow and exclude from awareness his past and ongoing developmental, emotional, and relational pain.

The case of Mr. S demonstrates how unconscious concerns and defensive motivations to manage those concerns can strongly influence a person's attitude toward assessment and treatment. Although each individual's specific dynamics will vary, we suspect that Mr. S is hardly alone in his longing for a medicalized label to account for distressing symptoms as opposed to considering their psychological meaning. We speculate that this is a factor in the rising incidence and prevalence of ADHD in recent decades. Concerns regarding the increased frequency with which children and adults are diagnosed with ADHD have been voiced in multiple contexts across the world (Harrison, 2006; Merten, Cwik, Margraf, & Schneider, 2017). But there are sociocultural and systemic factors also at play. Hinshaw and Scheffler's (2014) analysis revealed that when state and federal funding of schools in the United States was incentivized on the basis of standardized test performance, the frequency with which children were diagnosed with ADHD dramatically increased. The implication is that if families and school systems can get children diagnosed and quickly treated (with medication typically the first line intervention) for attentional problems, their scores will improve, and more funding will be secured. In our experience of conducting and supervising psychodynamically informed collaborative psychological assessment in a large healthcare center over the past two decades, we have observed similar referral patterns. Systematic review of referrals to our service from 2015 to 2018 revealed that the question of ADHD accounted for 42% of all of our referrals, with approximately half of those referred actually meeting symptom criteria and not better accounted for by other conditions.

We hypothesize that within our medical setting, the high frequency with which questions of ADHD arise in our population of largely psychiatric and primary care healthcare clinicians is related to multiple factors having to do with contemporary conceptual frameworks (e.g., the traditional biomedical model; (the current symptom-focused culture of mental health), market forces (productivity expectations, brief visits, emphasis on technique-oriented solutions) as well as patients' (like Mr. S's) and clinicians' unconscious motivations to downplay relational and intrapsychic factors, which can be painful and complex and take time to understand and resolve. Although the recent wave of implementation of IBH is in some ways encouraging, the consultative and treatment models espoused within this approach are predominantly behavioral or acceptance-based as opposed to those that take into account development, relational factors, unconscious motivation, and meaning. We are fortunate that in our particular IBH setting, we have been able to advocate with our administration to continue to have the opportunity to widen and deepen the scope of diagnostic inquiry by offering psychodynamically informed psychological assessment.

## Notes

1  Subsequently, we will refer to the student-supervisor team of Ms. Q and Dr. A as the assessors or evaluators.
2  In Barrie's original story, the rivalry between Peter Pan and Captain Hook is initiated when Peter feeds the Captain's hand to a crocodile. The crocodile relentlessly pursues the Captain, whose hand is replaced by the eponymous hook. Captain Hook seeks revenge on Peter Pan for his injury.

## References

Altmaier, E. M., & Tallman, B. A. (2013). Psychological assessment in medical settings. In K. F. Geisinger, B. A. Bracken, J. F. Carlson, J.-I. C. Hansen, N. R. Kuncel, S. P. Reise, & M. C. Rodriguez (Eds.), *APA handbooks in psychology. APA handbook of testing and assessment in psychology: Testing and assessment in clinical and counseling psychology* (vol. 2, pp. 285–302). Washington, DC: American Psychological Association.

American Psychiatric Association, DSM-5 Task Force. (2013). *Diagnostic and statistical manual of mental disorders: DSM-5™* (5th ed.). Washington, DC: Author. doi:10.1176/appi.books.9780890425596.

Barkley, R. A., Murphy, K. R., & Fischer, M. (2008). *ADHD in adults: What the science says.* New York: Guilford.

Barrie, J. M. (1957). *Peter Pan.* New York: Random House.

Birkin, A. (2003). *J.M. Barrie and the lost boys: The real story behind Peter Pan.* New Haven, CT: Yale University Press.

Bornstein, R. F. (2001). The impending death of psychoanalysis. *Psychoanalytic Psychology, 18*(1), 3–20. doi:10.1037/0736-9735.18.1.2.

Bram, A. D. (2015). To resume a stalled psychotherapy? Psychological testing to understand an impasse and reevaluate treatment options. *Journal of Personality Assessment, 97*(3), 241–249. doi:10.1080/00223891.2014.997824.

Bram, A. D. (2017). Reviving and refining psychodynamic interpretation of the Wechsler intelligence tests: The verbal comprehension subtests. *Journal of Personality Assessment, 99*(3), 324–333. doi:10.1080/00223891.2016.1236342.

Bram, A. D., & Peebles, M. J. (2014). *Psychological testing that matters: Creating a road map for effective treatment.* Washington DC: American Psychological Association. doi:10.1037/14340-000.

Busch, F. N., & Sandberg, L. S. (2014). Unmentalized aspects of panic and anxiety disorders. *Psychodynamic Psychiatry, 42*(2), 175–195. doi:10.1521/pdps.2014.42.2.175.

Conners, C. K., Erhardt, D., & Sparrow, M. A. (1999). *Conners adult ADHD rating scales.* New York: Multihealth Systems, Inc.

Conway, F., Lyon, S., Silber, M., & Donath, S. (2019). Cultivating compassion ADHD project: A mentalization informed psychodynamic psychotherapy approach. *Journal of Infant, Child, and Adolescent Psychotherapy, 18*(3), 212–222. doi:10.1080/15289168.2019.1654271.

Costa, Jr., P. T., & MacCrae, R. R. (2010). *NEO inventories for the NEO personality Inventory-3, (NEO PI-3), NEO five-factor Inventory-3 (NEO-FFI-3), NEO-PI-R: Professional manual.* Lutz, FL: Psychological Assessment Resources, Inc.

Dobmeyer, A. C. (2018). *Psychological treatment of medical patients in integrated primary care.* Washington, DC: American Psychological Association. doi:10.1037/0000051-000

Erikson, E. (1994). *Identity and the life cycle.* New York: Norton.

Finn, S. E., Fischer, C. T., &Handler, L. (2012). *Collaborative therapeutic assessment: A casebook and guide.* Hoboken, NJ: Wiley.

Gilmore, K. (2000). A psychoanalytic perspective on attention-deficit/hyperactivity disorder. *Journal of the American Psychoanalytic Association, 48*(4), 1259–1293. doi:10.1177/00030651000480040901.

Harrison, A. G. (2006). Adults faking ADHD: You must be kidding! *ADHD Report, 14*(4), 1–7. doi:10.1521/adhd.2006.14.4.1.

Hauser, R. M. (2002). *Meritocracy, cognitive ability, and the sources of occupational success.* Working Paper No. 98-07. Retrieved from University of Wisconsin-Madison Center for Demography and Ecology website: https://cde.wisc.edu/wp-content/uploads/sites/839/2019/01/cde-working-paper-1998-07.pdf.

Hinshaw, S. P., & Scheffler, R. M. (2014). *The ADHD explosion: Myths, medication, money, and today's push for performance.* New York: Oxford University Press.

Kivlighan, D. M., Goldberg, S. B., Abbas, M., Pace, B. T., Yulish, N. E., Thomas, J. G., … Wampold, B. E. (2015). The enduring effects of psychodynamic treatments vis-à-vis alternative treatments: A multilevel longitudinal meta-analysis. *Clinical Psychology Review, 40*, 1–14. doi:10.1016/j.cpr.2015.05.003.

Konstabel, K., Realo, A., & Kallasmaa, T. (2002). Exploring the sources of variations in the structure of personality traits across cultures. In R. R. McCrae & J. Allik (Eds.), *The Five-Factor Model across cultures* (pp. 29–52). New York: Kluwer Academic. doi:10.1007/978-1-4615-0763-5_3.

Kroenke, K., Spitzer, R. L., & Williams, J. B. W. (2001). The PHQ-9: Validity of a brief depression severity measure. *Journal of General Internal Medicine, 16*(9), 606–613. doi:10.1046/j.1525-1497.2001. 016009606.x.

Lerner, P. M. (2005). Red beavers and building bridges between assessment and treatment. *Journal of Personality Assessment, 85*(3), 271–279. doi:10.1207/s15327752jpa8503_03.

Lingiardi, V., & McWilliams, N. (Eds.) (2017). *Psychodynamic diagnostic manual: PDM-2* (second edn.). New York, NY: Guilford Press.

Matarazzo, J. D., & Goldstein, S. G. (1972). The intellectual caliber of medical students. *Journal of Medical Education, 47*(2), 102–111.

McCoy, K., Cummings, E. M., & Davies, P. T. (2009). Constructive and destructive marital conflict, emotional security and children's prosocial behavior. *Journal of Child Psychology and Psychiatry, 50*(3), 270–279. doi:10.1111/j.1469-7610.2008.01945.x.

McCrae, R. R., Yang, J., Costa, P. T., Dai, X., Yao, S., Cai, T., & Gao, B. (2001). Personality profiles and the prediction of categorical personality disorders. *Journal of Personality, 69*(2), 155–174. doi:10.1111/1467-6494.00140.

Merten, E. C., Cwik, J. C., Margraf, J., & Schneider, S. (2017). Overdiagnosis of mental disorders in children and adolescents (in developed countries). *Journal of Child and Adolescent Psychiatry and Mental Health, 11*(5). doi:10.1186/s13034-016-0140-5.

Meyer, G. J., Finn, S. E., Eyde, L. D., Kay, G. G., Moreland, K. L., Dies, R. R., … Reed, G. M. (2001). Psychological testing and psychological assessment: A review of evidence and issues. *American Psychologist, 56*(2), 128–165. doi:10.1037/0003-066X.56.2.128.

Meyer, G. J., Viglione, D. J., Mihura, J. L., Erard, R. E., & Erdberg, P. (2011). *Rorschach Performance Assessment System: Administration, coding, interpretation, and technical manual.* Toledo, OH: Rorschach Performance Assessment System, LLC.

Morey, L. C. (1991). *Personality assessment inventory professional manual.* Odessa, FL: Psychological Assessment Resources.

Morey, L. C., & Hopwood, C. J. (2007). *Casebook for the personality assessment inventory (PAI): A structural summary approach.* Odessa, FL: Psychological Assessment Resources..

Murray, H. A. (1943). *Thematic apperception test manual.* Cambridge, MA: Harvard University Press.

Musso, M., Hill, B., Barker, A., Pella, R., Jones, G., Proto, D., & Gouvier, W. (2011). Thought disorder subscale of the personality assessment inventory as a measure of self-reported ADHD symptoms in college students. *Archives of Clinical Neuropsychology, 26*(6), 470–567. doi:10.1177/1087054714548031.

Peebles, M. J. (2012). *Beginnings: The art and science of planning psychotherapy* (2nd ed.). New York: Routledge/Taylor & Francis Group.

Quirk, M. E. (1996). *How to learn and teach in Medical School: A learner-centered approach.* Springfield, IL: Charles Thomas Publisher.

Rapaport, D., Gill, M. M., & Schafer, R. (1946). *Diagnostic psychological testing: The theory, statistical evaluation, and diagnostic evaluation of a battery of tests* (vol. 2). Chicago, IL: The Year Book Publishers.

Robinson, P. J., & Reiter, J. T. (2017). *Behavioral consultation in primary care: A guide to integrating Services* (2nd ed.). New York: Springer.

Safran, J. D., & Kraus, J. (2014). Alliance ruptures, impasses, and enactments: A relational perspective. *Psychotherapy, 51*(3), 381–387. doi:10.1037/a0036815.

Sandford, J., & Sandford, S. E. (2019). *Integrated visual and auditory continuous performance test*—version 2 interpretation manual. Richmond, VA: BrainTrain.

Schafer, R. (1954). *Psychoanalytic interpretation in Rorschach testing: Theory and application.* Oxford: Grune & Stratton.

Schottenbauer, M. A., Glass, C. R., Arnkoff, D. B., & Gray, S. H. (2008). Contributions of psychodynamic approaches to treatment of PTSD and trauma: A review of the empirical treatment and psychopathology literature. *Psychiatry, 71*(1), 13–34. doi:10.1521/psyc.2008.71.1.13.

Schrank, F. A., Mather, N., & McGrew, K. S. (2014). *Woodcock Johnson-IV tests of achievement.* Rolling Meadows, IL: Riverside.

Schwartz, A. L. (2011). The temptations and distractions of assessing adult ADHD. *Society for Personality Assessment Exchange,* 23(1), 2–13.

Schwartz, A. L., & York, D. J. (2017). Strangers in a strange land: Is there a role for psychological assessment in integrated care? *Society for Personality Assessment Exchange,* 29(1), 2–11.

Shedler, J. (2010). The efficacy of psychodynamic psychotherapy. *American Psychologist,* 65(2), 98–109. doi:10.1037/a0018378.

Spitzer, R. L., Kroenke, K., Williams, J. B. W., & Lowe, B. (2006). A brief measure for assessing generalized anxiety disorder: The GAD-7. *Archives of Internal Medicine, 166*(10), 1092–1097. doi:10.1001/archinte.166.10.1092.

Stuewig, J., & McCloskey, L. A. (2005). The relation of child maltreatment to shame and guilt among adolescents: Psychological routes to depression and delinquency. *Child Maltreatment, 10*(4), 324–336. doi:10.1177/1077559505279308.

Watson, J., & Liljequist, L. (2015). Using the personality assessment inventory to identify ADHD-like symptoms. *Journal of Attention Disorders, 22*(11), 1049–1055. doi:10.1177/1087054714567133.

Wechsler, D. (2008). Wechsler *scale of intelligence—fourth edition* (WAIS-IV). San Antonio, TX: Pearson.

Wechsler, D. (2011). Wechsler *abbreviated scale of intelligence—second edition* (WASI-II). San Antonio, TX: NCS Pearson.

Widiger, T. A., Trull, T. J., Clarkin, J. F., Sanderson, C., & Costa, P. T., Jr. (2002). A description of the DSM-IV personality disorders with the five-factor model of personality. In P. T. Costa, Jr. & T. A. Widiger (Eds.), *Personality disorders and the five-factor model of personality* (pp. 89–99). New York: Kluwer Academic. doi:10.1037/10423-006.

World Health Organization. (1992). *International classification of diseases and related health problems* (10th rev., ICD-10). Geneva: Author.

Yuppa, D. P., & Meyer, F. (2017). When and why should mental health professionals offer traditional psychodynamic therapy to cancer patients? *American Medical Association Journal of Ethics, 19*(5), 467–474. doi:10.1001/journalofethics.2017.19.5.stas2-1705.

Zare, B. (2007). Evolving masculinities in recent stories by South Asian American women. *The Journal of Commonwealth Literature, 42*(3), 99–111. doi:10.1177/0021989407081671.

# 9 Psychoanalytic aspects of the fitness for duty psychological evaluation[1]

*Mark H. Waugh*

## Psychodynamic aspects of the fitness for duty psychological evaluation

Work is basic to peoples' lives. Employment supplies economic rewards for our life needs as well as social connections and avenues for finding purpose actualizing self-identity. In other words, work bridges several rungs of Maslow's (1943) well-known hierarchy of needs. The Russian novelist Tolstoy said, "One can live magnificently in this world if one knows how to work and how to love" (Troyat, 1967, p. 158). The psychoanalytically informed reader is familiar with Freud's maxim that life is reckoned within two domains: "love and work" (Erikson. 1950/1993, p. 265). In this chapter, we examine a specialized type of forensic psychological evaluation that focuses on the life domain of work. In so doing, we acknowledge the realms of "love and work" overlap, that they represent heuristic distinctions. The person, of course, is a whole.

The Occupational Fitness for Duty (FFD) psychological evaluation assesses specific work-related psychological domains. Furthermore, results from the FFD evaluation are frequently communicated in a focused, rather concise report. Generally, a dichotomous judgment of fit for duty or not fit for duty must be stated. However, much takes place behind the scenes to provide the rationale for this dichotomous decision. The requisites are technical knowledge, clinical skill and experience, and sound professional judgment. This spans proficiency and understanding of psychological assessment, personality science and theory, psychopathology, and the social processes and systems theory relevant to workplace organizational dynamics. As in much of clinical practice, qualities like the ability to think on one's feet, intellectual and professional flexibility, and the accrual of practical savvy from experience are invaluable in this high-stakes specialty practice. The psychological FFD assessor knows that psychodynamic principles also apply outside of the psychotherapeutic setting. Psychodynamic theory and empirical findings provide a platform for understanding people and their problems (Luyten, Mayes, Fonagy, Blatt, & Target, 2017), workplace interactions (Hirschorn, 1990; Levinson, 1959; Stapley, 2018), and group behavior (Bion, 1961). *Ipso facto*, psychodynamic conceptualization is a tool in the psychological FFD evaluation.

## Description of the setting: The unique nature of the psychological FFD evaluation I agree

The psychological FFD evaluation, also known as Occupationally Mandated Psychological Evaluation (OMPE; APA, 2018) is a type of forensic psychological evaluation. Thus, it differs from psychological and psychiatric evaluations performed in a healthcare setting. First, a forensic FFD evaluation typically serves the needs of the referring organization or entity (e.g., employer, agency, municipality, hospital, licensing board, etc.) as opposed to the individual patient. Second, the evaluation answers a psycho-legal question (i.e., fit for duty for the job) rather than, for example, informing differential diagnosis or treatment planning—although these issues may pertain to the FFD. Third, the forensic evaluation generally privileges assessor objectivity (Shuman & Zervopoulos, 2010). Furthermore, the psychological FFD evaluation differs from Industrial-Organizational (IO) psychological evaluations (Shorey, 2018). In the IO setting, psychometric assessment typically addresses personnel selection, organizational effectiveness, business performance, and similar matters.

The FFD evaluation arises when an individual's behavior creates concerns pertaining to workplace and/or public safety. There are many types of FFD evaluation. Examples include the pre-employment evaluation for public safety personnel (e.g., police officers, commercial airplane pilots, nuclear power reactor operators). The safety-sensitive nature of these jobs triggers mandates for FFD evaluations. The pre-employment psychological FFD evaluation takes place only after the candidate receives a conditional offer of employment. This is because the law does not permit employers to consider employee medical status unless specified public safety issues exist (and then only as a contingency to the hiring decision).

Another route to the psychological FFD evaluation is a "for cause" event. This occurs when the employer or agency strongly suspects psychiatric or psychological status (including substance use disorder or event) adversely affects the ability of the person to perform their job (or endanger workplace safety). The employer must establish a reasonable nexus with psychiatric/psychological functioning prior to referral because the FFD evaluation is a medical exam addressing fitness for the job. It cannot be used as a human resource intervention for "problem workers"—although the assessor may encounter situations where this seems to be the case. Examples of "for cause" FFD evaluations include licensing board referrals of impaired physicians and other health professionals, those arising in safety-sensitive industrial jobs, cases involving government security clearance infractions, and specialized military fitness and high-risk duty assignments. Employee threat assessments are also for cause FFD evaluations. These are largely driven by the imperative to ensure a safe workplace for employees. In every instance, these FFD evaluations are high stakes for the employee and for the employer.

The laws, regulations, and standards relevant to the specific job and setting organize the FFD evaluation. These range considerably and the assessor must stay informed on these issues. Such regulations and laws include those of the *American with Disability Act* (ADA), Occupational Safety and Health Administration (OSHA), Equal Employment Opportunity Commission (EEOC), *Civil Rights Acts of 1964, Title VII of the Rehabilitation Act of 1973*, and State statutes for Peace Officer certification—among others.

The fundamental psycho-legal construct organizing the FFD evaluation is whether the individual's psychological or psychiatric functioning interferes with the performance of the job (and/or workplace safety). The evaluator must always refer to the formal job description for the person being evaluated (Stone, 2000). This may be obtained from the referring human resource department or from other sources of occupational job descriptions (e.g., the U.S. Department of Labor; see https://www.bls.gov/ocs/ocsjobde.htm).

## Brief literature review on FFD evaluations

In addition to legal regulations and statutes, the FFD evaluator stays current on standards of practice and important trends in the field. Relevant sources of information include the American Psychological Association (APA) professional practice guidelines for occupationally mandated evaluations (APA, 2018), the International Chiefs of Police (IACP) guidelines for performing FFD evaluations (IACP, 2013), the American Psychiatric Association guidelines for psychiatric FFD of physicians (Anfang, Faulkner, Fromson, & Gendel, 2005), and the APA *Standards for Educational and Psychological Testing* (Eignor, 2013). This also includes knowledge of current research and practice implications regarding psychological testing instruments in the forensic context. We know, for example, that a positive impression management (PIM) response style often colors subjects' self-report in employment testing (Rosse, Stecher, Miller, & Levin, 1998) and similar situations where the demand to not be seen in a negative light is high. To contend with these operative contextual factors, specialized scales and approaches are available for major instruments such as the Minnesota Multiphasic Personality Inventory—2nd Edition (MMPI-2; Hathaway & McKinley, 1989), the Personality Assessment Inventory (PAI; Morey, 2007) and the Minnesota Multiphasic Personality Inventory-2-Restructured Form (MMPI-2-RF; Tellegen & Ben-Porath, 2011). This includes special testing instructions for the MMPI-2 (e.g., Butcher, Morfitt, Rouse, & Holden, 1997; Walfish, 2010), PAI norms for law enforcement settings (Lowmaster & Morey, 2012) and physician FFD evaluation (Brown, Iannelli, & Marganoff, 2017). For performance-based assessment, Ganellen (2008) discusses the Rorschach and Picano, Williams, and Roland (2006) describe innovative use of sentence completion measures in high PIM-demand situations. Katsavdakis, Gabbard, and Athey (2004) review the FFD evaluation for the population of impaired physicians.

A final proviso cannot be overlooked. The forensic context of the FFD colors everything. Greenberg and Shuman (1997, p. 50) contrast clinical and forensic evaluations and argue that an "irreconcilable conflict" exists between the role of clinician and forensic evaluator (see also Greenberg & Shuman, 2007). However, others contend this distinction is less axiomatic (Heltzel, 2007). The FFD evaluation is forensic in nature, but the skills involved in high-quality clinical assessment are directly relevant. In this regard, Mulay, Mivshek, Kaufman, and Waugh (2018) suggest clinician empathy serves the forensic evaluator well (see also Brodsky and Wilson, 2013). Mulay et al. (2018) reason that disciplined use of empathy may mitigate potential implicit bias between the evaluator and the person being evaluated, potentially foster the assessment process via a temporary, if limited, therapeutic alliance of sorts, and constitute a source of clinical information for the assessor (Lerner, 1990).

## Case background: "Dr. Ether"

We illustrate how clinical assessment findings coordinate with the operative psycho-legal question of FFD with an example of a potentially impaired physician. We call the patient "Dr. Ether," as he practiced anesthesiology and pain medicine, and thoroughly disguise all identifying features of the case while preserving the core psychological details. Typically, the FFD evaluation takes place in the assessor's office or at the employee's workplace. In the present case, Dr. Ether's psychologist asked if I would travel and evaluate her patient, knowing that I possessed an active license to practice and occasionally performed evaluations in their area. The psychologist and Dr. Ether were interested in the evaluation of fitness to practice medicine because of concerns about Dr. Ether's behavior. Dr. Ether had a history of previous treatment for alcohol abuse and voluntarily participated in monitoring by a medical advocacy organization serving impaired health professionals in his State (State Medical Foundation [SMF]). The official State Medical Licensing Board (SMLB) considered his license to practice medicine unrestricted and in good standing because of this monitoring arrangement. Dr. Ether told his psychologist and the SMF advocates about receiving a Restraining Order (RO) barring contact with his former spouse. Because the circumstances of the RO were very unusual and suggested possible delusional thinking, the SMF asked for a current FFD evaluation, and the referring psychologist and Dr. Ether believed this would be helpful. Dr. Ether voluntarily participated in the evaluation and he authorized results to be shared with his psychologist and the SMF. He also received the evaluation results and paid the fee for the assessment. It should be noted that in many FFD evaluations, the employer (who is the "client"), not the employee or patient, receives the results and pays the costs of the evaluation.

At the time of the assessment, Dr. Ether was 62 years old, practiced anesthesiology part-time in a local hospital, and ran an outpatient practice for medically assisted treatment of opioid disorders. One year ago, he and his (second) wife of six years divorced, and he acknowledged the loss of the marriage was very difficult. Four years ago, he received residential treatment for a 20-year history of alcohol abuse. Since completing treatment, he remained abstinent from alcohol and psychoactive substances. He participated in the SMF monitoring program, attended 12-step meetings two to three times per week, and participated in a weekly recovery-oriented support group for impaired professionals. He also participated in once-weekly individual psychotherapy.

Regarding his marriage, Dr. Ether said neither he nor his ex-spouse wished to separate. However, he claimed his ex-spouse was "compelled" to divorce for hidden, nefarious reasons. He explained that his former wife had been married three times and her second husband, who had been a politician in state government, had forced her to divorce Dr. Ether. This was reportedly done by threats to kill her children (by her first husband) if she did not leave Dr. Ether. Dr. Ether elaborated that the second husband had supposedly died in a car accident, but he was not deceased. Dr. Ether claimed that he staged his death to elude investigation over alleged criminal mismanagement of state funds. After the faked death, according to Dr. Ether, the second husband assumed a false identity as an accountant and sent surreptitious communications to Dr. Ether and his ex-spouse.

Dr. Ether explained that his "missions in life" were to practice medicine and rescue his ex-wife from the vengeful (but incognito) ex-husband. Dr. Ether repeatedly tried to communicate with his ex-wife, but she told him to stay away and obtained a court order to prevent his contact. Dr. Ether asserted he "knew" her actions were a sham enacted only to prevent her children from being killed by the accountant. Thus, seeking to reassure her, he continued to try to communicate with her. Contact was by telephone, "accidental" encounters in public, and sending signs he felt only she would recognize. These included leaving incidental objects on her porch and at her place of work. He also confronted the accountant in public on several occasions, accusing him of nefarious actions. Dr. Ether filed reports about his ex-wife's situation and the accountant with the local law enforcement authorities as well as the Federal Bureau of Investigation (FBI). He acknowledged his story sounded far-fetched, but he unwaveringly maintained it was true.

Importantly, outside of this specific area of his life, Dr. Ether's general behavior and professional conduct as an anesthesiologist and medical practitioner had not raised concerns. In his office practice, he counseled patients, led a mindfulness-based stress reduction addiction group, and prescribed buprenorphine and naloxone medications. He was very enthusiastic about his practice and said his life was about "saving people," inspired also by his spiritual convictions. Similarly, his privileges as a part-time anesthesiologist at the hospital where he worked, were unblemished. His psychologist, the SMF, the Human Resources (HR) department of the local hospital, and a license verification from the SMLB confirmed he enjoyed a strong reputation as a physician with no work performance problems. He had no legal history other than the recent RO barring contact with his ex-spouse and the local accountant (her alleged previous husband). For recreation, Dr. Ether enjoyed horseback riding, antique shopping, and studying Eastern religious philosophy.

In terms of early history, Dr. Ether, a Polish-American, was from a Midwestern industrial town. His father was a Second World War-era emigre from Poland and had worked as an industrial engineer, and his mother had been a homemaker. He had three siblings, all with professional careers. One sibling suffered from depression; otherwise, he denied psychiatric, alcohol, or substance problems in the family—but admitted his father occasionally "had too much to drink." Dr. Ether had been an excellent student, studying chemistry and philosophy at a selective Midwestern college and then earning his medical doctorate from the State university where he was also president of his medical school class.

## Rationale for the FFD battery

As noted, the first step in the FFD evaluation was to obtain informed consent and clarify the recipients of the evaluation results (i.e., himself, referring psychologist, and SMF). I wished to obtain as much collateral information as practical to supplement self-report and performance psychological assessment. Accordingly, I reviewed records from his past treatment center (including a recent follow-up psychiatric evaluation that noted emergent delusional-like beliefs), the referring psychologist, and the SMF advocacy counselor. In addition, the Human Resources Department where Dr. Ether worked part-time provided job requirements for a *medical physician* and *anesthesiologist* and a report on his work conduct. I administered a clinical interview and conducted a mental status examination of Dr. Ether. The interview focused on history, his recovery and treatment progress, current work and social relationships, how he coped with stress generally and about both previous marriages, and his current functioning for evidence of the soundness of personal judgment. In addition, I explored his ideas about his divorce and his ex-wife's alleged predicament with the persecuting accountant, carefully observing his behavior, reasoning, and affect as we discussed these topics. Following an extended two-hour clinical interview, I administered Dr. Ether the MMPI-2, PAI, and Rorschach Performance Assessment System (R-PAS; Meyer et al., 2011. The MMPI-2 and PAI provided forensic-defensible, broadband self-report assessment of personality and psychopathology variables and a rich suite of response validity indices. I chose to administer both instruments for several reasons. First, they differ in scale construction and how they represent psychiatric diagnostic syndromes. Second, their psychometric properties (Wise, Streiner, & Walfish, 2010) and predictive validities of their response style scales differ (Blanchard, McGrath, Pogge, & Khadivi, 2003). Given the forensic context of the evaluation, using multiple indices of under-reporting and constructs related to psychoticism seemed strategic. The R-PAS permitted performance-based assessment with well-validated variables pertaining to thinking and reasoning, perceptual accuracy and reality testing, investment in social relationships, and emotion and impulse control (Mihura et al., 2013), psychological constructs pertinent to the question of FFD.

The evaluation focused on the forensic question of fitness to practice medicine but establishing the psychiatric differential diagnosis was also important. To be considered fit to practice, a medical physician must have the requisite technical knowledge, background, experience, and a current license in good standing as well as be able to perform complex analyses of clinical and laboratory data, interventional procedures, and communicate with patients and professional staff in a complex, public safety-sensitive, and fast-paced environment. This requires strong cognitive skills, focus, and memory along with sufficient interpersonal skills, emotional controls, adequate assertiveness, independent functioning, and sound judgment.

## Summary of findings: Interview and test data

### Interview data

Dr. Ether was pleasant, mildly guarded, but seemed to warm up over time. He was cooperative, polite, and respectful if somewhat formal. He worked quickly and completed all procedures on the day of the interview. He provided a complete-sounding history which was consistent with collateral information. He brought a sign-in sheet evidencing attendance at 12-step meetings as well as a copy of the report from the recent follow-up psychiatric appointment at the residential treatment center. However, he stated he disagreed with the psychiatrist's opinion of Delusional Disorder and he became slightly agitated while making this point. In general, Dr. Ether exhibited an attitude of innocence and moral conviction and frequently asserted his commitment to helping his patients. When describing incidents and events associated with his ex-spouse and her alleged dire circumstances, Dr. Ether often became mildly passionate, but his speech and reasoning did not derail, and his demeanor was not problematic.

He denied symptoms of depression and anxiety but acknowledged his preoccupation with his ex-spouse's reported predicament. Dr. Ether showed no evidence of weakness in attention, reasoning, calculations, memory, or proverb interpretation. His speech and thinking were organized and goal-directed with no tangentiality or loose associations. He denied auditory or visual hallucinations and other aberrant experiences, but he added he "believed in synchronicity." He explained this idea with his spiritual beliefs which he said had become more "New Age" and important to him in recent years. He did not acknowledge any specific instances of anomalous experiences or a sense of psychological breakdown. He elaborately discussed his ex-spouse, her continuing love for him, her alleged status as an emotional hostage, and the incognito accountant (purportedly her second husband, having staged a fake death prior). He admitted these events sounded untrue, but asserted they were factual. He gave as evidence certain "signs" he perceived in his ex-wife's demeanor. He also cited his opinion the state medical examiner had never produced adequate documentation to substantiate the death of his ex-wife's second husband.

## Test data

The test data from the MMPI-2 and PAI were scored with the publishers' software. All psychometric validity scales indicated the self-report data were credible and interpretable. There was no evidence of symptom over-reporting or invalidating-levels of under-reporting as demonstrated by the following MMPI-2 (non-gendered)[2] scores: Infrequency (F) T = 43; Infrequency Psychopathology (Fp) T = 40; Lie (L) T = 52, Correction (K) T = 65, Superlative Self-Presentation (S) T = 66. Similarly, the PAI Positive Impression Management (PIM; T = 58) scale was not markedly elevated. As a point of reference, Brown et al. (2017) reported about 50% of a sample of physicians referred for FFD evaluation produced PAI PIM scales with T> 57, and Walfish (2010) found nearly 60% of professionals referred for FFD evaluation produced MMPI-2 under-reporting validity scales exceeding commonly recommended levels for interpretation. Dr. Ether's self-reports were regarded as acceptedly credible even if they conveyed a slightly positive tilt. Importantly, both the MMPI-2 and PAI showed no evidence of significant emotional or psychiatric symptoms on their main clinical scales. His highest MMPI-2 Clinical Scale (CS) elevations were as follows: Scale 3 Hysteria (Hy) T = 56; Scale 5 Masculinity-Femininity (Mf) T = 55; and Scale 6 Paranoia (Pa) T = 55. The MMPI-2 Restructured Clinical Scales (RCS) were all within normal limits (WNL) with Ideas of Persecution (RC6; T = 53) and Hypomanic Activation (RC9; T = 52) his highest scores, and Aberrant Experiences (RC8) very low at T = 39. Although these results were within normal limits, they also suggested a slightly optimistic and repressive style (Hy T = 56) curiously coupled with hints of a vigilant, sensitive cognitive style (Pa T = 55; Mf T = 55; RC6 T = 53). On the PAI, the few clinically significant elevations were Alcohol Problems (ALC) T = 64, Drug Problems (DRG) T = 58, and Stress (STR) T = 60. These minor elevations seemed to reflect the fact of his history of alcohol disorder and relatively mild to moderate current situational stress. The PAI also indicated he exhibited a generally warm, extraverted, and moderately assertive interpersonal style (Dominance [DOM] T = 58; Warmth [WRM] T = 64). Examining the PAI subscales for the Paranoia (PAR) and Schizophrenia (SCZ) scales, mild elevations were noted for Persecution (PAR-P; T = 55) and Psychotic Experiences (SCZ-P; T = 58). These results, relative to his other PAI scores, dovetailed with the concern over possible delusional thinking, yet they were subclinical in magnitude, normatively speaking. These were important findings and needed to be coordinated with multi-method assessment of his implicit functioning in the domains of reality testing, reasoning, affect control, and judgment. The Rorschach provided information in this regard.

On the Rorschach, Dr. Ether was cooperative and engaged, but produced a rather brief R-PAS record, particularly in light of his estimated Superior (or above) intellectual level (R = 18; Standard Score [SS] = 94).[3] Other pertinent R-PAS cognitive processing scores included Complexity (SS = 104), Synthesis (Sy SS = 105), Blends (SS = 109), and Human Movement (M SS = 110).

Given the moderate degree of cognitive complexity reflected in his responses and his known intellectual ability, this was viewed as evidence of a mild level of guardedness, akin to the findings from the MMPI-2 K and S scales and the PAI PIM scale. Dr. Ether was careful and deliberate in his responses, but they were not so brief, coarcted, or sparse to preclude interpretation.

The pivotal assessment questions with Dr. Ether concerned his capacity to perceive and test reality and to reason in a logical and consensual manner. The Rorschach method provides a strong evidenced-based tool for assessing these capacities and functions (Kleiger, 2017; Mihura et al., 2013). Relevant indices of perceptual accuracy and reasoning include Form Quality Minus Percent (FQ−%), the Ego Impairment Index-3 (EII-3), Thought & Perception Composite (TP-Comp), WD Minus Percent (WD−%), and Weighted Sum Cognitive Codes (WSumCog). Dr. Ether showed mild elevations on the TP-Comp (SS = 113), FQ−% (SS = 116), and WD-% (SS = 117) indices, whereas the EII-3 (SS = 105), WSumCog (SS = 107), and Severe Cognitive Codes (SevCog; SS = 94) were within normal limits. He also gave six responses coded for Level 1 cognitive codes (three Incongruous Combinations [INC1; SS = 126] and three Deviant Verbalizations [DV1; SS = 128]). The number of INC1 and DV1 codes in his record, while not indicative of major lapses in reasoning, are noticeable.

Normatively speaking, the degree of perceptual inaccuracy and the problems in reasoning suggested by these collective results are not particularly alarming. However, these findings need to be interpreted with respect to (a) the reported delusional-like beliefs, (b) his effort to convey a positive impression and be found FFD to practice, and (c) the relatively unelaborated Rorschach record (e.g., R = 18; Complexity SS = 104) despite his strong intellectual capacities. These points add interpretive weight to the admittedly modest glimpses of potentially problematic ego functioning reflected in his Rorschach record.

We now examine his single response to Card IX (R13), which was coded both FQ− and DV1. Dr. Ether stated, after a very long pause: "it's pretty … don't see shapes or forms … greenish part … no … [examiner then prompted him to respond] … a wasp's head with two big eyes and hooking-mouth and reddish wings on side." Despite prompting, he offered no further response to Card IX. In the Clarification Phase (CP), he simply said, "Head, hooking-mouth, wings" and handed back the card. Notable was his long delay—the first and only time this occurred on the test. He also emphasized how "pretty" the colors were, which was seemingly incongruous with his anxious hesitancy and the content that followed, suggesting defensive efforts to ward off unsettling feelings and content. Nudging from the examiner elicited the response of an aggressive thematic code (Aggressive Content [AGC]), referring to a predatory, cold-blooded insect and highlighting the vigilant eyes and (dangerous, piercing) oddly phrased "hooking-mouth" (a DV1 response). This DV1 response suggested a mild lapse in the integrity of his reasoning and communication, and the response reflected poor perceptual accuracy (FQ−). The full coding for R13 was v W SI Ad Sy—FC DV1 AGC ODL.

Interestingly, the response preceding the wasp of Card IX was of a "blue woman's girdle with laces in the center" (Card VIII, R12: D5 Cg, Sx o FC INC1)[4], and the five responses rattled off on Card X were simple, common details with sea animal and flower contents. From the interpretive frame of sequence analysis (Bram & Peebles, 2014; Peebles-Kleiger, 2002), we infer his lapse of ego functioning affecting both reality testing and reasoning on Card IX may have been stimulated by the preceding emotionally laden percept of a woman's undergarment (the blue girdle). But Dr. Ether then regrouped on Card X as he ticked off several rather neutral responses. We further note that he was activated across Cards VIII, IX, and X, offering 50% of his total responses (R8910% SS = 129) to the three chromatic cards (including four of his six total Level 1 cognitive codes). The problematic percept of the wasp on Card IX (R13), a response he had difficulty generating, conspicuously, was the only response on that card—followed by the five common detail (D) responses on Card X, by far the largest number of responses to any card. We surmise that Dr. Ether is sensitized to affect, responds with activation, and this may impinge on his reasoning to a mild degree. Furthermore, the sequence of faltering ego controls after his response of feminine, sexualized content takes on added salience in regard to the question of delusional thinking and his female love object. This observation is even more significant in view of his efforts to convey a positive impression, which would tend to suppress unconventional and negative-valenced responses. Nonetheless, these nuanced inferences must be considered with the context of the generally acceptable perceptual accuracy reasoning quality reflected in his record (e.g., EII-3 SS = 105; WSumCog SS = 107).

Dr. Ether's R-PAS record offers additional insights into his psychological functioning. Particularly informative are the strikingly elevated Oral Dependent Languages (ODL SS = 129), a relatively high number of achromatic color and shading determinants (YTVC' SS = 111), and several Clothing content responses (Cg SS = 119). Moreover, another determinant (not coded in the R-PAS) was notable and revealing. This is the *Form-Color Arbitrary* (FCarb) determinant found in the Rapaport, Gill, and Schafer (1968) system. FCarb responses apply color in an arbitrary way that is incompatible with the content. An example would be the response of "red beavers" to the location D1 on Card VIII where a percept of a four-legged animal is common and coded as a Popular response in the R-PAS (see Lerner, 1998, p. 157; Lerner, 2005).[5] Collectively, these and other signs and indicators in Dr. Ether's record point to an important axis of interpretation: the false self (Winnicott, 1965).

The concept of the false self was articulated by Winnicott (1965) and emphasized by other writers in the British Object Relations tradition. This idea refers to a developmental adaptation in response to insufficiently facilitating childhood experiences. Such experiences can lead to a characterological personality organization marked by an "as if" quality or façade aspect to the self. Authentic self needs and interests (the true self) remain hidden and nascent, and the individual's agency and identity orients to the other. This adaptation may be organized as a "caretaker self" (Winnicott, 1965, p. 142) style of relating. As such, the individual becomes focused on and sensitive to the needs of others, inclined to compliance, and may privately experience a sense of unreality to the self.

Lerner (1998; 2005) elaborated Rorschach signs that may flag the presence of a false self-structure. These include FCarb responses, Cg and mask contents, and the use of contours within shaded areas to form percepts (designated as Fc in the Rapaport et al. [1968] system). Notably, Dr. Ether offered two FCarb responses. These were the aforementioned "blue girdle" (Card VIII R12) and his Card VIII R10 response ("almost looks like a CT scan of the brain, in color; cerebellum and parietal lobes" [W An u CF INC1]). Let us consider these responses and their FCarb connotations in detail.

Indeed, some modern fashion undergarments come in colors, but considering Dr. Ether's age and the referent of his response was an old-fashioned item of clothing (i.e., a girdle), articulating the response as a "*blue* girdle" is not expectable. Similarly, a CT scan is a black and white image, not colored (as are PET and fMRI scan images), a fact that he would be aware of as a physician. That he attributed incompatible color in both responses suggests the color aspect of the stimulus was passively incorporated into his percept, consistent with the characterological compliance (and unreal sense) of the false self, according to Lerner (1998; 2005).

At times Dr. Ether traced contours within the shading features (shading as location in R-PAS; Fc per Rapaport et al., 1968) of inkblots to produce percepts, another sign suggestive of false self-dynamics (Lerner, 1998). He furthermore produced three additional Cg responses beyond the "blue girdle" (i.e., "blousy-dress" [Card I]; "high-heeled boot types, white colors, waistcoats" [Card II]; "old-style bonnet, gowns" [Card VII]). Lerner (1998) argues each of these indicators (FCarb, shading contours, Cg content) can signify a false-self posture. With Dr. Ether's Rorschach, we have a brief record but replete with Lerner's (1998) Rorschach false-self indicators. Additionally, the many ODL responses in his record (SS = 129) are striking. The ODL score has extensive construct validity (Bornstein & Masling, 2005) and is viewed as an indicator of implicit dependency needs. Despite Dr. Ether's self-reported interpersonal assertiveness (PAI DOM T = 58), self-image of a professional leader (medical school class president; practice founder), and valued role as family provider, the elevated ODL suggests he experiences significant disavowed and/or unmet needs for nurturing and caretaking.

Dr. Ether had declared in the interview his life missions were to care for people, to cure illness and suffering, and to rescue his ex-wife. One might speculate these consciously held life missions belied underlying self-needs hidden under the cloak of a caretaking identity. This is consistent with Modell's (1975) formulation of the illusion of self-sufficiency that underlies (false) self-disorders, an adaptation sometimes seen in perfectionistic and high-achieving individuals. That Dr. Ether's brief record contained ample shading, texture, and achromatic color responses (SS = 111) adds credence to the inference that underlying anxiety and dysphoria plagued his adjustment despite his self-report of psychological well-being and selfless dedication to others. Integrating the inferences from FCarb, YTVC', Cg, and ODL indicators, we see a man whose strong dependency needs are disavowed and enacted in false-self caretaking of others, representing a vertical split[6] in his self-functioning (Kohut, 1979; Goldberg, 2013). Given this psychodynamic, we hypothesize Dr. Ether was uncommonly vulnerable to the loss of his marital relationship. We additionally speculate he was inclined to idealize his love objects as evidenced by the emotional distancing conveyed in his several Cg responses: the "*angels* in blousy-gowns" on Card I, *French* waiters in high-heeled boot types and waistcoats" on Card II, "women in *daguerreotype ... old-style* bonnets, gowns" on Card VII, and "blue *girdle* with laces" on Card VIII.

## ICD-10 and PDM-2 diagnoses

Dr. Ether's *International Statistical Classification of Diseases and Related Health problems* (ICD-10; World Health Organization, 2010) diagnoses included:

F22: Delusional Disorder Erotomanic and Persecutory type[7]
F10.10: Alcohol Use Disorder, in sustained remission.

It is known that Delusional Disorder can occur in people who otherwise function in an acceptable manner. This was the case with Dr. Ether. Dr. Ether showed no history or evidence of other psychotic disorders, including bipolar disorder, schizophrenia, schizotypal personality disorder, neurocognitive disorders, and obsessive-compulsive disorder—all of which need to be ruled out for Delusional Disorder. Because of his encapsulated but persistent and apparently unfounded belief that his ex-spouse continued to love him, despite evidence to the contrary and upon which he acted out, suggested erotomania. He was diagnosed with Persecutory type because he believed his ex-wife's previous husband, having falsified his death and assumed a new identity, was conspiring against both him and his ex-wife. His Alcohol Use Disorder was viewed as in sustained full remission, supported by a robust recovery program.

Multiaxial diagnoses using the *Psychodynamic Diagnostic Manual, Second Edition* (PDM-2; Lingiardi & McWilliams, 2017) and the Psychodiagnostic Chart (PDC; Gordon & Bornstein, 2018) were as follows:

**Level of personality organization**: straddling Borderline and Neurotic ranges
**Personality syndromes (P Axis)**: Dependent Personality Pattern (counter-dependent converse manifestation) and probable Narcissistic, Covert Type of Personality
**Mental functioning (M Axis)**: Mild impairments in mental functioning[8]
**Symptom patterns (S Axis)**: Delusional Disorder
**Implications and recommendations**: The forensic conclusion

The bottom-line forensic psychological diagnostic opinion was that Dr. Ether was fit for duty to practice as a medical doctor. Coordinating the relative strengths and deficits observed from his history, in the collateral information, on interview, and from psychological assessment justified this conclusion. Although his functioning was highly problematic in relation to his previous romantic relationship, his Delusional Disorder symptoms did not significantly encroach on his general cognitive functioning, work-related social communication and relationships, or general reasoning and judgment. The psychological report emphasized the importance of keeping his concerns and feelings about his ex-spouse entirely separate from his physician duties (and not acting on the beliefs), and recommended continued psychotherapy, support group attendance, and indefinite monitoring by the SMF.

## Assessment feedback

As the examining psychologist traveled from another state to perform the evaluation, feedback was given in the form of a brief summary of impressions at the end of the day's assessment and later in a subsequent telephone discussion (after Dr. Ether and his psychologist had reviewed the written report). Dr. Ether listened intently to the summary of results, stipulated he disagreed with the diagnosis of Delusional Disorder, but expressed relief that the bottom line was he was FFD. He also said that the time and care taken in the psychological evaluation made him feel "listened to." Other than the diagnosis, he said he agreed with all observations in the psychological report (which focused largely on the FFD issues rather than some of the more inferential psychodynamics). The therapist received extended feedback which generally confirmed his understanding of the case. The feedback also empowered the therapist to reinforce the idea that although Dr. Ether was FFD, he needed to contain his concerns about his ex-wife to protect his professional life from being undermined.

## Assessor reflections: Psychodynamics, stalking, and Delusional disorder

The FFD evaluation of Dr. Ether was challenging. His job had substantial responsibility and public safety implications. The stakes were high for him, the public, and the evaluator. As to his delusional beliefs and behavior, he acknowledged they seemed far-fetched, but he nonetheless firmly believed them true (and sometimes acted on them). But these symptoms did not seem to adversely affect his behavior otherwise—as confirmed by interview, collateral data, and the generally spared ego functioning reflected in the psychological testing. Despite the suggestions in the Rorschach data of relatively mild lapses in thinking and reasoning as well as a personality organized within a false-self adaptation, these findings did not rise to a forensically actionable level. To understand Dr. Ether and further probe the question of FFD, we now ask: What is Delusional Disorder?

Delusional Disorder is a rare condition with a lifetime prevalence estimated at 0.2% (DSM-5; APA, 2013b). The syndrome is as old as psychiatry—as well as the record of human medical maladies (Berrios & Kennedy, 2002). In the early 19th century, Jean Etienne Dominique Esquirol may have been the first to delineate the syndrome of paranoia, which he termed partial psychosis (Opjordsmoen, 2014). Both Emil Kraepelin and Eugene Bleuler distinguished it from schizophrenia (*Dementia Praecox*) and manic-depressive psychosis, delineating a pure paranoid syndrome Kraepelin called *Verrücktheit*, also distinct from paranoid schizophrenia (*Paranoide Formen Dementia Praecox*) (see Kendler, 2018; Kelly, Kennedy, & Shanley, 2000). Delusional Disorder is defined in recent DSMs by the presence of encapsulated delusions that do not seriously impair psychosocial functioning and no or minimal other positive symptoms of psychosis (e.g., Schneiderian First-Rank Symptoms [FRS]). The DSM-5 lists five subtypes: Erotomanic, Grandiose, Jealous, Persecutory, and Somatic (APA, 2013b). Importantly, the condition also may exist in the absence of a pronounced paranoid personality or cognitive style such as described by Shapiro (1965/1999). Given its rarity, less scientific research has been published on the condition, and discussions of psychological test patterns associated with Delusional Disorder are rare. Notable exceptions are the case reports by Exner and Edberg (2005) and Acklin (2018), although they are not necessarily "pure" cases of Delusional Disorder. Kleiger (2017) also provides a discussion of Rorschach assessment in non-schizophrenic paranoia.

A subset of Delusional Disorders is known as *misidentification syndromes*. Examples include *Capgras syndrome*, the belief that a person has been replaced by a double, first described by Capgras and Rebul-Lachaux (1923, cited in Ellis, Whitely, & Luaute, 1994), and the *Fregoli* delusion, the belief that a known person is disguised as a different person (Courbon & Fail, 1927). Contemporary scientific psychopathology views misidentification syndromes as having a neuropsychiatric axis. Various medical conditions and neurological disorders have been linked to the development of misidentification syndromes. In some cases, abnormalities in the right cerebral hemisphere and the fusiform gyrus area (the seat of prosopagnosia, the inability to recognize faces) have been found (Ramachandrian, 1995; McKay & Dennet, 2009).

The eloquent biographer of neurological case histories, Oliver Sacks (1998), described prosopagnosia in the *Man who Mistook his Wife for a Hat* as well as other misidentification syndromes in various writings. Oliver Sacks emphasized that neurological disorders do not occur in a vacuum. That is, the person who experiences a neurological disorder has a specific personal history and set of psychodynamics which have developed within unique family interactions and cultural contexts. Neurological disorder may impinge on personality functioning, and the individual's emotional response to the effects of neurological changes felt in his or her life derives not only from the actual neuropsychological deficit but also from personal psychodynamics and history. McKay and Dennet (2009) and Bortolotti (2015) describe how delusions, irrespective of their putative neuropsychiatric genesis, can serve motivational and defensive functions. That is, delusions essentially become psychologically adaptive ego defenses (A. Freud, 1966/1992).

In this regard, it helps to reflect on the observation that erotomania, although marked by grievous mis-steps down a proverbial "rabbit hole" of the mind, nonetheless emerges from that universal experience about which the bards and poets speak, that is, love. Love and its gifts are the ground of human existence. For Freud, love was half of the famous dictum "to love and work" (Erikson, 1950/1993), and love is the currency of British object relations theorists like Winnicott (1965) and figural in contemporary psychodynamic attachment theory.[9] Scholars and artists alike have long recognized the preeminence of love in the panoply of human experience, an emotion inextricably connected with self, longing, and loss. Erotomania is a derivative maladaptation of love wherein the psychodynamics of blind spots, narcissism, and shame impinge on select areas of ego functioning (Kelly, 2018; Bortolotti, 2015; McKay, Langdon, & Coltheart, 2005). Shakespeare (1600/2005) said, "love is blind and lovers cannot see the pretty follies that themselves commit" (*Merchant of Venice*, 2.6.36). Love, fears of loss, the desire to be special, jealousy, wishes to control the fate of relationships and forestall grief—these can be psychological building blocks of erotomania.

The case of Dr. Ether features elements of erotomania and, very interestingly, a quasi-Fregoli delusion as well as obsessional stalking behavior. Meloy, Rivera, Siegel, Gothard, Nalmark, & Nicolini and colleagues (2000) studied empirical correlates of obsessional stalking. They found stalking tends to be linked with attachment pathology, non–antisocial personality disorders, average or above-average intellectual resources, and substance abuse. Also, a greater risk of violence occurs with prior sexual intimacy, but the risk is decreased if psychosis is present (Meloy & Gothard, 1995; Meloy et al., 2000; Mohandie et al., 2006). The case of Dr. Ether involves several of these correlates: an insecure attachment pattern, a false-self structure and counter-dependent personality pattern, prior alcohol disorder, strong intellectual resources, and psychosis (despite adequate ego functioning outside of his area of psychological vulnerability [i.e., delusions about his ex-spouse and alleged persecutor]). In addition, there were hints of a possible neuropsychological diathesis in his presentation. The assessment did not include neuropsychological studies, and his medical history was not significant for neurological or other relevant medical conditions. However, we note that Dr. Ether became directionally "lost" in trying to find the office where the assessment took place (although it was in a readily accessible medical complex). This is a very soft and not uncommon neurological sign, nor was Dr. Ether evaluated for prosopagnosia. Yet, given his Delusional Disorder, it is tempting to speculate on a possible neuropsychological vulnerability as assumed in modern two-component theories of delusion formation which posit a neuro-cognitive scaffold upon which faulty meaning systems elaborate (Freeman, 2007; Coltheart, Langdon, & McKay, 2010). Perhaps Dr. Ether carried such a neuropsychological diathesis. If so, this may have set the stage for a motivated, compensatory, and self-protective delusional complex to emerge out of the felt devastation of object loss. Struggling to maintain his identity as a needed caretaker in the face of rejection and loss, he may have undergone a disorienting, hyper-salient experience that threatened self-cohesion. From such fractured self-experience, we surmise Dr. Ether may have woven delusional beliefs from the threads of his personal life experiences and personality dynamics, organizing a fragile peace within himself.

## Notes

1  The author wishes to thank Lorrie G. Beevers, PhD, Jed Yalof, PsyD., and Anthony Bram, PhD for helpful comments on earlier drafts of this chapter.
2  In employment-related settings, the use of non-gendered T scores is preferred to avoid basing test interpretations on gender-related variables, a demographic that employers legally cannot use in hiring and personnel actions.
3  Dr. Ether recalled his college SAT score was about 1300; this corresponds psychometrically to a SS of 123 and 94thpercentile.
4  Discussion of the rationale for the coding of INC1 for Dr. Ether's R12 and its significance is found below.
5  The FCarb response may be viewed as a subset of the INC1 coding in the R-PAS. Note also the R-PAS Manual provides an example INC1 response that resembles Lerner's (1998, p. 157) "red beavers" illustration of the FCarb: "red lion" (Meyer et al., 2011, p. 120).
6  The psychodynamic term *vertical split* contrasts with the traditional concept of repressed unconscious material (*horizontal split*). The term was introduced by Kohut and refers to mental contents that are disavowed but not fully outside of conscious awareness. Gabbard (2002) offers examples from the popular TV series *The Sopranos*. The lead character, Tony Soprano, lives the life of a concerned, tender father figure and devoted husband who idealizes his wife. Yet, he simultaneously works as a Mafia gangster and conducts numerous extra-marital affairs. He disavows these seemingly contradictory ways of living in his self-image.
7  With a continuous course and severity of "moderate" on the "Delusions" item of the *Diagnostic and Statistical Manual-5th edition* (DSM-5; American Psychiatric Association, 2013b (Clinician-Rated Dimensions of Psychosis Symptom Severity scale (C-RPSS; American Psychiatric Association, 2013a). This DSM-5 index is used to provide a dimensional characterization of psychotic symptoms.
8  His relatively spared mental functioning capacities reflected benefits of the encapsulated nature of his S Axis disorder, with otherwise generally strong intellectual and psychosocial functioning and cognitive reserve.
9  John Lennon and Paul McCartney has something to say about love in 1967.

## References

Acklin, M. W. (2018). Using R-PAS in a criminal responsibility evaluation. In J. L. Mihura & G. J. Meyer (Eds.), *Using the Rorschach performance assessment system (R-PAS)* (pp. 187–204). New York: Guilford.
American Psychiatric Association. (2013a). *Clinician-rated dimensions of psychosis symptom severity*. Retrieved from https://www.psychiatry.org/psychiatrists/practice/dsm/educational-resources/assessment-measures.
American Psychiatric Association. (2013b). *Diagnostic and statistical manual of mental disorders (DSM-5®)*. Arlington, VA: American Psychiatric Publishers.

American Psychological Association. (2018). Professional practice guidelines for occupationally mandated psychological evaluations. *The American Psychologist, 73*(2), 186–197.

Anfang, S. A., Faulkner, L. R., Fromson, J. A., & Gendel, M. H. (2005). The American psychiatric association's resource document on guidelines for psychiatric fitness-for-duty evaluations of physicians. *Journal of the American Academy of Psychiatry and the Law, 33*(1), 85–88.

Berrios, G. E., & Kennedy, N. (2002). Erotomania: A conceptual history. *History of Psychiatry, 13*(52), 381–400.

Bion, W. R. (1961). *Experiences in groups and other papers*. London: Tavistock Publications. [Reprinted London: Routledge 1989].

Blanchard, D. D., McGrath, R. E., Pogge, D. L., & Khadivi, A. (2003). A comparison of the PAI and MMPI-2 as predictors of faking bad in college students. *Journal of Personality Assessment, 80*(2), 197–205.

Bornstein, R. F., & Masling, J. M. (2005). The Rorschach oral dependency scale. In R. F. Bornstein & J. M. Masling (Eds.), *Scoring the Rorschach: Seven validated systems* (pp. 135–157). Mahwah, NJ: Erlbaum.

Bortolotti, L. (2015). The epistemic innocence of motivated delusions. *Consciousness and Cognition, 33*, 490–499.

Bram, A. D., & Peebles, M. J. (2014). *Psychological testing that matters: Creating a road map for effective treatment*. Washington, DC: American Psychological Association.

Brodsky, S. L., & Wilson, J. K. (2013). Empathy in forensic evaluations: A systematic reconsideration. Behavioral Sciences & the Law, 31(2), 192–202.

Brown, K. P., Iannelli, R. J., & Marganoff, D. P. (2017). Use of the personality assessment inventory in fitness-for-duty evaluations of physicians. *Journal of Personality Assessment, 99*(5), 465–471.

Butcher, J. N., Morfitt, R. C., Rouse, S. V., & Holden, R. R. (1997). Reducing MMPI-2 defensiveness: The effect of specialized instructions on retest validity in a job applicant sample. *Journal of Personality Assessment, 68*(2), 385–401.

Coltheart, M., Langdon, R., & McKay, R. (2010). Delusional belief. *Annual Review of Psychology, 62*, 271–298.

Courbon, P., & Fail, G. (1927). Illusion of Frégoli syndrome and schizophrenia. *Bulletin de la Société Clinique de Médicine Mentale, 15*, 121–124.

Eignor, D. R. (2013). The standards for educational and psychological testing. In K. F. Geisinger, B. A. Bracken, J. F. Carlson, J.-I. C. Hansen, N. R. Kuncel, S. P. Reise, & M. C. Rodriguez (Eds.), *APA handbooks in psychology. APA handbook of testing and assessment in psychology: Test theory and testing and assessment in industrial and organizational psychology* (vol. 1, pp. 245–250). Washington, DC: American Psychological Association.

Ellis, H. D., Whitley, J., & Luauté, J. P. (1994). Delusional misidentification. The three original papers on the Capgras, Fregoli and inter-metamorphosis delusions. *History of Psychiatry, 5*(17), 117–118.

Erikson, E. H. (1950/1993). *Childhood and society*. New York: WW Norton & Company.

Exner Jr., J. E., & Erdberg, P. (2005). *The Rorschach: A comprehensive system*. New York: John Wiley & Sons Inc.

Freeman, D. (2007). Suspicious minds: The psychology of persecutory delusions. *Clinical Psychology Review, 27*(4), 425–457.

Freud, A. (1966/1992). *The ego and the mechanisms of defence*. London: Karnac Books.

Gabbard, G. (2002). *Psychology of the Sopranos: Love, death, desire, and betrayal in America's favorite gangster family*. New York: Basic Books.

Ganellen, R. J. (2008). Rorschach assessment of malingering and defensive response sets. In C. B. Gacono & B. Evans (Eds.), *The handbook of forensic Rorschach assessment* (pp.89–119). New York: Routledge.

Goldberg, A. I. (2013). *Being of two minds: The vertical split in psychoanalysis and psychotherapy.* New York: Routledge.

Gordon, R. M., & Bornstein, R. F. (2018). Construct validity of the psychodiagnostic chart: A transdiagnostic measure of personality organization, personality syndromes, mental functioning, and symptomatology. *Psychoanalytic Psychology, 35*(2), 280–288.

Greenberg, S. A., & Shuman, D. W. (1997). Irreconcilable conflict between therapeutic and forensic roles. *Professional Psychology: Research and Practice, 28*(1), 50–57.

Luyten, P., Mayes, L. C., Fonagy, P., Blatt, S. J., & Target, M. (Eds.) (2017). *Handbook of psychodynamic approaches to psychopathology.* New York: Guilford.

Hathaway, S. R., McKinley, J. C., & MMPI Restandardization Committee (1989). *MMPI-2: Minnesota multiphasic personality Inventory-2: Manual for administration and scoring.* Minneapolis, MN: University of Minnesota Press.

Heltzel, T. (2007). Compatibility of therapeutic and forensic roles. *Professional Psychology: Research and Practice, 38*(2), 122–128.

Hirschhorn, L. (1990). *The workplace within: Psychodynamics of organizational life* (vol. 8). Boston, MA: MIT Press.

International Association for Chiefs of Police. (2013, July). *Psychological fitness for duty evaluation guidelines.* Retrieved from https://www.theiacp.org/sites/default/files/all/p-r/Psych-FitnessforDutyEvaluation.pdf.

Katsavdakis, K. A., Gabbard, G. O., & Athey, G. I. (2004). Profiles of impaired health professionals. *Bulletin of the Menninger Clinic, 68*(1), 60–72.

Kelly, B. D., Kennedy, N., & Shanley, D. (2000). Delusion and desire: Erotomania revisited. *Acta Psychiatrica Scandinavia, 102*(1), 74–76.

Kelly, B. D. (2018). Love as delusion, delusions of love: erotomania, narcissism and shame. *Medical Humanities, 44*(1), 15–19.

Kendler, K. S. (2018). The development of Kraepelin's mature diagnostic concepts of paranoia (die Verrücktheit) and paranoid dementia praecox (dementia paranoides): A close reading of his textbooks from 1887 to 1899. *JAMA Psychiatry, 75*(12), 1280–1288.

Kleiger, J. H. (2017). *Rorschach assessment of psychotic phenomena.* New York: Routledge.

Kohut, H. (1979). The two analyses of Mr. Z. *International Journal of Psycho-Analysis, 60*(1), 3–27.

Lerner, P. M. (1990). The clinical inference process and the role of theory. *Journal of Personality Assessment, 55*(3–4), 426–431.

Lerner, P. M. (1998). *Psychoanalytic perspectives on the Rorschach.* Hillsdale, NJ: The Analytic Press.

Lerner, P. M. (2005). Red beavers and building bridges between assessment and treatment. *Journal of Personality Assessment, 85*(3), 271–279.

Levinson, D. J. (1959). Role, personality, and social structure in the organizational setting. *The Journal of Abnormal and Social Psychology, 58*(2), 170.

Lingiardi, V., & McWilliams, N. (Eds.) (2017). Psychodynamic diagnostic manual: Second edition (PDM-2). New York: Guilford.

Lowmaster, S. E., & Morey, L. C. (2012). Predicting law enforcement officer job performance with the personality assessment inventory. *Journal of Personality Assessment, 94*(3), 254–261.

Maslow, A. H. (1943). A theory of human motivation. *Psychological Review, 50*(4), 370–396.

McKay, R. T., & Dennett, D. C. (2009). The evolution of misbelief. *Behavioral and Brain Sciences, 32*(6), 493–510.

McKay, R. T., Langdon, R., & Coltheart, M. (2005). "Sleights of mind": Delusions, defenses, and self-deception. *Cognitive Neuropsychiatry, 10*(4), 305–326.

Meloy, J. R., & Gothard, S. (1995). Demographic and clinical comparison of obsessional followers and offenders with mental disorders. *American Journal of Psychiatry, 152*(2), 258–263.

Meloy, J. R., Rivers, L., Siegel, L., Gothard, S., Nalmark, D., & Nicolini, J. R. (2000). A replication study of obsessional followers and offenders with mental disorders. *Journal of Forensic Sciences, 45*(1), 147–152.

Meyer, G. J., Erard, R. E., Erdberg, P., Mihura, J. L., & Viglione, D. J. (2011). *Rorschach performance assessment system: Administration, coding, interpretation, and technical manual.* Toledo, OH: Rorschach Performance Assessment Systems, L.L.C.

Mihura, J. L., Meyer, G. J., Dumitrascu, N., & Bombel, G. (2013). The validity of individual Rorschach variables: Systematic reviews and meta-analyses of the comprehensive system. *Psychological Bulletin, 139*(3), 548–605.

Modell, A. H. (1975). A narcissistic defence against affects and the illusion of self-sufficiency. *International Journal of Psycho-Analysis, 56*(3), 275–282.

Mohandie, K., Meloy, J. R., McGowan, M. G., & Williams, J. (2006). The RECON typology of stalking: Reliability and validity based upon a large sample of North American stalkers. *Journal of Forensic Sciences, 51*(1), 147–155.

Morey, L. C. (2007). *Personality assessment inventory (PAI): Professional manual.* Odessa, FL: Psychological Assessment Resources.

Mulay, A. L., Mivshek, M., Kaufman, H., & Waugh, M. H. (2018). The ethics of empathy: Walking a fine line in forensic evaluations. *Journal of Forensic Psychology Research and Practice, 18*(4), 320–336.

Opjordsmoen, S. (2014). Delusional disorder as partial psychosis. *Schizophrenia Bulletin, 40*(2), 244–247.

Peebles-Kleiger, M. J. (2002). Elaboration of some sequence analysis strategies: Examples and guidelines for level of confidence. *Journal of Personality Assessment, 79*(1), 19–38.

Picano, J. J., Williams, T. J., & Roland, R. R. (2006). Assessment and selection of high-risk operational personnel. In C. H. Kennedy & E. A. Zillmer (Eds.), *Military psychology: Clinical and operational applications* (pp. 353–370). New York: Guilford.

Ramachandran, V. S. (1995). Anosognosia in parietal lobe syndrome. *Consciousness and Cognition, 4*(1), 22–51.

Rapaport, D., Gill, M. M., & Schafer, R. (1968). *Diagnostic psychological testing.* New York: International Universities Press.

Rosse, J. G., Stecher, M. D., Miller, J. L., & Levin, R. A. (1998). The impact of response distortion on preemployment personality testing and hiring decisions. *Journal of Applied Psychology, 83*(4), 634–644.

Sacks, O. (1998). *The man who mistook his wife for a hat.* New York: Simon & Schuster.

Shakespeare, W. (1600/2005). The merchant of venice. In S. Wells & G. Taylor (Eds.), *The Oxford Shakespeare: The complete works* (2nd ed.). New York: Oxford University Press.

Shapiro, D. (1965/1999). *Neurotic styles.* New York: Basic Books.

Shorey, H. S. (2018). Introduction to the special issue on the role of personality assessment in consulting to organizations. *Journal of Personality Assessment, 100*(5), 493–497.

Shuman, D. W., & Zervopoulos, J. A. (2010). Empathy or objectivity: The forensic examiner's dilemma? *Behavioral Sciences and the Law, 28*(5), 585–602.

Stapley, L. F. (2018). *Individuals, groups and organizations beneath the surface: An introduction.* New York: Routledge.

Stone, A. V. (2000). *Fitness for duty: Principles, methods, and legal issues.* Boca Raton, FL: CRC Press .

Tellegen, A., & Ben-Porath, Y. S. (2011). *MMPI-2-RF: Minnesota multiphasic personality Inventory-2 restructured form: Technical manual.* Minneapolis, MN: University of Minnesota Press.

Troyat, H. (1967). *Tolstoy.* New York: Doubleday Publishing.

Walfish, S. (2010). Reducing MMPI-defensiveness in professionals presenting for evaluation. *Journal of Addictive Diseases, 30*(1), 75–80.

Winnicott, D. W. (1965). Ego distortion in terms of the true and false self. In D.W. Winnicott (Ed.), *The maturational processes and the facilitating environment: Studies in the theory of emotional development* (pp. 140–157). Oxford: International Universities Press.

Wise, E. A., Streiner, D. L., & Walfish, S. (2010). A review and comparison of the reliabilities of the MMPI-2, MCMI-III, and PAI presented in their respective test manuals. *Measurement and Evaluation in Counseling and Development, 42*(4), 246–254.

World Health Organization. (2010). *International statistical classification of diseases and related health problems* (10th Revision). Geneva: World Health Organization.

# 10 Teaching a model of formulation for psychoanalytic assessment reports

*Christina Biedermann*

Psychological assessment is, most simply, an effort to describe a patient's capacities and vulnerabilities based on the administration, scoring, and integrated interpretation of evidence-based measures. Psychological testing facilitates clarification of diagnoses, development of clinical formulations, prediction of behaviors, and design, evaluation, and refinement of psychological interventions. To do so, psychologists sift through, organize, and communicate the vast amount of information available from the testing situation. This information includes, at the very least, patients' test scores and behaviors during the assessment process, as well as, from a psychoanalytic perspective, the thematic content of patients' speech (Bram, 2017), patients' attitudes (transferences) to the testing situation and assessor (Schafer, 1954), and the assessors' attitudes (countertransferences) to the patient (Schactel, 1966). Assessors compare patients' performances to normative samples as well as to other scores within the patients' own test batteries. Psychoanalytic assessors also consider patients' metaphors and associations. They are interested in how each patient uniquely receives and responds to testing stimuli (Bram, 2017; Schafer, 1954), with the premise that there is meaningful data available beyond the test scores, including unconscious material that presents in both language and action (Bram, 2017; Yalof, 2020). Assessors must then organize their conclusions and present them in ways that report readers, from patients to families to colleagues, can understand and use. As a primary vehicle for feedback, the psychological test report is thus a culmination of a considerably involved process. Crafting it is a complex task to practice as well as to learn.

There are many strategies for teaching the mechanics of organizing and writing psychological test reports (e.g., Bram & Peebles, 2014; Eriksson & Maurex, 2018; Tallent, 1966; Wiener & Costaris, 2012); however, few focus on the ways psychoanalytic theory in particular might inform and enhance the process. In this chapter, I discuss a way in which the psychoanalytically informed teacher of psychological assessment might help students create accessible, useful reports. After discussing the main issues associated with teaching psychoanalytic report writing in shifting educational and clinical landscapes ambivalent about psychoanalysis (Downing, Lubin, & Yalof, 2018), I offer a three-part, psychoanalytically informed model that facilitates the report writing process and then present a clinical illustration. The model is designed to assist students in developing and organizing theoretically derived inferences into easily understood narratives. As such, it equips students to describe complex clinical phenomena accessibly and to make useful clinical recommendations. Patients should ultimately be able to recognize themselves in test reports and fully understand their implications. This requires that students move beyond just descriptive, scores-based hypotheses or abstract, theory-driven inferences, instead integrating and presenting both in terms understandable in the context of the patient's lived experience. For example, the concept of oral dependency (Abraham,1924) is a psychoanalytic term incorporated into contemporary assessment practice (Bornstein, 1996; Meyer, Viglione, Mihura, Erard, & Erdberg, 2011). Using this term in a report, however, would be obtuse and might be experienced as shaming or nonspecific. Instead, writing about a patient's desire to be cared for, how this desire elicits feelings of dependency, how these dependent feelings affect interpersonal relationships and the patient's experience of them, and how the patient protects herself from these feelings are fair-minded and understandable statements (Harty, 1986).

Teaching this type of translation and creating test reports that use it effectively is easier said than done, especially in contemporary educational and clinical climates. Although there has been some decline in the use of psychological assessment since the inception of managed care, the large majority of psychologists believe it is valuable in informing psychodiagnostic and treatment planning efforts (Wright et al., 2017) and an important part of the profession of psychology's identity (Norcross & Karpiak, 2012). Given the widespread need and respect for psychological assessment as well as the somewhat daunting nature of the task, it is curious that, in general, training in personality assessment is lacking. Though reports vary about whether didactic assessment training in graduate clinical psychology programs is increasing (Ready & Veague, 2014) or decreasing (Belter & Piotrowski, 2001), it is clear that performance-based measures are being taught less (Piotrowski, 2015a, 2017) while cognitive and self-report measures are being taught more (Mihura, Roy, & Graceffo, 2017) and that there is insufficient opportunity for graduate students to practice the assessment skills they learn before internship (Mihura et al., 2017). Without adequate exposure to performance-based measures, students lack the education and training necessary to perform true multi-method assessments and to write fully integrated reports, both of which are considered basic competencies by the American Psychological Association (Kaslow, 2004; Krishnamurthy et al., 2004).

Further, without adequate training in assessment during their graduate education, students are not prepared to take advantage of opportunities to develop those skills during internship training. As of the early 2000s, internship training directors commonly found students knew little beyond the fundamentals of psychological assessment (Clemence & Handler, 2001; Stedman, Hatch, & Schoenfeld, 2001). Stedman et al. (2001) found that internship directors believed only 25% of students began an internship with sufficient assessment report writing experience. More recently, Piotrowski (2015a) suggested internship settings may be increasingly abandoning expectations of competency in projective (i.e., performance-based) techniques in particular. When assessment training at the predoctoral level is compromised, it then also undermines advanced supervised experience at the postdoctoral level. As fewer and fewer early-career professionals enter practice competent in true multi-method assessment, the field risks losing a valuable educational and clinical tool.

Although there is no comprehensive data outlining why programs teach what they do, the trend toward breadth at the cost of depth in assessment training (Mihura et al., 2017) suggests it might, in part, be a matter of students' time (Piotrowski, 2015b). It simply takes time to master the complex knowledge base necessary to practice psychological assessment competently. Doing so requires specialized knowledge in psychometric theory, culturally informed theories of intelligence and human cognition, theories of human development and personality, and ethics pertaining to assessment practice, as well as the skills necessary to select, administer, score, interpret, and communicate about a wide variety of assessment measures. Krishnamurthy and colleagues (2004) go further, adding the abilities to assess intervention outcomes; to evaluate the multiple roles and contexts within which clients and psychologists function and their impact on assessment activity; to establish, maintain, and understand collaborative professional relationships that provide the context for psychological assessments; and to understand the relationship between assessment and intervention. If personality assessment is considered an isolated skill and opportunities to integrate it into graduate clinical psychology education early are missed, the sprawling scope of the knowledge base and the time needed to master it may later be considered in conflict with other coursework and supervised clinical experience. It simply takes too much precious time to learn it all. Moreover, as personality assessment is used less and less outside of forensic and inpatient settings since the implementation of managed care (Wright et al., 2017), a logical solution to the competition for graduate students' time and attention would be to focus on subjects and skills most immediately and definitively applicable. This may be particularly true in scientist-practitioner and clinical science programs, in contrast to practice-focused programs (Mihura et al., 2017).

However, many assessment skills are far from specialized, and approaching them as such overlooks the potential to teach them in more integrated ways that develop not only assessment-related skills but also fundamental, non-assessment clinical skills requiring the integration of theory and practice, including, for example, case formulation. There are opportunities to introduce psychological testing from the beginning of advanced undergraduate study through early graduate curricula when students are beginning to learn theories of perception and motivation, affect, and interpersonal schemas, as well as to analyze clinical interchanges between clinicians and patients. In each of these domains, instructors first attempt to break down complex experience into component parts. This emphasis on components is the first step in a complex educational process wherein students eventually begin using theory to integrate discrete data points into overarching constructs and then to apply them clinically. The process of breaking experience down into component parts is precisely the territory and strength of psychological testing, and early exposure facilitates such learning. Children's responses to the Rorschach test (Rorschach, 1927; Meyer et al., 2011), for example, show the development of cognitive skills; dysphoric Thematic Apperception Test (TAT; Murray, 1943) stories demonstrate depressed patients' difficulties expressing and managing affects; and clocks drawn by patients with hemispheric brain injury show visual-spatial impairment in ways that simply cannot be described. In addition to teaching these kinds of phenomena, early exposure to the ways psychological tests demonstrate these component parts might also ultimately make learning assessment-specific skills more efficient. If students learn the concepts behind the mechanics of administration first, they can then place those more rote efforts into richer conceptual frameworks and more quickly approach the complex task of re-integrating discrete data points into overarching constructs. With its focus on the integration of cognitive and emotional processes, use of interpersonal behavior as data, attention to language, and recognition of both conscious and unconscious motivations for behavior, psychoanalytic theory is particularly suited to the task of re-integration (Rapaport, Gill, & Schafer, 1968; Schachtel, 1966; Schafer, 1954).

Writing psychological assessment reports is a vehicle through which students practice this re-integration. Just as integrating assessment and non-assessment coursework facilitates learning in both domains, learning how to write test reports refines case formulation, clinical feedback, and professional writing skills. In test reports, students must organize and translate testing data into accessible, individualized narratives outlining patients' strengths and weaknesses. Effective test reports are written professionally, persuasively, and appropriately for the range of those who might read them (Appelbaum, 1970). Appelbaum stated:

> The objective ... is to set, and continue in motion, a process of understanding and development. With recognition of his reader's wishes, impulses, and needs in mind, the [assessment] test report writer, as a psychologist, selects and organizes his facts, chooses his style, and couches his opinions in ways that make it possible for the reader to get what the reader wants.
>
> (p. 352)

With its attention to language, metaphor, and the effects of speech, psychoanalytic theory is particularly useful toward these ends. Psychoanalytic theory offers possibilities to persuasively and accessibly describe phenomenon beyond what is offered in atheoretical frameworks that rely on descriptive, scientific, or research-based language (Appelbaum, 1970; Sugarman, 1991; Sugarman & Kanner, 2000).

However, there are different ways to think about theory in relation to assessment (Blais & Hopwood, 2017), and there may be ambivalence about applications of psychoanalytic theory in particular (Downing, Lubin, & Yalof, 2018). Reports organized around atheoretical, science-driven constructs rather than theoretically derived constructs seem to align with contemporary ideals of evidence-based practice and the scientific objectivity assumed therein. Psychological assessment reports based only on quantitative scores may appear more compelling, valid, or trustworthy. However, while the trend toward evidence-based practice may be a valuable invitation for applied research, it has also been criticized as a cultural phenomenon that has been misinterpreted, reified, and used to exclude effective ways of conceptualizing and treating patients, particularly aspects of patients that may not be so easily quantified (Shedler, 2018). The same is true in psychological assessment. Over-focusing on test scores, limiting conclusions to scores-based interpretations, and organizing test reports around only these data points comes at a cost. If strictly interpreted, it risks excluding information gleaned from behavioral observations, including, for example, interactions with the assessor that often directly relate to patients' functioning outside of the testing situation. Further, data interpretation and report writing without a unifying theory of personality lacks complexity and nuance and often leaves divergent data points unaccounted for. Pages of unintegrated scores and scores-based interpretations leave readers adrift, without an organized narrative in which to recognize the patient. Students taught to write these kinds of reports miss the learning opportunities in knitting together scores into more complete pictures of human beings and writing about them creatively and professionally.

## A psychoanalytic report writing model

Alternatively, theoretically informed assessment and report writing is the use of personality theory to organize and deepen the interpretation of assessment data. It parallels similar contemporary efforts to integrate theory with psychiatric diagnosis in the publication of the *Psychodynamic Diagnostic Manual, Second Edition* (*PDM-2*; Lingiardi & McWilliams, 2017) as a complement to the *Diagnostic and Statistical Manual of Mental Disorders, Fifth Edition* (*DSM-V*) (American Psychiatric Association, 2013), as well as the development of the Alternative Model of Personality Disorders (Morey et al., 2007). Using theories of personality, particularly psychoanalytic theories, to develop and deepen psychological testing is certainly not new. *Diagnostic Psychological Testing* (Rapaport et al., 1968) is a classic in the field of psychoanalytic assessment, and theories of personality have informed the development of many contemporary psychological measures. The NEO Personality Inventory-3 (NEO PI-3; McCrae & Costa, 2010) incorporates theoretically informed research into its conceptualization of narcissism, for example, and the Rorschach Performance Assessment System (R-PAS; Meyer et al., 2011) includes well-validated, theoretically derived measures of dependency and object relations (Bornstein, 1996;

Urist, 1977). Contemporary efforts to develop transtheoretical models of data interpretation include Bram and Peebles' (2014) application of Peebles' concept of underlying developmental disruption (2012). Bram and Peebles use this conceptualization to organize test data so as to identify patients' underlying troubles and draw out useful treatment implications. Blais and Hopwood (2017) offer three transtheoretical conceptual models (i.e., the transtheoretical model of personality, the quantitative psychopathology-personality trait model, and the interpersonal situation model) to teach the relationship between multimethod assessment and personality systems, diagnostic complexity and test selection, and the integration of test data and patient-assessor interactions.

Here, I offer a three-part, psychoanalytically informed model to facilitate the integration of theory and data in a way at once simple enough for beginning assessment students to grasp and open enough to accommodate the complexity more advanced practitioners bring to the task. While it is an approach aimed at facilitating the teaching of psychological test report writing, it is also applicable to clinical work more generally, as a simple means of efficiently organizing clinical information, developing useful case formulations, and shaping effective clinical writing.

While widely applicable, the model presented here is derived from psychoanalytic theory. Within psychoanalysis, there are many traditions, each offering a perspective on psychic development and conscious and unconscious functioning across the lifespan. Like psychological assessment, psychoanalysis was developed based on observations of behavior and language and provides a means of conceptualizing and articulating human experience. Many writers have discussed the application of psychoanalytic ideas to psychological assessment (Bram, 2017; Bram & Yalof, 2015; Kissen, 1986; Kleiger, 1997; Lerner, 1998, 2005, 2007; Schachtel, 1966; Yalof & Rosenstein, 2014; Yalof, 2016, 2019). These applications focus on the interaction of cognition, affect, intrapsychic conflict, and defenses, as well as character adaptation. Psychoanalytic ego psychology, in particular, lends itself to organizing the types of data psychological testing yields. With interests in patients' reality testing and capacities to delay gratification, it is no surprise the pioneers of psychodiagnostic testing, David Rapaport, Merton Gill, and Roy Schafer, emerged from the ego psychological tradition (Rapaport, 1950a, 1950b, 1953; Rapaport et al., 1968; Schafer, 1954).

Borrowing from ego psychology's focus on patients' defensive responses to psychic trouble and the character styles these processes shape, one might organize clinical data using three basic questions. When taken together, the questions coalesce into a convenient three-part model. Though particularly helpful for beginning students faced with the daunting task of organizing often-overwhelming amounts of data, even advanced practitioners benefit from returning to simple models when complexity threatens clarity. Whereas psychological assessment offers a systematic approach to breaking down complex information, psychoanalytic theory, and this model as an application of it, offers a structure within which to reintegrate it. Rather than simply focusing on convergent or otherwise easily organized data, this approach also affords the assessor the opportunity to make sense of seemingly incongruent data (Bram & Peebles, 2014). Psychoanalysis allows for conscious and unconscious motivations to be at odds, acknowledges both traits and states, and recognizes the ways in which people function differentially across contexts (Bromberg, 1996). Facilitating systematic integration of ostensibly incongruent data points is a unique contribution of psychoanalytically informed psychological assessment (Bram & Peebles, 2014).

### A model in three questions

Three questions organize this approach to report writing: (a) What is the primary problem? (b) How is the patient dealing with it? and (c) Where do these efforts leave the patient? Slightly elaborated, the questions evolve: What is causing the patient trouble? How is the patient managing, coping, or defending against those difficulties? And, what are the outcomes, or costs and benefits, of the patient's efforts? As the more advanced report writer articulates the patient's primary problem, they also might address what particular contexts or stressors evoke or mitigate it, before addressing ranges in the patient's efforts to manage and the strengths and weaknesses such efforts yield in terms of the patient's daily functioning. In this way, the model can be learned quickly and elaborated to accommodate and organize increasing levels of complexity as students' knowledge bases develop.

**What is the primary problem?** In isolating the primary problem, the first question narrows the field to what is most relevant to understanding the particular patient being assessed. Psychoanalytic theory offers an array of possible constructs, including, for example, intrapsychic conflict, ego functioning, object relations, and the cohesiveness and functioning of self-states (Pine, 1998).

**How is the patient dealing with it?** The second question guides the student to consider the patient's efforts to manage the trouble. Here, too, in its study of defenses, interpersonal process, and the functions of action and speech, psychoanalysis offers multiple options, and ego psychology, in particular, offers a sequential way of organizing them. First, there is a problem, then a defensive response. This sequence lends itself to the beginning construction of an accessible narrative.

**Where do these efforts leave the patient?** The third question then guides the report writer to consider the consequences of the patient's reactions. The writer can discuss the patient's strengths and vulnerabilities and make precise recommendations. This patient-centered approach facilitates the development of recommendations tailored to the patient's unique challenges and resources in order to promote more adaptive means of addressing the primary trouble. Treatment recommendations might include identifying particular areas of conflict to address in psychotherapy, skills-building programs to develop compromised ego functions, or group psychotherapy to help patients learn about the roles they play and more adaptive possibilities. Test scores are only included in the narrative insofar as they are evidence for conclusions; otherwise, they threaten to distract and disrupt the narrative. Lists of test scores can be included as addenda but this is a stylistic consideration where professionals might differ.

## Molly: A case example

What follows are excerpts from a disguised case that illustrate the model. A family therapist referred Molly (pseudonym) to me for a psychological assessment. She had been working with the family on an outpatient basis for nearly a year and a half. The referral questions included clarification of Molly's struggle to take up her life in developmentally appropriate ways, Molly's psychiatric diagnosis, the function of Molly's drug and alcohol abuse, and treatment recommendations. Molly was interested in the assessment to get a holistic assessment of her situation, to better understand her unique cognitive capacities, and to learn why other people's thoughts about her "defined" her. Molly completed the following tests: Minnesota Multiphasic Personality Inventory—Second Edition (MMPI-2; Butcher, Dahlstrom, Graham, Tellegen, & Kreammer, 1989), Rorschach Performance Assessment System (R-PAS; Meyer et al., 2011); Thematic Apperception Test (TAT; Murray, 1943), Repeatable Battery for the Assessment of Neuropsychological Status (RBANS; Randolph, 1998), Reynolds Intellectual Screening Test—Second Edition (RIST-2; Reynolds & Kamphaus, 2015), and the Wisconsin Card Sorting Test (WCST; Heaton, Chelune, Talley, Kay, & Curtiss, 1993).

Based on my conceptualization of Molly through the three-question model and my effort to use the structure of the report to illustrate Molly's primary problem and means of solving it, I organized Molly's test report in the following way. First, I used fairly standard subsections to orient the reader and meet ethical requirements: Identifying Information, Referral Questions, Methods of Assessment, Behavioral Observations and Comments on Validity, and Relevant History. However, then, in a section entitled "Integrated Summary of Findings," I shifted to adopt the scaffolding provided by the three questions. A section devoted to "Treatment Recommendations" followed.

As organized by the model, my review of the test data suggested Molly's primary trouble was disordered thinking, which then created intolerable affective and interpersonal experiences. Molly's performance on self-report and performance measures provided convergent evidence about the vulnerabilities in her thinking and the conditions under which it became acutely destabilized. From a psychoanalytic perspective, this might be described as a problem in ego functioning, particularly reality testing, that undermined Molly's ability to manage her internal experience. Molly's substance abuse was then conceptualized as her best effort at managing. The testing data suggested Molly was abusing substances to several ends, including as a means of destroying her mind and, potentially, of killing herself. In conceptualizing Molly's actions as solutions to problems in her thinking and their aftermath, this basic formulation structured the test report. In this way, psychoanalytic theory and the model I have derived from it allowed me to integrate discrete data points into a comprehensive, usable, data–informed narrative.

The following excerpts from the test report illustrate the ways in which I expanded upon this basic conceptualization and presented it to the reader. Consistent with a teaching model in which students demonstrate how they derive inferences so their teacher might evaluate their inferential processes, at the risk of cluttering the text, I have included references to the data supporting my conclusions.

### Test Report Excerpt 1: What is Molly's primary problem?

The quality of Molly's thinking is variable. Although at times she is able to perceive the world around her accurately, more often, she is confused and unable to maintain her thinking under duress. Molly's scores on cognitive and intellectual measures, including the RIST-2, WCST, and RBANS, were generally within the Average range. Any deviations (RIST-2 Coding SS = 5 [Borderline Impaired]; Story Recall SS = 7 [Low Average]) were clearly related to distractions secondary to internal distress. Molly, for example, began crying about an unrelated social situation while completing the Coding subtest, and she was less accurate in encoding emotionally evocative stimuli than less stimulating items on the Story Recall subtest. Thus, the ego functions, or psychological capacities, assessed by these kinds of cognitive tests, including attention, memory, and executive functioning, were essentially intact but vulnerable to internal distractions.

Rather, it seems that baseline disturbances in Molly's perceptual capacities, including perceptual accuracy and integration, causality, reality testing, and narrative coherence underlie Molly's vulnerability to losing access to her cognitive resources (R-PAS TP-Comp SS = 142, WSumCog Scaled Score [SS] = 148, SevCog Scaled Score SS = 144; FQ-% SS = 117, WD-% SS = 120; MMPI-2, Scale 8 [Schizophrenia] T = 113). Molly's thoughts, experiences, and feelings often lose shape and blend into one another (R-PAS EII-3 SS = 143). On TAT Card 14, for example, Molly described a woman who looks down to find that "[s]he has a shape she has never truly distinguished before." The character was then flooded with light, sounds, and smells and began wondering, "Where was she?" "Who was she?" and "Who is she?" Without basic stability in her identity and perceptual experience, Molly is vulnerable to losing track of her thoughts and why things are happening as they are; she is intermittently aware of this trouble. Molly ended several TAT stories bizarrely and abruptly when she was pressed beyond her capacities to stay organized. She started Card 13MF, for example, with a man leaving his bride to go to work, before he then heard warnings of robots being on the loose; his cab was then held up by "thousands of bikers." As she ended her story, Molly commented, "Maybe it's not the most normal day. That's why he always told himself to hold fast. I was so close to writing a normal story until the … robots. I didn't even mean to."

Molly is quite guarded, confused, suspicious, and suffers impaired concentration (R-PAS V-Comp SS = 113; MMPI-2 Scale 6 [Paranoia] T = 101 and Scale 8 [Schizophrenia] T = 113). Her distress (R-PAS YTVC' SS = 133) further compounds her struggles to think logically and to perceive situations accurately on a consistent basis (R-PAS EII-3 SS = 143). Molly generally denies these feelings, instead either adopting a counterphobic bored or saccharine stance. On TAT Card 2, she told a story about a woman who took psychedelic mushrooms and endured eight hours of her mind being "bended and pulled, pinched and pushed" and otherwise tortured. The character, however, then re-emerged into a world of shining suns and chirping birds, before Molly added, "The mind is sound." Similarly, on TAT Card 5, a woman struggled whether to trust her senses when she thought she heard an intruder. She ultimately pursued the noise only to find an owl, bear, and small pig inexplicably perched on top of a book. Molly adopted an abrupt and bizarre ending to the story to distance herself from the questions she had about the accuracy of her perceptions.

While Molly sometimes prides herself in the depth and clarity of her thinking, more often she feels self-critical, confused, defective, vulnerable, and socially inadequate (R-PAS MOR SS = 146; TAT Card 1, wherein a boy cannot play the notes he wants). In addition to these depressive concerns, Molly often feels agitated, as if she is spinning and might fall apart (MMPI-2 Scales 6 [Paranoia] T = 101, Scale 9 [Hypomania] T = 94). She often experiences these concerns in her body (R-PAS An SS = 128; MMPI-2 Scale 1 [Hypochondriasis] SS = 90, Scale 3 [Hysteria] T = 91). Living in this state of agitated depression pains Molly (R-PAS Y SS = 126). She feels ashamed and angry, and fears that when angry she may not always be able to control herself. Like the fluidity in her thinking, Molly's feelings often blend into one another so that at times she struggles to differentiate between them (R-PAS C Blend SS = 117). She is without an effective means of modulating these experiences and fearful of exploding. She ended TAT Card 18GF with a cold-blooded murder and Card 7BM with an explosive argument. Though others might provide Molly an anchor in this maelstrom and she exhibited strong dependent longings (R-PAS Texture [T] SS = 138, ODL% SS = 135), during the clinical interview and on the TAT (Card 1, wherein a mother wants to replace her needful son) she described her dependency needs as troublesome and feared they would incur emotional "debt."

Molly's confusion about her thoughts and feelings not only affect her experience of herself in the world, but also her perceptions of the social world (R-PAS M- SS = 113). Further, as she maintains distance from others, her perceptions go unchecked, deepening her fear of being burdensome. Across nine TAT stories, only one story involved interaction between people, and it was the story of a mother wanting to replace her disappointing, needful son with a new baby (TAT Card 1). When Molly does approach others, it is in the context of close relationships in which she becomes most confused about the origin of her thoughts and feelings. For example, after an altercation on TAT Card18GF, a character somehow became her own mother. Recognizing the confusion but unable to clarify, Molly hesitated and then added, "That's alright."

### Test Report Excerpt 2: How is Molly dealing with the primary problem?

Molly uses several means of managing her confusion and upset. Psychologically, she demonstrated a range in how she handles what troubles her (R-PAS MC Scaled Score = 124). She uses intellectualization and humor, distraction and magical thinking, as well as more profound bouts of denial in which she simply tries to "unsee" the trouble. In her TAT stories, she consistently retreated into confusing and bizarre fantasy worlds to distance herself from, if not completely forget, obviously distressing events. On Card 1, a mother's rejection of her son involved sending the son off to immigrate, after which the mother warmly shook her head, smiled, and thought about how much she loved her son and his careless ways. Molly's substance abuse is functional in this way too, as it facilitates these more sweeping efforts to wipe out her difficulties and quell her panic.

Troubled by depending on others, Molly works remarkably hard to check and control her thinking. Although she sometimes can control her thinking, she is more often unsure and faced with her dependency on others. Molly needs others to clarify her thinking and provide structure to her mind (R-PAS T SS = 138, ODL% SS = 135). Though she wishes she could more easily use others to help her and feel more socially accepted (clinical interview), she dismisses, denies, or otherwise conceals her longing for fear of being judged or rejected, just as the son on the aforementioned TAT story (TAT Card 1). In Molly's fantasy world, she is more socially connected, even admired (R-PAS M SS = 122; TAT Card 1; clinical interview). The rejected boy in TAT Card 1 becomes a great composer after joining forces with a sprite. Here too, Molly's substance abuse is facilitative. Using drugs enables Molly to withdraw into these worlds and feel connected therein.

All of these efforts, however, are ultimately ineffective, and Molly eventually opts to either withdraw further or explode, discharging in action what otherwise feels overwhelming (TAT Cards 18GF and 7 BM). Whereas most of Molly's substance abuse seems to mitigate her agitation and provide escape, in contrast, her use of alcohol is disinhibiting. Molly seems to use alcohol to facilitate discharge of her unbearable confusion and feelings so she might return to less agitated, more organized states.

### Test Report Excerpt 3: Where do Molly's efforts leave her?

Together, Molly's range in her capacities to see the world as others do (R-PAS P SS = 96) and her propensity to hide her struggles create the appearance her thinking processes are clearer than they are. Alone with the extent of her trouble, she is agitated, confused, and afraid (TAT Cards 5 and 14). Under the press of these emotions, Molly's logic is further strained. Although Molly's escape into fantasy and the substance abuse that promotes it may afford temporary relief from her confusion and isolation, these concerns inevitably return and plague her. She becomes increasingly confused while sober, ruminative about others (R-PAS V-Comp SS = 119, PHR Proportion SS = 134, M- SS = 113), and suspicious about their motivations (MMPI-2 Scale 6 [Paranoia] T = 101; TAT Card 5). In Molly's experience, relationships move from being cooperative to devastating very quickly and without apparent warning (R-PAS COP SS = 134, PHR Proportion SS = 134; TAT 18GF).

Molly's confusion about her thoughts and feelings and the ways in which her efforts to manage consistently fail ultimately leaving her in a serious bind. It is at this point, when Molly is exhausted, hopeless, still confused, and not able to turn to others, that she is most at risk for self-destructive behavior. Self-destruction, including more passive actions like putting herself in harm's way while under the influence, promises to destroy her mind and, thus, eclipse the primary source of her trouble, as well as to end her suffering. Molly endorsed some suicidality during her clinical interview and on self-report measures (MMPI-2 items), as well as concerning confusion and magical thinking about the finality of death (TAT Card 18GF). For example, after the aforementioned altercation on TAT Card 18GF, the character who was killed ultimately walked out of the situation.

## Conclusion

In offering a model for psychological test report writing, I join recent efforts to develop accessible models to organize (Blais & Hopwood, 2017) and present psychological testing data (Bram & Peebles, 2014; Wiener & Costaris, 2012). Here, I propose a psychoanalytically informed framework based on principles of ego psychology, particularly the premise that patients respond to psychic trouble in ways that ultimately coalesce into characteristic ways of being in the world. The model I propose breaks this premise down into three questions and organizes them sequentially: (a) What is the primary problem? (b) How is the patient dealing with it? and (c) Where do these efforts leave the patient? Analyzing and discussing testing data in this way also reflects ego psychology's emphasis on sequences in thought and behavior.

While even advanced practitioners of psychological testing occasionally benefit from returning to simple models in the midst of complexity, accessible models around which to orient are particularly valuable for beginning students of assessment for whom the sheer amount of data generated in psychological testing can be overwhelming. The three questions comprising the model proposed here simplify the field and provide a scaffolding upon which to present findings. They can then be elaborated to accommodate students' emerging competencies. Far from assessment-specific, this means of organizing clinical information also facilitates fundamental non-assessment clinical skills, including case conceptualization, clinical feedback, and professional clinical writing. As such, learning to formulate and write about assessment data in this way is an efficient and economic teaching tool. It develops students' capacities to understand and communicate about human functioning effectively and accessibly and, ultimately, to think about their patients more fully. In this way, it "set[s], and continue[s] motion, a process of understanding and development" (Appelbaum, 1970, p. 352), both for the students learning to write test reports and for those that read them.

# References

Abraham, K. (1924). A short study of the development of the libido, viewed in the light of mental disorders. In E. Jones. (Ed), *Selected papers of Karl Abraham, M.D.* (pp. 418–502). London: Hogarth Press.

American Psychiatric Association. (2013). *Diagnostic and statistical manual of mental disorders* (5th edn). Washington, DC: American Psychiatric Publishing.

Appelbaum, S. (1970). Science and persuasion in the psychological test report. *Journal of Consulting and Clinical Psychology, 35*(3), 345–355. doi:10.1037/h003010.

Belter, R. W., & Piotrowski, C. (2001). Current status of doctoral-level training in psychological testing. *Journal of Clinical Psychology, 57*(6), 717–726. doi:10.1002/jclp.1044.

Blais, M., & Hopwood, C. J. (2017). Model-based approaches for teaching and practicing personality assessment. *Journal of Personality Assessment, 99*(2), 36–145. doi:10.1080/00223891.2016.1195393.

Bornstein, R. (1996). Construct validity of the Rorschach oral dependency scale: 1967–1995. *Psychological Assessment, 8*(2), 200–205. doi:10.1037/1040-3590.8.2.200.

Bram, A. D. (2017). Reviving and refining psychodynamic interpretation of the Wechsler intelligence tests: The verbal comprehension subtests. *Journal of Personality Assessment, 99*(3), 324–333. doi:10.1080/00223891.2016.1236342.

Bram, A. D., & Peebles, M. J. (2014). *Psychological testing that matters*. Washington, DC: American Psychological Association.

Bram, A. D., & Yalof, J. (2015). Quantifying complexity: Personality assessment and its relationship with psychoanalysis. *Psychoanalytic Inquiry, 35* (Suppl. 1), 74–97. doi:10.1080/07351690.2015.987595.

Bromberg, P. (1996). Standing in the spaces: The multiplicity of self and the psychoanalytic relationship. *Contemporary Psychoanalysis, 32*(4), 509–535. doi:10.1080/00107530.1996.10746334.

Butcher, J. N., Dahlstrom, W. J., Graham, J. R., Tellegen, A. M., & Kreammer, B. (1989). *The Minnesota multiphasic personality Interview-2 (MMPI-2) manual for administration and scoring*. Minneapolis, MN: University of Minneapolis Press.

Clemence, A., & Handler, L. (2001). Psychological assessment on internship: A survey of training directors and their expectations for students. *Journal of Personality Assessment, 76*(1), 18–47. doi:10.1207/S15327752JPA7601_2.

Downing, D., Lubin, M., & Yalof, J. (2018). *Teaching, training, and administration in graduate psychology programs. A psychoanalytic perspective*. Latham, MD: Rowman & Littlefield Publishing Group.

Eriksson, Å., & Maurex, L. (2018). Teaching the writing of psychological reports through formative assessment: Peer and teacher review. *Assessment and Evaluation in Higher Education, 43*(8), 1924–1301. doi:10.1080/02602938.2018.1459470.

Harty, M. K. (1986). Action language in the psychological test report. *Bulletin of the Menninger Clinic, 50*(5), 456–463.

Heaton, S. K., Chelune, G. J., Talley, J. L., Kay, G. G., & Curtiss, G. (1993). *Wisconsin card sorting test manual: Revised and expanded.* Odessa, FL: Psychological Assessment Resources.

Kaslow, N. J. (2004). Competencies in professional psychology. *American Psychologist, 59*(8), 774–781. doi:10.1037/0003-066X.59.8.774.

Kissen, M. (Ed.) (1986). *Assessing object relations phenomenon.* New York: International Universities Press.

Kleiger, J. H. (1997). Rorschach shading responses: From a printer's error to an integrated psychoanalytic paradigm. *Journal of Personality Assessment, 69*(3), 342–364. doi:10.1207/s15327752jpa6902_7.

Krishnamurthy, R., VandeCreek, L., Kaslow, N. J., Tazeau, Y. N., Miville, M. L., Kerns, R. (2004). Achieving competency in psychological assessment: Directions for education and training. *Journal of Clinical Psychology, 60*(7), 725–739. doi:10.1002/jclp.20010.

Lerner, P. M. (1998). *Psychoanalytic perspectives on the Rorschach.* Hillsdale, NJ: The Analytic Press.

Lerner, P. M. (2005). Red beavers and building bridges between assessment and treatment. *Journal of Personality Assessment, 85*(3), 271–279. doi:10.1207/s15327752jpa8503_03.

Lerner, P. M. (2007). On preserving a legacy: Psychoanalysis and psychological testing. *Psychoanalytic Psychology, 24*(2), 208–230. doi:10.1207/s15327752jpa8503_03.

Lingiardi, V., & McWilliams, N. (Eds.) (2017). *Psychodynamic diagnostic manual* (2nd ed.). New York: Guilford Press.

McCrae, R. R., & Costa, P. T. (2010). *NEO inventories for the NEO personality Inventory–3 (NEO PI-3), NEO five-factor inventory–3 (NEO FFI-3) and NEO personality inventory–revised (NEO PI-R): Professional manual.* Lutz, FL: Psychological Assessment Resources, Inc.

Meyer, G. J., Viglione, D. J., Mihura, J. L., Erard, R. E., & Erdberg, P. (2011). *Rorschach performance assessment system: Administration, coding, interpretation, and technical manual.* Toledo, OH: Author.

Mihura, J. L., Roy, M., & Graceffo, R. A. (2017). Psychological assessment training in clinical psychology doctoral programs. *Journal of Personality Assessment, 99*(2), 153–164. doi:10.1080/00223891.2016.1201978.

Morey, L. C., Hopwood, C. J., Gunderson, J. G., Skodol, A. E., Shea, M. T., Yen, S. (2007). Comparison of alternative models for personality disorders. *Psychological Medicine, 37*(7), 983–994. doi:10.1017/S0033291706009482.

Murray, H. (1943). *Thematic apperception test manual.* Cambridge, MA: Harvard University Press.

Norcross, J. C., & Karpiak, C. P. (2012). Clinical psychologists in the 2010s: 50 years of the APA division of clinical psychology. *Clinical Psychology: Science and Practice, 19*(1), 1–12. doi:10.1111/j.1468-2850.2012.01269.x.

Peebles, M. J. (2012). *Beginnings* (2nd ed.). New York: Psychology Press.

Pine, F. (1998). The four psychologies of psychoanalysis and their place in clinical work. *Journal of the American Psychoanalytic Association, 36*(3), 571–596. doi:10.1177/000306518803600301.

Piotrowski, C. (2015a). Clinical instruction on projective techniques in the USA: A review of academic training settings 1995–2014. *SIS Journal of Projective Psychology and Mental Health*, *22*(2), 83–92.

Piotrowski, C. (2015b). On the decline of projective techniques in professional psychology training. *North American Journal of Psychology*, *17*(2), 259–266.

Piotrowski, C. (2017). Thematic apperception techniques (TAT, CAT) in assessment: A summary review of 67 survey-based studies of training and professional settings. *SIS Journal of Projective Psychology and Mental Health*, *24*(1), 3–17.

Randolph, C. (1998). *The repeatable battery for the assessment of neuropsychological status*. San Antonio, TX: The Psychological Corporation.

Rapaport, D. (1950a). On the psycho-analytic theory of thinking. *International Journal of Psycho-Analysis*, *31*, 161–170.

Rapaport, D. (1950b). *Organization and pathology of thought*. New York: Columbia University Press.

Rapaport, D. (1953). On the psycho-analytic theory of affects. *International Journal of Psycho-Analysis*, *34*(3), 177–198.

Rapaport, D. M., Gill, M. M., & Schafer, R. (1968). *Diagnostic psychological testing* (rev ed.). New York: International Universities Press.

Ready, R. E., & Veague, H. B. (2014). Training in psychological assessment: Current practices of clinical psychology programs. *Professional Psychology: Research and Practice*, *45*(4), 278–282. doi:10.1037/a0037439.

Reynolds, C. R., & Kamphaus, R. W. (2015). *Reynolds intellectual assessment scales (RIAS-2) and the Reynolds intellectual screening test (RIST-2) professional manual*. Lutz, FL: Psychological Assessment Resources.

Rorschach, H. (1927). *Rorschach test-psychodiagnostic plates*. Cambridge, MA: Hogrefe Publishing Corp.

Schachtel, E. (1966). *Experiential foundations of Rorschach's test*. New York: Routledge.

Schafer, R. (1954). *Psychoanalytic interpretation in Rorschach testing*. New York: Grune & Stratton.

Shedler, J. (2018). Where is the evidence for "evidence-based" therapy? *Psychiatric Clinics of North America*, *41*(2), 319–329. doi:10.1016/j.psc.2018.02.001.

Stedman, J. M., Hatch, J. P., & Schoenfeld, L. S. (2001). Internship directors' valuation of preinternship preparation in test-based assessment and psychotherapy. *Professional Psychology: Research and Practice*, *32*(4), 421–424. doi:10.1037/0735-7028.32.4.421.

Sugarman, A. (1991). Where's the beef? Putting personality back into personality assessment. *Journal of Personality Assessment*, *56*(1), 130–144. doi:10.1207/s15327752jpa5601_12.

Sugarman, A., & Kanner, K. (2000). The contribution of psychoanalytic theory to psychological testing. *Psychoanalytic Psychology*, *17*(1), 3–23. doi:10.1037/0736-9735.17.1.3.

Tallent, N. (1966). Clinical communication and the psychodiagnostics process. *The Canadian Psychologist,* *7a*(3), 197–208. doi:10.1037/h0083101.

Urist, J. (1977). The Rorschach test and the assessment of object relations. *Journal of Personality Assessment*, *41*(1), 3–9. doi:10.1207/s15327752jpa4101_1.

Wiener, J., & Costaris, L. (2012). Teaching psychological report writing: Content and process. *Journal of School Psychology*, *27*(2), 119–135. doi:10.1177/0829573511418484.

Wright, C. V., Beattie, S. G., Galper, D. I., Church, A. S., Bufka, L. F., Brabender, V. M., & Smith, B. L. (2017). Assessment practices of professional psychologists: Results of a national survey. *Professional Psychology: Research and Practice*, *48*(2), 73–78. doi:10.1037/pro0000086.

Yalof, J. (2016). Transferential and countertransferential aspects of multicultural diversity in psychological assessment and psychotherapy: A case illustration highlighting race and gender. In V. M. Brabender & J. L.Mihura (Eds.), *Handbook of gender and sexuality in psychological assessment* (pp. 373–395). New York: Routledge.

Yalof, J. (2020). When the assessor's limits are tested: Enactments and the assessment frame in psychological testing. *Journal of Personality Assessment, 102*(4), 573-583. https://.org/10.1080/00223891.2019.1613241.

Yalof, J., & Rosenstein, D. (2014). Psychoanalytic interpretation of superego functioning following CS readministration procedures: Case illustration. *Journal of Personality Assessment, 96*(2), 192–203. doi:10.1080/00223891.2013.836528.

# 11 Conclusion

*Jed A. Yalof*

We conclude by returning to the quotation (Schafer, 1954) with which we began this book:

> No matter how helpful a clinical tool it may be, a psychological test cannot do its own thinking. What it accomplishes depends upon the thinking that guides its application. This guiding thought is psychological theory, whether explicit and systematized or implicit and unsystematized.
>
> (p. xi)

Each chapter endeavored to illustrate how psychodynamic thinking can be woven into the inference process of psychological assessment across a wide range of professional settings. First and foremost, psychologists of any theoretical orientation must respect the ability of referral source, patient, and any other potential audience to understand the findings. When it comes to psychoanalytic theory, this is no easy task. Psychoanalytic theory, with its history of elegant but abstract concepts (Ahktar, 2009) requires psychoanalytic assessors to subordinate the temptation of assuming a common understanding of terminology to the priority of communication. The end goal here, however, is collaboration, the translation of abstract to concrete, and in the end, utility and applicability of the report.

Assessments also mandate synthesis of many points of reference, including the array of data that arrives through tests and measures, patient-examiner/behavioral observations, the client's history, the assessor's self-reflection, and thoughts about the manner in which the reader might experience the report. Each impacts the writer's attitude toward what to say, how to say it, when to say it, what to emphasize, and what to minimize. In the end, aims are measured by outcomes. For test reports, outcomes emerge in response to such questions as: Was it helpful and applicable? Did it raise useful questions for further consideration? Were findings contextualized such that conditions under which behavioral manifestations are likely to occur made clear within the limits of reasonable expectation? If, for example, there are difficulties learning academically, what are they, when do they most often occur most, how and when can accommodations be offered, how does one think through a cadre of tests and measure to organize so much information? How do these insights help us further understand the fit between learning inefficiencies, symptoms, psycho-dynamic conflicts, and overall psychosocial adjustment? Without high skill in cognitive, academic, and personality testing, a void remains in understanding the overall clinical picture. Similarly, these questions can be raised and answered, as we saw, when there are medical problems, neuropsychological problems, outpatient or residential psychiatric care, forensic, and personnel settings. These skills can also be taught in the classroom.

Moving back to our opening quotation, we recognize how the experience and sophistication of psychoanalytic assessors can preserve the richness of an intellectual/clinical base and utilize it in a way that remains targeted to setting. In each chapter, thinking is explicated, data are integrated, and writing is readable. What comes next? We think that the greatest gift that an assessor steeped in psychoanalytic theory can bring to a report is the ability to operationalize and concretize theory, as well as make theory accessible to different professional audiences.

## References

Akhtar, S. (2009). *Comprehensive dictionary of psychoanalysis*. London: Karnac.
Schafer, R. (1954). *Psychoanalytic interpretation in Rorschach testing*. New York: Grune & Stratton.

# Index

relatedness and 140; characteristics of 139; custody evaluations and 98, 108; defenses and 144; forensic evaluation and 123–124; interpersonal style and 90; report writing and 31; self-perception and 121; therapeutic alliance difficulties and 140
Narcissistic Personality Disorder (NPD) 139
NEO-Personality Inventory—Third Edition (NEO-PI-3) 131–132, 173
neurological disorders 162
neuropsychological assessment: ADHD and 28–54, 59; feedback and 52–53; personality assessment and 24n1; psychoanalytic mindset and 28–29, 32, 54–55; report writing and 29–31; *see also* Ms. T (case study)
Nicolini, J. R. 163

object relations 120–121, 173
obsessional stalking behavior 163
Occupational Fitness for Duty (FFD) psychological evaluation: assessor reflections and 161; "for cause" events and 150; feedback and 161; forensic evaluation and 149–164; impaired physicians and 151–152; law enforcement and 150–151; pre-employment 150; psychodynamic assessment and 149–150; rationale for FFD battery 154–155; regulations and standards for 150–151; report writing and 149; workplace/public safety and 150–151; *see also* Dr. Ether (case study)
Occupationally Mandated Psychological Evaluation (OMPE) 150
Occupational Safety and Health Administration (OSHA) 151
Olesen, N. W. 100
oral dependency 170

PAI *see* Personality Assessment Inventory (PAI)
PAI-A *see* Personality Assessment Inventory, Adolescent (PAI-A)
paranoia 80, 90, 119, 156, 162
Parent & Teacher forms and Behavioral Rating Inventory of Executive Functions, Second Edition (BRIEF-2) 62
Patient Health Questionnaire (PHQ-9) 127, 133
PDM-2 *see* Psychodynamic Diagnostic Manual, The (PDM-2)
Peebles, M. J. 14, 20, 131, 174

performance-based measures: ambiguous-demand 35, 42; FFD evaluation and 151, 154; graduate training in 170; guardedness and 19; logical thinking and 11–12; performance difficulties and 131; personality assessment and 132; reality testing and 11; reasoning and reality testing 9–10
performance difficulties 65–67, 131
personality assessment 24, 170–171, 173–174
Personality Assessment Inventory (PAI): assessment for ADHD 37, 42, 131–132, 134; FFD evaluation and 151, 154, 156–157; in forensic settings 118–119; self-report measures and 131; symptomatology and 132
Personality Assessment Inventory, Adolescent (PAI-A) 62
Picano, J. J. 151
Piotrowski, C. 171
positive impression management (PIM) 151
post-traumatic stress disorder (PTSD) 17, 90
Primary Care Behavioral Health (PCBH) model 127
primary care settings *see* medical practice settings
private practice: assessment applications in 7–8; custody evaluations and 95–96; neuropsychological assessment in 28; psychodynamic assessment in 6–8; psychotherapy and 7; referrals and 6–8; *see also* Joshua (case study)
Prodromal Questionnaire-16 (PQ-16) 10
psychic distress 127
psychoanalysis: custody evaluations and 95–111; neuropsychological assessment and 28–29, 32, 54–55; psychic development and 174; psychodynamic assessment and 185–186; psychological testing and 1–2, 174; report writing and 169–175; suicide and 124; transference/countertransference and 97
*Psychoanalytic Interpretation in Rorschach Testing* (Schafer) 1
psychoanalytic report writing model: accessibility and 180–181; integration of seemingly incongruent data and 175; organization of clinical data in 174–175; personality assessment and 173–174; three questions in 175–176; *see also* Molly (case study); report writing
psychodynamic assessment: ADHD and 126–127; clinical empathy and 127;

thought disorders: emotional regulation and 88–89; psychodynamic assessment and 81–84; psychological testing and 11–12; rationale for assessment battery 9–10

*Title VII of the Rehabilitation Act of 1973* 151

Tolstoy, L. 149

TOMAL-2 *see* Test of Memory & Learning, Second Edition (TOMAL-2)

Trail Making Test 36, 39

transference-countertransference: empathy and 110; patient-examiner relationship and 10; psychoanalysis and 53, 97–98; psychological assessment and 124; relational contexts and 78; report writing and 30; therapist identification and 124; treatment teams and 79–80

trauma: affect regulation and 43; domestic violence and 135–136; murder and 123; physical abuse and 35; post-traumatic stress disorder (PTSD) and 17, 90; as underlying developmental disruption (UDD) 16–17, 21

Trauma History Questionnaire (THQ) 10

treatment-centered diagnosis 6, 20–21

underlying developmental disruption (UDD): maladaptive character patterns as 17–18; paradigms of 131, 174; psychodynamic assessment and 6; structural weaknesses as 14–15; trauma as 16–17, 21

vertical split 160, 164n6

WAIS-IV *see* Wechsler Adult Intelligence Scale-Fourth Edition (WAIS-IV)

Walfish, S. 156

Walters, M. G. 100

Waugh, M. H. 3, 152

WCST-CV4 *see* Wisconsin Card Sorting Test—Computer Version 4 (WCST-CV4)

Wechsler Abbreviated Scale of Intelligence—Second Edition (WASI-II) 131, 133

Wechsler Adult Intelligence Scale-Fourth Edition (WAIS-IV): assessment of ADHD and 35; assessment of cognitive factors in 10, 16, 19; assessment of learning disabilities and 36; assessment of thought disorder and 11–12; experience of self and other 46; feedback and 23; intelligence testing and 37–38; in residential/hospital-based settings 78; self-criticism and 18; thought organization and 81, 83–84

Wechsler Individual Achievement Test, Third Edition, Essay Composition (WIAT-III) 62

Wechsler Intelligence Scale for Children, Fifth Edition (WISC-V) 62–64, 66

WIAT-III *see* Wechsler Individual Achievement Test, Third Edition, Essay Composition (WIAT-III)

Wide Range Assessment of Memory and Learning, 2nd ed.(WRAML2) 36, 39–40

Williams, T. J. 151

Winnicott, D. W. 158, 163

Wisconsin Card Sorting Test—Computer Version 4 (WCST-CV4) 36, 40–41

WISC-V *see* Wechsler Intelligence Scale for Children, Fifth Edition (WISC-V)

WJA-IV *see* Woodcock-Johnson Tests of Academic Achievement, Fourth Edition (WJA-IV)

WJOL-IV *see* Woodcock-Johnson Tests of Oral Language, Fourth Edition (WJOL-IV)

Woodcock-Johnson Tests of Academic Achievement, Fourth Edition (WJA-IV) 36, 41, 62, 131, 133

Woodcock-Johnson Tests of Oral Language, Fourth Edition (WJOL-IV) 62–63

WRAML2 *see* Wide Range Assessment of Memory and Learning, 2nd ed.(WRAML2)

Yale Child Study Center 96

York, D. 3

For Product Safety Concerns and Information please contact our EU
representative  GPSR@taylorandfrancis.com
Taylor & Francis Verlag GmbH, Kaufingerstraße 24, 80331 München, Germany

www.ingramcontent.com/pod-product-compliance
Lightning Source LLC
Chambersburg PA
CBHW050710280326
41926CB00088B/2918